THE HIT MEN

And The Kid Who Batted Ninth

THE HIT MEN

And The Kid Who Batted Ninth

BIGGIO, VALENTIN, VAUGHN & ROBINSON

Together Again in the Big Leagues

by David Siroty

DIAMOND COMMUNICATIONS
Lanham • South Bend • New York • Oxford

THE HIT MEN
And The Kid Who Batted Ninth

BIGGIO, VALENTIN, VAUGHN & ROBINSON

Together Again in the Big Leagues

Copyright © 2002 by David Siroty

All rights reserved. No part of this book may be used
or reproduced in any manner whatsoever
without the written permission of the publisher.

10 9 8 7 6 5 4 3 2 1

Manufactured in the United States of America

Published by Diamond Communications
An Imprint of the Rowman & Littlefield Publishing Group
4720 Boston Way
Lanham, Maryland 20706
Distributed by National Book Network

Website: www.diamondbooks.com
To order through The National Book Network:
800-462-6420

Library of Congress Cataloging-in-Publication Data

Siroty, David, 1963-
   The hit men and the kid who batted ninth : Biggio, Valentin, Vaughn & Robinson : together again in the big leagues / by David Siroty.
    p. cm.
   ISBN 1-888698-43-8
   1. Biggio, Craig. 2. Vaughn, Mo, 1967-   . 3. Valentin, John. 4. Robinson, Marteese. 5. Baseball players—United States—Biography. 6. Seton Hall University—Alumni and alumnae—Biography.   I. Title: Hit men. II. Title.
  GV865.A1 S5155 2001
  796.357'092'273--dc21

2001047094

Contents

Acknowledgements vii
Foreword xi
Introduction xiii

1987
1. "The Hit Men" Are Born 3
2. No One Ever Found the Ball 19

Growing Up
3. The Next Doug Flutie Turns to Baseball 27
4. A Fire Sent Him to Baseball .35
5. A Pull Hitter Because of the Right Field Dogs 41
6. Baseball Was His First Love .47

Going Pro
7. Draft Day Tension 57
8. Biggio and Robinson Join the Pro Ranks 64
9. Former Walk-On Joins the Red Sox Chain 73
10. Norwalk Pair Goes in the First Round 84

The Minor Leagues
11. Mom, Can You Keep a Secret? 95
12. Not One of the Chosen Few 106
13. Three Teammates Play Their Way to Pawtucket 121

The Major Leagues
14. Biggio Gets There First 139
15. Norwalk Boys Make It to Boston 152
16. Val Gets There Too 174
17. Back in the Game 184

Leaving a Legacy
18. Following in Their Footsteps 201

Helping Children with Cancer
19. Biggio and the Sunshine Kids 207
20. Baseball is Put in Perspective 215
21. This One's for Jason 224
22. Donations 236

Conclusion
23. Together Again 241
    About the Author 248

To Jill —   We can do whatever we imagine

ACKNOWLEDGMENTS

I do not remember the first time I mentioned the idea of writing this book, but Marteese Robinson says it was in 1987 right after he had his photo taken for *Sports Illustrated*'s "Faces in the Crowd." I apparently told him that he and his Seton Hall teammates, especially Craig Biggio and Mo Vaughn, were so dominant on the collegiate baseball scene that I should write a book about them. I do not remember that moment, but Marteese swears I had a gleam in my eye.

I do know that writing this book was a dream for many years. I wrote a few pages in the early 1990s and, each time Biggio and Vaughn made the All-Star team or John Valentin blasted another dramatic home run, I got the itch.

It took a while, but finally I was determined to make my dream a reality, and I visited Craig at Shea Stadium in 1999. As we sat in the visitor's dugout, I was sweating, nervous that I was really going to ask Craig for his blessing. I had butterflies, not because he might say no, but because when he said yes there would be no turning back. As I knew he would be, Craig was all for the idea. Mo and John were next. They were equally excited to help.

I cannot thank Craig, Mo, John, and Marteese enough for allowing this book to happen. They were all extremely open and available and spent hours with me, sometimes hours they really did not have. Once I got going, I was persistent and they had to endure late-night phone calls, faxes, cell phone interruptions, and locker room meetings. But they never complained. I have told them time and time again how thankful I am to them. I want to do it again. Thank you.

As helpful as the players were, I never could have done this project without their families. The Biggio family: Johnna, Lee, Gwen, and Terry, not to mention the always kind, helpful, and patient Patty. The Valentin family: Davina, Arnold Sr., Arnold Jr., Liz, and Marie, who openly shared their heartwarming stories. The Vaughn family: Shirley, Leroy, Catherine, and Donna, who since I met them have made me feel like one of their own. The Robinson family: Betty Robinson, Wayne and Debbie Naylor, and Charlene Robinson, who could never do enough for me.

Former Seton Hall players Dana Brown, John Sheppard, and Kevin Morton were just as important as the families. Dana helped any way he could and lifted my spirits time and time again with his enthusiasm and attitude. Kevin and John provided valuable insight and spent hours giving me stories and background I needed. Another former college athlete, Bryan Wilson, who grew up with Mo, was also vital to the book's completion.

I am also grateful to Sue Leader, whom the Vaughns consider to be part of their family, for spending several emotional hours with me reliving her son Jason's life. Sue, along with Alexandria Valentin and Julian Zagars, gave a human face to childhood cancer.

The members of the Seton Hall Athletic Department, then and now, helped any way they could. To mention a few: John Paquette, Joe Quinlan, Mark Berard, Sal Petruzzi, Jeannie Fritzen, John Wooding, Marie Wozniak, Tracy King, Jeff Andriesse, Larry Keating, Keith Meyers, the late John Murphy, Sue and Richie Regan, John Levitt, Sheila Noecker, Carolyn Goeckel, Robin Cunningham, Peg Hefferan, Pat Elliott, Joe Del Rossi, Kathy Cardillo, Betty Murphy, Peggy Davis, Jimmy O'Donnell, Paul Huegel, Jeff Fogelson, Mike Sheppard Sr., Ed Blankmeyer, Nick Bowness, Fred Hopke, Chris Buckley, Jeff Goldberg, Mike Cocco, Rob Sheppard, and Phil Cundari.

Thanks also to my colleagues at Saint Peter's College: Ed Rhodes, Fred Cranwell, Katya Wowk, and Pauline Heaney.

I got help from the staff of several teams in Major League Baseball: Larry Babcock [Anaheim Angels]; Kevin Shea [Boston Red Sox]; Rob Matwick, Warren Miller, and Todd Fedewa [Houston Astros]; Bill Stetka [Baltimore Orioles]; Bart Swain

[Cleveland Indians]; Rick Cerrone, Jason Zillo, and Monica Yurman [New York Yankees]; Howard Starkman [Toronto Blue Jays]; Jay Horwitz, Marc Levine, and Stella Fiore [New York Mets]; Larry Shenk and Leigh Tobin [Philadelphia Phillies] and Brian Bartow, Brad Hainje, and Melody Yount [St. Louis Cardinals]. Matt Gould and Josephine Impastato provided valuable assistance at Major League Baseball as did Steve Fortunato and Meleata Smalls at Major League Baseball Productions, and James Martin at the Baseball Assistance Team. I also want to provide a plug for a web site I used religiously for research: www.baseball-reference.com.

Speaking of research, I relied heavily on several people who work at the minor league level: Bill Wanless [Pawtucket Red Sox]; Chris McKibben [New Britain Rock Cats]; Jim Riley [Huntsville Stars]; Adam Fox [Modesto A's]; Chris Smith [Asheville Tourists]; Steve Lenox [Staten Island Yankees]; Kyle Richardson [Wichita Wranglers]; Matt Herring [Buffalo Bisons]; Rick Cerone and Dave Popkin [Newark Bears]; and Ken Cail [Nashua Pride]. I also received assistance from John Wylde [Wareham Gatemen]; Don Carlile [Topeka Capitols]; Jay Virshbo [Howe Sportsdata] and Dave Fanucchi [USA Baseball].

I also got help from Gregg Sarra [*Newsday*], Jim Hague [*Hudson Reporter*], Dennis Johnson and Greg Phillips [Fox Sports Net], Darren Gaskins [Jackie Robinson Foundation], Brian VanderBeek [*Modesto Bee*], Louriann Mardo-Zayat, Dave Schofield, Todd Snyder [ESPN], Dave Kaplan [Yogi Berra Museum], and the late Brent Rutkowski who took his lunch breaks to research articles in the *New Britain Herald*.

John Morris, who wrote his book *Bullet Bob Goes to Louisville* after playing seven years in the major leagues, could not do enough for me. His guidance, suggestions, and editing tips helped make this a valuable experience. John brought my idea to Jill Langford and Shari Hill at Diamond Communications. Jill took a chance on a first-time author and I cannot thank her enough for the guidance she provided. I also want to thank ESPN's Bob Ley for taking the time to write the foreword. Ever since I met Bob back in 1987, he has always provided assistance whenever I have called. This time was no exception, even as his Emmy-winning *Outside the Lines* show has grown to a weekly event.

I was also lucky enough to have great friends who gave me the encouragement to write this book. Steven Borger, Tony and Jennie McIntosh, Connie and Bruce Hartman, Jay and Melanie Williams, along with my "lawyer" Bonnie Nathan and her husband Noah, were part of this from the very beginning. Steve Smith, who took the cover and back cover photos, went above and beyond the call of duty time and time again. Dean Diltz, Joe Favorito, John Stallings, Larry Baumann, Helen Strus, Charlie McCarthy, the entire Yazdan clan, Rich Levinson, Pat Scanlon, and the Krasnoo, Morello, Gargiulo-Dombroski, MacKenzie, and Ellsworth families have also been extremely supportive.

Special thanks to my parents, Margo and Bob Siroty, my sisters, Beth and Hedy, and brothers-in-law, Larry Smith and Glen Reed, along with my in-laws Bobbi and Joel Reed. My grandmothers, Louise Arens and Gertie Bauman, along with my aunts and uncles, Sandy Rosner, Mike and Sherry Rubin, Ron and Cindy Bauman, Bruce and Diana Reed, Arnold and Bonnie Arens, and all of their kids — Amy, Bob, Pam, Dan, Hank, Roberta, Marci, Deb, Dave, Keith, Karen, Delphine, Matt, Ethan and Heather have never stopped being excited about the book.

Finally I have to thank my wife Jill. For a solid year I was either thinking about or writing the book for hours at a time. Basically, Jill was married to *The Hit Men and The Kid Who Batted Ninth*. No conversation ever strayed more than a second or two away from the book. She knew how important it was to me and did everything she could to help. Without her love and constant support I'm not sure you would be reading this today.

I hope you will enjoy reading this book as much as I enjoyed writing it.

D.S.

FOREWORD

All too often the love of the game gets buried under the digits and the dollars. I see it every day.

The names Mo Vaughn, Craig Biggio, and John Valentin are more likely to conjure up their combined $150 million in contracts, rather than an appreciation of what brought them to this point. The irony is that Marteese Robinson's road to the big leagues is more incredible than those of his three teammates.

They all share something very special. It is a legacy of a love of the game burning so fiercely that it cuts through chilling early-spring Jersey afternoons, or finds the joy in stealing time on the gym floor to long toss before being booted by the hoop guys, or sparks players to recruit fans to come see (for free, no less) players who years later would truly be household names.

That's what baseball means at Seton Hall. It begins with the fierce faith and pride of Mike Sheppard, who has given his life to his school and his sport. He has created less a "program" than a family, in the truest sense of the word.

I know, because I've seen it first hand. I was there when Shep first took over as head coach. It is impossible to be in the presence of this former Marine (believe me, you are reminded) and not be inspired to live his motto, "Never lose your hustle."

Our radio station, WSOU, was (and still is) housed in Walsh gym. I remember one day encountering workmen loading large pieces of lumber into the gym. "Gee, what's all that stuff?" I asked. "Outta my way, this stuff's heavy. It's the Roller Derby track." Shep was fundraising again. Good intentions alone weren't going to get you those AB's in the Florida sun.

I chuckle now at the campaign in the mid-'80s publicizing Vaughn, Biggio, and Robinson as "The Hit Men." This, on the campus where the fictional Tony Soprano is said to have attended class for a semester and a half.

The world is now infected with Jersey Chic. But those of us before the deluge — even from my time in the mid-'70s — fondly recall the rakish pride we all took in Pirate baseball, the hardscrabble excellence that sprouted at Owen Carroll Field. On one side of the diamond, The Bubble, a bulbous and very white inflatable dome. To the other, a driveway, lined with that most precious of commodities — on-campus parking.

When we weren't broadcasting the games, we were enjoying them as fans. And more. In fact (Shep, you can correct me here if you want, but you might ruin a good story), I recall one game against St. John's when our loyal and loud contingent ragged the Redmen's pitcher so long, so hard, so creatively, and so mercilessly, that the poor pitcher tried to flip us a surreptitious digit. Trouble was, he was on the rubber at the time. Balk. Run scores. It was my only collegiate RBI.

That's the kind of family that envelops Seton Hall baseball. It nurtured Mo, Craig, John, and Marteese. It continues today.

Just like that ball Mo blasted at Muzzy Field. I saw that, too. And I still don't believe it.

— Bob Ley,
ESPN Sportscaster
Seton Hall Class of '76

INTRODUCTION

It had been a long night. Most of these off-season banquets were. But this one had been more enjoyable than most for Major League Baseball stars Craig Biggio, John Valentin, and Mo Vaughn who sat on the dais, happy to be there. Nine years after leading the 1987 Seton Hall University Pirates to the school's first Big East title, they, along with their coach, Mike Sheppard Sr., had just been enshrined into the school's Athletic Hall of Fame.

CBS Sports' Jim Hunter, the Master of Ceremonies and Class of '82, wrapped up the night's dinner by wishing everyone a safe drive home. But no one wanted to leave. The crowd of more than 400 who attended the January 24, 1996, event wanted more and Seton Hall baseball's most prized possessions were more than willing to oblige. As a line quickly formed, they smiled and signed away. Balls, magazines, cards, and programs. Every now and then they posed for a photo.

"Wasn't there another guy who was pretty good on your college team?" one fan asked. "The guy who led the country in hitting?"

"Hey, where is Marteese?!" Vaughn yelled with a smile, but more than half seriously. "He should be here!" He certainly should have been.

Instead, Marteese Robinson was at work, 2,500 miles away. He had the night shift — 9 PM-to-7 AM. Just like the fans in line, he was also collecting autographs. Not of major leaguers, but of law breakers. He was in Scottsdale, Arizona, working as a detention officer for the Scottsdale Police Department. If jail were a hotel, Robinson was your friendly front-desk employee. But it was not "Sign right here and we'll get you to your room." Instead, Robinson had the troublemakers sign their booking record and escorted them to their jail cell.

"I didn't even know about the dinner," Robinson said. "They didn't invite me. I was mad when I found out. I should have been there. We were together for a great season and we should have always been linked together. I know they made it to the major leagues and I didn't, but the school's Hall of Fame should be about what we did in college. What we did in college was truly awesome and I will always remember it that way."

He was talking about the 1987 Seton Hall baseball team that went down in history as having one of the most potent offenses in NCAA lore. The Pirates hit .355 for the season and scored 11.4 runs a game, the fourth-highest production in NCAA history. Eight players from that team signed professional contracts, with four —Biggio, Vaughn, Valentin, and briefly Kevin Morton — advancing to the major leagues. Robinson eventually got there too, although his name is never mentioned on any big league roster or, for that matter, in any encyclopedia or website devoted to the game's highest level.

They were among a long list of stars who played baseball at "The Hall," a small Catholic school nestled tightly on the South Orange-Newark, New Jersey, border. So many players had signed pro contracts after playing at the school that it should have been called a "baseball factory." But that was not the case. That title was held by schools on the West Coast and down south which had tremendous facilities and weather that allowed them to practice outside the minute NCAA rules allowed.

But baseball in the Northeast is a tough proposition. The average temperature in February in New Jersey is 35 degrees, rising to 45 degrees in March and finally, to a baseball-considerate 51 degrees in April before spring comes in May.

"One thing about those guys — Valentin, Biggio, and Vaughn — those guys are all winners," former Boston Red Sox and current Houston Astros manager Jimy Williams said during the 2000 season. "They are very competitive and like to compete in big games. They are durable, they play with pain. These kids are all from the East. They're tough kids. You also think about [Jeff]

Bagwell, he's like that. These guys don't have the opportunity as youngsters to play as many games as kids in the South and West Coast because of the weather."

Vaughn echoed his former manager's sentiments. "We had to be tough," the Anaheim Angels first baseman said about his college days. "No one plays baseball in the snow, but I remember one game when we not only played in the snow, but our offense was so tough we were crushing balls through the snow flakes."

But Vaughn also knows it was not the weather that made them tough. It was their coach, Mike Sheppard. Sheppard is one of the nation's most respected coaches. Through the 2001 season, the "Old Man," as his players and five children call him, was 916-446-10 in 28 years. He has seen 77 players sign pro contracts with 11 advancing to the big leagues.

"He was a military sergeant," said former New York Yankees catcher Rick Cerone, Sheppard's first major leaguer, who played at Seton Hall from 1972-75. "He was tough, demanded an awful lot to the point that it was a little crazy." Sheppard, who admits to using physical contact as a motivator in his early years, had toned down his act by 1987. But he still was a disciplinarian who wanted the game played a certain way.

"We relied on each other to pick each other up," remarked Dana Brown, one of the eight players off the 1987 squad to sign a pro contract. "We would stay up in the dorms and tell stories about Shep. The guy could be vicious. But off the field he was a great guy who really cared for us. He taught you to be a great person. He also taught you to how to win because he made you hate losing so badly."

Looking back, Brown and the rest of his 1987 teammates realized that Sheppard did something right. While sending four players from one college team to the major leagues was not a rare occurrence, finding a Northeast school on the list certainly was.

"That year was special and we didn't even know it," Valentin said years later while playing for the Boston Red Sox. "We were an East Coast team. March came and we were playing in the snow. Coach Sheppard made sure we knew that all of those other teams played in warm weather and had better facilities than us, but we would always outwork them."

Following is a list of collegiate teams in the 1980s that sent four or more players to the major leagues off of one team. Seton Hall is the only one of the 32 teams not considered a traditional college power from a warm, or at least moderate, climate:

1980 Wichita State Shockers
(NCAA Tournament participants): Joe Carter; Don Heinkel; Charlie O'Brien; Bryan Oelkers; Phil Stephenson.

1981 Wichita State Shockers
(NCAA Tournament participants): Joe Carter; Don Heinkel; Charlie O'Brien; Bryan Oelkers; Phil Stephenson

1982 Arizona Wildcats
Tom Barrett; Kevin Blankenship; Casey Candaele; Jack Daugherty; Ed Vosberg; Kevin Ward

1982 Texas Longhorns
(NCAA College World Series participants): Mike Brumley; Roger Clemens; Spike Owen; Calvin Schiraldi

1982 Wichita State Shockers
(NCAA Runnerup): Don Heinkel; Charlie O'Brien; Bryan Oelkers; Russ Morman; Phil Stephenson

1983 Arizona Wildcats
Jack Howell; Joe Magrane; Ed Vosberg; Kevin Ward

1983 Texas Longhorns
(NCAA National Champions): Billy Bates; Mike Brumley; Roger Clemens; Bruce Ruffin; Calvin Schiraldi

1984 Arkansas Razorbacks
Kevin Campbell; Jeff King; Les Lancaster; Pat Rice

1984 Arizona State Sun Devils
(NCAA College World Series participants): Barry Bonds; Mike Devereaux; Doug Henry; Oddibe McDowell

1984 Florida State Seminoles
(NCAA Tournament participants): Luis Alicea; Mike Loynd; Jody Reed; Paul Sorrento

1984 Mississippi State Bulldogs
(NCAA Tournament participants): Jeff Brantley; Will Clark; Rafael Palmeiro; Bobby Thigpen

1984 Texas Longhorns
(NCAA College World Series participants): Billy Bates; Dennis Cook; Bruce Ruffin; Greg Swindell

1985 Arizona State Sun Devils
Mike Benjamin; Barry Bonds; Mike Devereaux; Doug Henry

1985 Florida Gators
(NCAA Tournament participants): Dave Eiland; Jeff Fischer; Scott Lusader; Mike Perez; Steve Rosenberg; Scott Ruskin; Mike Stanley

1985 LSU Tigers
(NCAA Tournament participants): Albert Belle; Mark Guthrie; Eric Hetzel; Barry Manuel; Clay Parker; Jeff Reboulet; Jack Voigt

1985 Mississippi State Bulldogs
(NCAA College World Series participants): Jeff Brantley; Will Clark; Rafael Palmeiro; Bobby Thigpen

1985 Texas Longhorns
(NCAA Runnerup): Billy Bates; Dennis Cook; Bruce Ruffin; Greg Swindell

1985 UCLA Bruins
Jeff Conine; Torey Lovullo; Alex Sanchez; Todd Zeile

1986 Arkansas Razorbacks
(NCAA Tournament participants): Kevin Campbell; Jeff King; Jim Kremers; Mike Oquist; Scott Pose; Pat Rice

1986 LSU Tigers
(NCAA College World Series participants): Albert Belle; Jim Bowie; Mark Guthrie; Barry Manuel; Jeff Reboulet; Jack Voigt

1986 UCLA Bruins
(NCAA Tournament participants): Jeff Conine; Eric Karros; Torey Lovullo; Alex Sanchez; Todd Zeile

1987 Arizona Wildcats
(NCAA Tournament participants): Chip Hale; Gil Heredia; Kenny Lofton; J.T. Snow

1987 LSU Tigers
(NCAA College World Series participants): Albert Belle; Mark Guthrie; Barry Manuel; Ben McDonald; Russ Springer; Jack Voigt

1987 Seton Hall Pirates
(NCAA Tournament participants): Craig Biggio; Kevin Morton; John Valentin; Mo Vaughn

1987 UCLA Bruins
(NCAA Tournament participants): Jeff Conine; Bob Hamelin; Eric Karros; Alex Sanchez

1988 Arizona Wildcats
Lance Dickson; Trevor Hoffman; Kenny Lofton; J.T. Snow

1988 LSU Tigers
John O'Donoghue; Keith Osik; Curt Leskanic; Ben McDonald; Russ Springer

1988 Stanford Cardinals
(NCAA National Champions): Brian Johnson; Mike Mussina; Stan Spencer; Ed Sprague

1988 Wichita State Shockers
(NCAA College World Series participants): Greg Brummett; P.J. Forbes; Dave Haas; Mike Lansing; Pat Meares; Eric Wedge

1989 Arizona Wildcats
(NCAA Tournament participants): Lance Dickson; Trevor Hoffman; Kenny Lofton; J.T. Snow

1989 LSU Tigers
(NCAA College World Series participants): Curt Leskanic; Ben McDonald; John O'Donoghue; Chad Ogea; Keith Osik; Russ Springer

1989 Wichita State Shockers
(NCAA National Champions): Greg Brummett; P.J. Forbes; Mike Lansing; Pat Meares; Eric Wedge

Seton Hall, besides being the only Northeast school on the list, is also the only one that was not a regular participant in the NCAA College World Series. In fact, the last Northeastern team to make it to Omaha was the 1986 Maine Bears, led by shortstop Mike Bordick, and they advanced largely because the system was still designed to allow a team from the region to participate.

With one exception from 1975-86, the NCAA had a Northeast Regional which brought conference champions to one site to play for a bid to the College World Series. This bracket automatically allowed a team from the region to advance to Omaha; Maine was usually the school which advanced, winning in '81, '82, '83, '84, and '86. But in 1987, the NCAA began to treat its baseball tournament like it's basketball's March Madness to ensure that the game's best teams were included. So that year, while the Northeast Regional still existed, it was played in Atlanta with Georgia Tech, Georgia, and Michigan included, while Seton Hall was sent to the South I Regional in Huntsville, Alabama.

Chris Monasch, commissioner of the America East Conference and a member of the 2001 NCAA Baseball Tournament Selection Committee, understands the frustrations the Northeast college teams have, but realizes the seeding system is best for the college game. "Each conference champion, along with 34 at-large teams, are still included in the tournament, but by seeding, you ensure that the best teams have the best chance to make it to the College World Series. Before 1987, many of the nation's best teams, traditionally from the West Coast and South, did not even make the NCAA Tournament. That is how the basketball tournament once was, but when that tournament changed to include the best teams, the tournament became extremely successful and grew in interest. The same thing has happened with the baseball tournament."

The 1987 Seton Hall Pirates helped the sport grow in popularity. The talent level was impressive, considering Biggio, Valentin, and Vaughn have each already played 10 or more seasons in the big leagues and they were not even the best players on the team. That title, hands-down went to Marteese Robinson who hit .529 as the nation's top hitter. "Marty was the best," Vaughn said in 2000. "We all knew it. He ran like a deer. He hit with power. He drove in runs. Defensively he was very smooth."

The major leagues were supposed to be a certainty for him. But it never happened that way. Instead Robinson watched from the sidelines as his former teammates — Biggio, Valentin, and Vaughn — took the teachings of Mike Sheppard all the way to stardom in the the major leagues.

IN MEMORY

*In memory of Seton Hall University students
Frank Caltabilota, John Giunta, and Aaron Karol
who lost their lives
in the tragic January 19, 2000, Boland Hall fire.*

1987

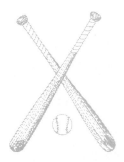

"THE HIT MEN" ARE BORN

CHAPTER 1

Few, except for the players and coaches, along with their family, friends, and an occasional fan, paid much attention to baseball in the Northeast. The sport was a poor stepchild to college basketball, with a season that started during the winter and finished to an empty campus after final exams. The games were rarely televised and daily newspapers provided only brief blurbs, scores, and an occasional story. Seton Hall, even though it boasted one of the most successful baseball programs around, fell into that black hole. But, in reality, baseball should have been King at Seton Hall.

The 1987 season began with Seton Hall 201-622-16 all-time. Baseball was the school's first sport started in 1863 with a 20-16 win over Fordham. To that point, the school had 75 winning seasons, 18 NCAA Tournament appearances, five College World Series visits and 20 major league players. Even the school's athletic nickname stemmed from baseball. Back on April 23, 1931, Seton Hall used a five-run ninth inning to beat Holy Cross. The next day, the Newark *Evening News* article read, "One of the sportswriters was so excited in the turn of events that he exclaimed with disgust, 'That Seton Hall team is a gang of Pirates.'"

Although easily the school's most successful sport with only three losing seasons in a half-century, baseball was played in a vacuum. Basketball, which had a storied tradition with a national title in the '50s, came first. P.J. Carlesimo's team was rising in the ranks. His Pirates had just advanced to the 1987 NIT, the school's first postseason trip in 11 years. In another year it would be the school's first NCAA Tournament bid. Two more years until the 1989 Final Four.

"Shep had some great teams," Carlesimo, who left Seton Hall in 1994 to coach the Portland Trail Blazers, said in late December 2000 while working as an NBA analyst for NBC. "I always enjoyed the relationship between the basketball program and Shep's players. "They were always very supportive of our teams and we were the same way towards them. It was fun getting to know the guys and watching them play."

Seton Hall head baseball coach Mike Sheppard Sr. and his players understood the attention basketball received.

But baseball was not even a close second. The soccer team got more respect, having just finished seventh in the nation. To make it even more insulting to the baseball players, the soccer team played on the outfield of their field — Owen T. Carroll Field — named after the former baseball coach. Fall baseball practice was forced to take a backseat to soccer. It was as if Europe's passion had overtaken "America's Pastime." The players griped that the women's basketball team also came before them.

"We had to share our field with the soccer team," Houston Astros star Craig Biggio later remembered in an article for an Astros game program, "and the batting cages with the fencing team and the cheerleading squad. While I was there, we built our own pitching mounds. It would be easy to get frustrated, but Coach Sheppard holds it all together." Biggio failed to mention the baseball team back then washed their own uniforms and worked as the grounds crew, even if it meant beating the coming rains with 3 AM tarp duty.

"Craig had mastered the fact that baseball was never given its due here and that we still had to overcome it," Sheppard said. "He would tell me, 'Fuck 'em, Coach. Let's just win. We can overcome anything.'"

Sheppard could not understand the school's indifference to baseball, especially because the sport brought in revenue. Considering Sheppard had only 15 scholarships to give and more than 75 players annually attended opening practice, baseball brought in at least 60 students a year paying tuition, room and board. That was at least $500,000 a year.

"I pushed a lot for the program," Sheppard said. "A lot of people didn't like that, but I am driven because I care so much about Seton Hall and have so much passion for baseball and the program. I was bleeding blue before Tommy Lasorda ever came along."

Sheppard, the program's glue, came from the old school. He was demanding and relentless. He hated mental mistakes. After one of his infielders made three errors in the same inning, Sheppard tossed an empty bucket onto the field and yelled at his mistake-prone player, "Here! See if you can catch a ball with this!"

"If I'm not on your ass, I didn't see potential," Sheppard said. "When I was a kid, if I came home from a game and went 3-for-5, my father would say I did well, but let's talk about the two at-bats you did not get a hit on. That is my job as a coach to point out the things a player needs to do to improve."

"My old man's philosophy is to eliminate mistakes," said John Sheppard, the coach's middle son of three who played second base on the 1987 team. "If you go 4-for-4, he wants to talk about the mistakes you made in the field. That type of coaching style is not popular with a lot of people, but our group appreciated it because we all wanted to get better every day."

His stars understood and explained Sheppard's actions to the younger players. "Biggio would get three hits," Sheppard said, "and say, 'Jeez, he's on my ass to get the fourth one. What is wrong with that? That's what will make us great players.' "

The players had conflicting views about their coach who acted differently on and off the field. "He is a no nonsense leader," 1987 center fielder Dana Brown said. "When you come here to play for Shep, if you don't love the game, you're not gonna make it. There were times we wanted to grab the guy by the throat and squeeze him to death."

At the same time, he cared for his players greatly and tried to mold them into quality young men. "He taught us respect," Biggio said after his 13th major league season. "Respect who you are. Respect the game. Respect your family. If you have respect, you will do the right thing."

When Sheppard and his Pirates began practicing for the 1987 season, they did not meet on green grass under a hot sun as you would expect a college baseball team to do. After all, this was the Northeast in the middle of winter. Instead they met in the school's "baseball complex." A dusty, dungeonesque room in the basement of 2,000-seat Walsh Gymnasium. The batting cages featured torn netting hanging on wires strung across the 40 x 120 foot room. The pitchers worked their arms next door in a cramped 70-foot expanded closet. Only two could possibly throw at a time. The team could only long toss in the upstairs gym.

Throwing had to be completed by 3 PM because of basketball practice. The baseball team also competed for floor space with athletic department staff pick-up basketball games. The players adjusted. They simply threw over the administrators. One time they played. "We had to be careful," Vaughn said, "because if Shep found out he would kill us. It was the baseball team against the athletic department. They played every day, every day. But we crushed 'em."

Besides sneaking in a quick game of hoops, the Pirates got in shape by running in the cold. They practiced baserunning in the snow. It was not baseball "like it oughta be," but still, Sheppard was excited about the season. He had eight starters returning, although his two best pitchers from the 1986 32-26 club, eventual major leaguer Rich Scheid and Doug Cinnella, both signed pro contracts after their junior years.

The 1987 infield was solid. Six-foot-one, 180-pound junior first baseman Marteese Robinson, who was voted a Freshman All-America by *Baseball America* and the Big East Freshman of Year, was returning from an injury-shortened 1986 season. Robinson hit .394 his rookie year, but only .287 as a sophomore.

Robinson's best friend, second baseman John Sheppard, hit .325 in 1986 after transferring from North Carolina. His double play partner, 6'1" sophomore John Valentin was one of the smoothest fielders Sheppard ever coached. A walk-on surprise, Valentin hit .296 as a rookie with only 10 strikeouts. He went 6-for-9 in the Big East Tournament and was named to the

All-Tournament team. Junior Jeff Riggs played the hot corner.

The outfield — Brown, left fielder Pete Petrone, and senior right fielder Ralph Soto — was a speedy bunch.

The designated hitter was 6'0", 200-pound freshman Maurice "Mo" Vaughn. A four-year starter in football, basketball and baseball at Trinity-Pawling [NY] School, Vaughn was athletic, but still an unproven commodity.

Biggio, a 5'11" junior catcher, would captain the Pirates and guide a young pitching staff. He hit .351 with 43 RBI the previous year with 42 stolen bases and earned All-Big East honors.

"Our one-to-five spots are loaded with power," Sheppard told the *Star-Ledger*'s Ed Barmakian. "Biggio can do it all. We also have some guys who can fly. We've always been a running team. Whether you're fast or not, you better learn how to run when you come here."

A mid-February, five-game, season-opening trip to Miami was the first time the Pirates would step foot on an actual baseball diamond not covered in snow. And, as Sheppard said, they were ready to run. Seton Hall stole 20 bases during the trip and rookie Vaughn made an immediate impact. Vaughn, who Sheppard called a "lefty Don Baylor," smacked two two-run homers in an 11-5 win over national power Miami.

The Pirates returned home 3-2, and again practiced indoors, with an occasional trip outside when the temperature went above freezing. They flew south again on March 14, this time to Orlando and the Central Florida/Burger King Classic where they won eight straight.

Robinson went 23-for-34 in the tournament to win MVP honors. Not a bad week for a guy who many thought was done for his career after suffering a major injury the year before in a 6-5, 13-inning win at Tulane. "Val [Valentin] went into the six hole and tried to bounce the ball in the grass so it would skip to me," Robinson remembered. "It took a bad hop and came up and would have hit me in the face, but I put my glove up to keep it in front of me. It was the only thing I could do. The base runner, Tookie Spann, a football player, I'll never forget his name, hit my arm. I was screaming and yelling and I could see our trainer, John Levitt, running towards me, but it seemed like it took him

45 minutes to go the 30 feet from the dugout." Robinson was hospitalized. Sheppard and his wife Phyllis rushed to his side and helped make a decision on surgery with a long distance call to Robinson's mother. Robinson remained in New Orleans with Sports Information Director John Wooding. The team went home as Robinson's season was lost. Medical report: Broken wrist; broken forearm; 10 screws; two metal plates.

"No one actually came out and said it, but I don't think a lot of people thought I would come back," Robinson, who now proudly showed off an enormous scar on his right forearm, told Barmakian before the season. "When I was in the hospital, the guy I roomed with had been in a car accident and he almost lost both his legs. After seeing what he went through, I would look down at my arm and figure it wasn't so bad. He told me not to give up and gave me the inspiration I needed to come back."

"It seems strange to say, but in some ways, what happened to Marty turned out to be positive," Sheppard said in the same article. "He got on a weight program and came back stronger. In my opinion, he's the best defensive first baseman in college baseball. No one stretches and picks up a ball in the dirt like he does."

Offense. Defense. Robinson was back and his fast start re-lit his effervescent, room-lighting smile. "I got off to a pretty good start this season," he said. "After my injury last season, I worked with weights. John Morris helped me with my hitting. When I was at Seton Hall Prep, I saw John Morris hit a 450-foot home run and we talked about hitting," Robinson said. "He always told me to hit line drives and not try for home runs. I watched him and copied his whole stance. He still comes here in the fall and works with me."

Morris, who would play for the St. Louis Cardinals in 1987, was one of many former Seton Hallers who returned to campus each winter. Yankees catcher Rick Cerone and Braves pitcher Charlie Puleo, who both led Seton Hall to the 1974 and 1975 College World Series, along with Pat Pacillo, then a rookie pitcher on the Reds, were part of the tradition-rich Seton Hall program who always seemed to be around.

"I would go back to Seton Hall during the off-season and work with the guys," Cerone said in 2001. "I worked with the catchers a bit, but mostly I wanted to get my work in. To them, though, I was the guy who brought them the new shoes and batting gloves. During the course of a major league season you acquire a lot of gear and every year when I would work out at Seton Hall I would bring back a lot of stuff for the guys. It was like Christmas for those guys. "

Cerone appreciated what the Seton Hall players were going through. They had a coach who was as rugged as they came. "Shep taught us that you had to be tough to play baseball even though it is a game that you use your head more than your body. You had to be physically and mentally tough. You had to battle the elements. It is tough to play baseball in March and April in New Jersey. He's not an X and O's guy. He believed in discipline."

Although Sheppard, who admits that his first few years at Seton Hall were a bit too Woody Hayes-like, had calmed down, he still had what he called "the fire in his belly." That intensity fit perfectly with his 1987 squad which raced to a 16-3 start. They cracked the Top 20 for the first time in three years, 16th in the *Collegiate Baseball* poll, but celebrated by blowing a late lead and losing to Fairleigh Dickinson, 8-7.

The FDU loss had Biggio angry. A three-hour bus trip to Siena two days later did nothing to change his spirits. Before the Pirates built an 8-1 fifth inning lead, Biggio's emotions spilled over. Robinson, who had singled, was being kept close with a series of pick-off tries which ended with harder and harder whacks to his helmet. Starter Jeff DiNuzzo was quietly resting his arm in the dugout, watching. With the two dugouts jawing at each other over the hard tag, Biggio turned to DiNuzzo and yelled, "When that fucking guy comes up, you better fucking throw at him. Nobody is going to do that to us!!" The next inning, the first baseman was dusted. Biggio smiled. Respect earned. His mood brightened. A 9-4 win also helped.

Biggio was the undisputed leader, but it was not always that way. "Craig came to us as the worst defensive catcher I had ever seen," Sheppard said. "But he is a hard worker and he made himself into one of the best catchers in the East. Without him I don't know where we would be."

"Craig was fierce," Vaughn said later. "He was our captain. He ran the team. He even coached us in the fall season when we had split-squad games. He was so fast and played the game so hard. As the DH, I would sit in the dugout and watch him beat guys down the line backing up groundballs at first."

The day before the FDU loss, Sheppard spoke at the season's first New Jersey College Baseball Writers and Coaches Association meeting at the Town Pub in nearby Bloomfield. He was all smiles. "There were 25 scouts out there," he said about an earlier 14-1 win at Monmouth, "as many as I've ever seen at a game.

"You can't walk Biggio because he can run and you don't want to walk him with Mo Vaughn coming up next. He's the guy who really came along for us in Florida. He's really mature for a freshman, I just hope he can keep it up." To this point, the Pirates had a team batting average of .361 with 93 stolen bases in 102 tries. Robinson was leading the nation with a .580 average and had 14-straight stolen bases, Biggio .400 with 14-of-15 swipes, and Vaughn .473 with 29 RBI.

Sheppard, bubbling with excitement, took some ribbing from his peers not used to big smiles and unbridled enthusiasm from the drill sergeant-like guy. "I'm not getting soft," Sheppard said. "I like these kids." He would like them even more after a 14-4 pasting of in-state rival Rutgers which was led by Brown's childhood friend, sophomore center fielder Eric Young. It was Brown who had convinced the football wide receiver to also play baseball at Rutgers. It turned out to be a good career move for the future major league star.

Seton Hall then beat Fordham, moved to 15th in the nation at 19-4, and saw Robinson featured in *USA Today*. "Maybe I should break everyone's arm," Sheppard joked to writer Roscoe Nance. Then he got serious in talking about the .582-hitting Robinson who also had nine homers, 44 RBI, and a 22-game hitting streak. "He's not resting on his laurels. I've seen guys like this before. They get two hits and then they coast. Not this guy. He always wants to get a hit or steal a base. He keeps in the back of his mind what it was like not to play."

Biggio and Vaughn drew Robinson's praise. "Without those guys, I wouldn't be in the position I'm in." Although Robinson was humble, the spotlight still focused on him. *Collegiate Baseball* named him its National Player of the Week after an "average" few days. He went 7-for-12 with two homers and six RBI during the span.

"I've never seen anyone like Marteese," *Collegiate Baseball* managing editor Lou Pavlovich said. "His statistics are so shocking, it's like testing a lightning rod after it's been struck." But Robinson and the Pirates suffered a power failure. Hated St. John's handed them their only shutout loss of the season, 7-0. Terry Bross, a 6'10" basketball forward for Coach Lou Carnesecca, who eventually pitched in the major leagues, helped limit the Pirates to just two infield hits. Robinson's hitting-streak ended at 22.

The Pirates then took 4-of-5 on a road trip and Vaughn took his turn in the spotlight. The first freshman to hit cleanup at Seton Hall since Cerone in 1973, Vaughn started his career hitting .111 in the fall practice season. He learned first-hand how demanding Sheppard could be.

"We didn't like our coach at all," Vaughn said years later. "He was the toughest man we ever faced, but as you look back on it, he was the best thing to happen to us. He was tough love. He wanted you to be the best you could be. We all tried to bend the rules, no doubt. He'd bring us in the office and tell us if we didn't do things right, we wouldn't play. He knew playing was the only satisfaction we had."

But Sheppard took the game away when he suspended Vaughn for a month during the fall season for missing mandatory study hall. The veterans were not surprised by the punishment. "He doesn't let you play if your grades slip or if you're not running or doing what you need to," Biggio said. Valentin added, "Shep is a constant. He's always the same. He is really, really tough. College is a time when you could stay out late, go out, miss class. But he has a really tight rope on us."

But during the winter, after he reinstated Vaughn, Sheppard recognized he needed to do some yard work at Owen T. Carroll Field to take advantage of the freshman's strength. For years a big tree sat behind the right field fence. If a home run ball hit the tree and bounced back, the ball was in play. No home run.

"The power in his bat caused me to cut the tree's limbs," Sheppard explained to Barmakian. "It was the first time I used a power saw."

Vaughn, however, would face no such obstacles once the "real" spring season began. He showed his skills by hitting three homers in a 16-8 second-game win at Georgetown. The players called the final one a "bomb." "One of the parents showed me where it landed," Sheppard said. "I'm a football official, so I know how to walk out a yard at a time. The ball cleared the right field fence and then went over another fence before landing on a softball diamond. He hit it so far it just seemed like a moment in time. The sign said 480 feet at the point it went over the fence." Sheppard's best guess? 540 feet.

"I got around Craig and Marty and the three of us talk hitting all the time," Vaughn said showing the maturity Sheppard spoke about earlier in the season. "Being around them has helped me a lot. Not only have I learned a lot from them, but hitting between them in the lineup really helps me too. Pitchers can't pitch around you when you're batting between two major league prospects."

"Mo was a hitter," Biggio said. "He is a student of the game. He watched and he listened and he talked about hitting. He had a passion for it."

It was now time for some self-promoting by the Pirates and left-hander John Brogan, a junk ball thrower, was their P.T. Barnum. The Pirates knew they were good and, like any performers, wanted enthusiastic audiences. Brogan took photos of his teammates, created promotional flyers and plastered them all over campus.

One of Brogan's creations declared Biggio, Vaughn, and Robinson were "The Hit Men." The Yankees had just come off a 90-win season led by All-Star first baseman Don Mattingly. Mattingly's Nike "Hit Man" poster was popular in the New York area. Brogan stole the idea and convinced Seton Hall's talented trio to dress as gangsters. Biggio stood in the middle wearing sunglasses. Vaughn stood to his left and Robinson to his right. Robinson looked like a natural. His hat tilted to the right and his black suit fit flawlessly. Even the way he held his fake machine gun looked the part, perhaps an omen of where his career would take him. "They really liked the idea of getting dressed in their suits," Brogan said. "They never thought anything of it. All we wanted to do was try to get more people to the games."

Ironically, the Pirates did not know what it was like to draw crowds. They had not yet played on campus. A botched sodding effort at Owen T. Carroll Field kept them on the road with home games played at nearby parks. They came home on April 20 against Georgetown and Robinson took care of the welcome home party. He went 7-for-8 in the opening doubleheader with three homers and six RBI. The 16th-ranked Pirates were 26-6 with Robinson hitting .551 just over halfway through the season. He was hitting 48 points higher than any other collegian and was dead even with the all-time NCAA mark set by New Mexico's Keith Hagman in 1980.

"I've never before seen a college kid go through such a hot streak," Yankees scout Joe Di Carlo said. "His batting average is legitimate. He's whacking everything for line drives with power."

The Pirates were cruising at 9-1 in the Big East Southern Division mark, but Sheppard was not satisfied with his .340-hitting club which was scoring just under 10 runs a game. His son John certainly did not escape criticism from the equal-opportunity motivator. "Our sixth and seventh guys have to hit with men on base," the head coach said. Guess whose son hit sixth?

But Robinson, John Sheppard's best friend, had no problem generating offense. With more than a month to go, Robinson already had a school-record 86 hits. Biggio was curious when he approached a member of the school's sports information staff and asked, "What would Marteese's average be if he did not get a hit the rest of the season?" The two sat down at a calculator and figured Robinson, who was hitting .551 at the time, would need just one hit in his next 60 at-bats to ensure a .400 average. "That is really amazing," Biggio said shaking his head.

The Pirates were 31-7 when Brogan unveiled "The Hit Men" campaign on campus. The flyer, which had Robinson's first name misspelled "Martese," was also displayed at the weekly media luncheon.

Bill Kennedy Jr., the sports editor for the *Elizabeth Daily Journal*, was intrigued. He attended the Pirates' game later that afternoon in South Orange and asked Brogan for the original photo which he used under a banner headline — "Robinson, Biggio, Vaughn are 'The Hit Men.'"

"So, when the Pirates defeated New York Tech, a very good Northeast Division I baseball team, 17-2, yesterday, it figured that "The Hit Men" would have been satisfied with their work — a total of six hits and four RBI," Kennedy observed. "They were not." He watched as Vaughn threw postgame batting practice to Biggio before the two reversed roles. They probably did not need the extra work. Robinson was hitting .559, Biggio .397, and Vaughn .395. Together — 212 hits, 40 homers, 173 RBI.

"The Hit Men" photo the *Daily Journal* used turned out to be the only one to survive much past the photo shoot. "We took about 15 pictures," Brogan said, "and I left them on our bus after we lost at St. John's. I left everything, the negatives and the envelope. I still have the pictures of the other flyers, but not 'The Hit Men.'"

As Kennedy pointed out, the Pirates never quit. An afternoon game the day Kennedy's article came out proved it. The Pirates were a bit too relaxed on the bus ride to Pace University, spending the time ribbing Biggio, Vaughn, and Robinson about the photo and article.

Pace, which came in five games above .500, used a five-run fourth to build a 10-2 lead. After the inning's third out, Biggio stormed off the field, ripped off his catcher's equipment and screamed for teammates to huddle up. They did as told. Biggio yelled loudly, but clearly: "Let's get going! Right now!" And the Pirates played follow the leader. Biggio hit a three-run homer. His roommate, Scott Napolitano, a reserve utilityman, added another three-run home run. Fifteenth-ranked Seton Hall scored 20-straight runs to improve to 33-7.

Seton Hall was a legitimate threat to win the national title. "Many of the previous national champions have been great base stealing teams," Pavlovich said. "Arizona, Texas and Miami have all been great on the bases." So was Seton Hall. The Pirates combined hitting prowess with a running attack that led the nation with 4.94 thefts per game.

It all came together on May 6 when the Pirates crushed Brooklyn College at Owen T. Carroll Field, 21-0, for Sheppard's 500th win. The skipper, in his 15th year at Seton Hall, was 500-199-5. He became only the fourth active coach in the Northeast to reach the milestone. The Pirates presented him with a bottle of champagne and an autographed game ball.

Sheppard also received congratulatory telegrams from Vice President and former Yale baseball player George Bush, and New Jersey Governor Thomas Kean. Big leaguers Cerone and Morris also sent notes.

"I've always been in love with this game," the coach said. "The one regret I had was that my father died before I really got going in coaching. He coached me in Junior PAL and he was the one who taught me to keep a book on mistakes. If I swung at a bad ball and got a hit, he would remind me that I was swinging in the pitcher's zone instead of mine."

Sheppard's father Bill also taught his son an important life lesson. "He told me to never lose your hustle. I took what I learned in baseball and made it a lesson in life. Always do the best you can, don't sit back and expect things to happen. Go out and make them happen."

Never lose your hustle. Four words to describe the Seton Hall baseball program. The motto is repeated constantly by Sheppard who even ends his voice mail greeting with the phrase. "Never lose your hustle is not only physical, it is mental too," Sheppard said describing his core belief. "You can do more things mentally in this great game of baseball than you can do physically. We teach our guys to run to the grass, not to the base. We have a 10-step-rule on tag plays. When the outfielder makes the catch, you are going to run 10 hard steps. That might make the outfielder hurry the throw and blow it. We teach guys to run out the back end, meaning, when you hit a single, don't watch the ball. Get the hell out of the box and run hard, home to first. Some guys might only turn it on if they see they have a chance for a double. But we want you to pressure the outfielder right away and you better be running hard out of the box."

Never lose your hustle has also come to symbolize life after baseball for his players. "Our guys will never quit," Sheppard continued. "Never lose your hustle might mean getting a sale and never taking no for an answer. It means waking up early in the morning and working late into the night. Basically, it is a motto for success. It pumps me up when I hear from my old players and they tell me how happy they were that I taught them to never lose your hustle. So many of them have done so well. They thank me to teaching them how to work hard."

Sheppard grew up in the Vailsburg section of Newark, just a half mile from Seton Hall, with three older brothers. His mother died when he was four and the lack of a female influence was visible at an early age. "It was a tough household," Sheppard said. "There was no woman around to soften things up. We had to rely on mental and physical toughness. I always thought I could settle everything with these [fists]. My father was the kind of guy that you knew he loved you, but if you screwed up you got his left hook."

Sheppard attended all-male Seton Hall Prep, a high school then on the university's campus, where he earned three varsity letters in a Hall of Fame career. He turned down a minor league offer with the Cubs from scout Ralph DiLullo, choosing instead to stay on campus at the University.

"I took a scholarship; it was the first baseball one they offered in a long time," Sheppard said. Sheppard went on to captain the swimming, soccer, and baseball teams, where he caught for Coach Owen Carroll. Carroll had pitched for the Detroit Tigers, New York Yankees, Cincinnati Reds, and the Brooklyn Dodgers.

Following graduation in 1958, Sheppard followed many of his childhood friends into the Marines and rose to the rank of captain. "I learned in the Marines that if you do the little things correctly the big things will follow. You had to pay attention to detail. I also learned about respect. Our platoon sergeant said, 'I don't care if you like me, but you will respect me.'"

Once out of the Marines, Sheppard did not have professional baseball as an option. He had dislocated both shoulders during his college career and his strong arm never regained its early power.

Instead he began his coaching career as an assistant at

Newark's St. Benedict's Prep. He also assisted at nearby Barringer High and Our Lady of the Valley. He got his first head coaching job at Vailsburg High in 1965. Success came quickly that year with a 17-1 mark and a state title.

In 1973, Sheppard took over the Seton Hall coaching reigns from Carroll. "I played football and baseball," Sheppard said. "My coaching style comes from the guys who taught me, tough guys who thought nothing of banging you on the helmet or hitting you in the stomach if you ran the wrong play. I always thought coaches were tough guys who stayed out there in the wind and the cold with you. I always had the feeling that they would never ask you do something that they wouldn't do themselves. That is how I coach. I'll never ask you to do something that I didn't already do. If it is something new it would have to be something that I would still do if the roles were reversed."

The hard-charging Sheppard took his first Seton Hall team to the NCAA District II playoffs with a 22-8 record. By 1987 he had never had a losing season, and had guided Seton Hall to 14 straight postseason tournaments.

Number 15 was just days away. The 1987 Pirates went on the road to Villanova. A combined score of 61-13 gave Seton Hall a three-game sweep and the top-seed in the Big East Tournament. "This is the kind of team that if we score 31 runs one day [as they did against Villanova], we want to go out and score 32 the next," Biggio told Barmakian. "We keep hearing that people on the West Coast and down South are questioning the competition we play. Well, we want to prove everyone wrong. We've set out to make believers out of everybody."

There was no denying they knew about Robinson. He was named the Big East Player of the Year after hitting .545 with 16 homers and 85 RBI during the regular season. "If, indeed, there are three better hitters in college baseball today, their names must be Cobb, Carew and Williams," wrote *Star-Ledger* columnist Jerry Izenberg.

Sheppard earned the league's Coach of the Year Award and Vaughn, who came into the postseason hitting .421 with 26 homers, was the Freshman of the Year. Biggio settled for All-

Conference honors with his .417 average and was joined on the squad by Robinson, Vaughn, Brown, and pitcher Rick Vichroski.

No One Ever Found the Ball

Babe Ruth, Fred Lynn, Jim Rice, and Wade Boggs all played in historic Muzzy Field in Bristol, Connecticut — a 4,900-seat, wooden ballpark built in 1912. Ruth came through on barnstorming trips, while the later Red Sox stars all played their Double-A ball with the Bristol Sox. But by the end of the 1987 Big East Tournament, it was not the past that people were talking about, but the present, primarily Seton Hall freshman Mo Vaughn.

Future major league pitcher Rafael Novoa opened the tournament at Muzzy with 15 strikeouts to lead Villanova past St. John's. An excited crowd waited anxiously for 41-8 Seton Hall to meet 23-15 Connecticut. UConn was having its best season since going to the College World Series a decade earlier. "It was a big game for UConn," pitcher Charles Nagy, a future Cleveland Indians All-Star, said. "We had not been in the tournament in a long time. We had a good team. Seton Hall had the guy who led the country in hitting. They had an unbelievable team. Everyone was looking forward to that game. We knew if we could beat those guys then...

"We had never played a night game before. It was a stadium. It was a lot more people we were used to playing in front of. It was tournament time. It was really exciting and the guys were really excited about it." The game was on live television in New York and New England.

Nagy, the league's Pitcher of the Year as a rookie, struck out Biggio and Vaughn, to the delight of the 1,500 partisan UConn fans, in the first. But Vaughn got major revenge in the third. "It was a high slider," Vaughn said. "I had two strikes on me and I was just trying to go back up the middle."

With two on, Vaughn launched a 1-and-2 Nagy offering deep to right. It was not just another long, long home run where no outfielder moves. It was more than that. Vaughn could only stand and watch. The Big East Rookie of the Year took Nagy deep. Really, really deep. The ball was climbing as it reached the right-field fence, kept going over the huge, majestic pine trees that gave the historic ballpark its intimate feeling, over the light towers and towards the sky. Most assumed Vaughn's 27th homer of the season landed, but no one knew where. Not even television replays could catch its re-entry point. No one ever found the ball.

"Was that a shot or what?" stunned UConn coach Andy Baylock said. "If you're a baseball purist it was pretty. It was high and deep and he hit it off a good man. When he hit it, you almost expected fireworks to go off as the ball sailed higher and higher and then disappeared."

"I remember striking him out the first time and then I threw him the same pitch the next time he came up and that is when he hit the home run," Nagy said of the pitch he called a curve. "I kind of hung it the second time and he crushed it. It was one of those majestic shots. At that park, right field wasn't really that far. And they had these pine trees that were really tall and it was night time and it was pitch-dark. Seeing the white ball going up was something out of the movies, like *The Natural.* He hit it really well and it kept going, going, going and going into the darkness." All Nagy could do was say, "Shit."

With Muzzy Field located just down the road from ESPN's Bristol studios, one Seton Hall alum was showing his Pirate Pride. "A bunch of us came over to Muzzy and we were enjoying a great day of baseball," ESPN broadcaster Bob Ley said. "Someone had smuggled in a six pack of Rolling Rock, the official beverage of choice. It was a nice day in a jewel of a ball park. Mo then hit his blast. I don't think it has landed yet. It was quite possibly the longest home run I had ever seen. It was a masterpiece. It was a Monet."

Word of Vaughn's work quickly spread to nearby New

Britain, Connecticut, where future big leaguers Pete Harnisch and Jeff Bagwell, from Fordham and Hartford, respectively, were playing in the ECAC Tournament. "We're in the middle of our tournament and some scouts and fans came over to our games after going to the UConn-Seton Hall game," said Jay Williams, who was running the ECAC Tournament. "They came up to our press box and couldn't wait to describe what they had just seen." "They were talking about how Mo's home run went over the trees in right field. So many people said it was the longest home run they had ever seen. It was kind of like a big-fish story, because everyone had it longer than the next guy, but when we saw highlights of it, it was awesome."

"I still hear about that home run from my friends and family," Nagy said a dozen years later by phone from the Cleveland Indians clubhouse in Jacobs Field. "They love to get on me about it. It's still talked about in New England."

The Pirates erupted again in game two. They battered Villanova's pitching staff and the Big East recordbooks with 17 hits, five doubles and 29 total bases in an 18-1 romp. The Wildcats then came through the loser's bracket the next day with a win over St. John's and earned a rematch with the Pirates. This time it would not be so easy. The 13th-ranked Pirates trailed 7-5 in the eighth before rallying for a 10-7 win and Seton Hall's first Big East title.

> "It was a nice day in a jewel of a ball park. Mo then hit his blast. I don't think it has landed yet. It was quite possibly the longest home run I had ever seen. It was a masterpiece. It was a Monet."
>
> — Bob Ley, ESPN Broadcaster

"It was a very emotional tournament," Robinson told Barmakian. "I think some of the pressure is off, but we're not satisfied. All this does is make us hungry." Seton Hall knew they would go on the road for the NCAA Tournament. The NCAA had decided there would be a Northeast Regional, but it would be played in Georgia.

"I don't think it is fair to the people of the Northeast, not being able to see their teams play," Sheppard said in a postgame press conference. "I just hope they keep the teams from the

Northeast together." Sheppard also reflected on his team and its chances in the NCAA Tournament. "This team has more power and speed than any team I've had, but we are going to need pitching."

Sheppard did not get his wish to remain near home as the Pirates, now ranked 12th nationally with a 44-8 mark, were assigned to the South I Regional in Huntsville, Alabama, where they would open against the Auburn Tigers. Sixth-ranked Arkansas, 13th-ranked Clemson, West Virginia, and Middle Tennessee State rounded out the regional. Not a local team in the bunch.

Auburn was led by two future major league stars, sophomore stopper Gregg Olsen, who was 10-1 with 10 saves, and freshman first baseman Frank Thomas, who entered the regional with a .353 average, 20 homers, and 59 RBI.

"Being a team from the East, they're going to look down on us," commented Robinson, who was still leading the nation with a .540 average. "Teams from the West and the South don't think we can compete because we're from the East. We'll go in with something to prove. As long as we don't swing at bad pitches, we're going to score some runs. We can hit against anybody."

"I don't think we realized how good they were," Arkansas coach Doug Clark said years later. "When you're playing down here, and you get an Eastern team in your region, I'm not saying you overlook them, but they don't play in the SEC. And yet, being in coaching, you respect them. We've been in regionals where the Eastern teams have played 30-to-40 games and we've played our 60 games. They have to stay inside, they have to fight the elements up there. It takes those guys time to get going."

Because Auburn, the 40-16 SEC runner-up, was the in-state favorite, the media wanted some information about their New Jersey opponent. Word quickly spread about "The Hit Men." By the time the Pirates flew to Atlanta and on to Huntsville, Biggio, Vaughn, and Robinson were celebrities. "When we got off the plane in Alabama, everyone was asking for 'The Hit Men,' " Brogan said. "The writers and photographers all wanted them. It was amazing."

The *Huntsville Times* ran a posed photo of Biggio, Robinson, and Vaughn taken at the airport and ran it alongside Bob Mayes article titled "Hit Men Eye Tiger Contract." "Armed with blazing bats," Mayes wrote, "The Hit Men arrived in Huntsville Tuesday afternoon, looking, gunning for a championship in the NCAA South I Regional that would propel them into the College World Series in Omaha." Mayes quoted *Baseball America* editor Allan Simpson. "They unquestionably have the best 1-2-3 hitting punch in the country in Robinson, Vaughn, and Biggio," Simpson said. "I don't think any team in the country approaches them."

"They scare me to death," Auburn coach Hal Baird told Mayes. "I've never seen a team with the combination of speed and power they have. We have two or three guys who can run and another two or three who can hit with power. But we don't have anyone with the combination they have."

The Pirates entered Thursday's tournament opener with one member of their double-play combination suffering from the flu. John Sheppard was left at the hotel with a 103-degree fever, so Valentin moved over to second, a position he had never played before, and Victor DiPasquale was inserted at short. The Pirates did not miss a beat. After a four-hour rain delay, the Pirates showed Baird why he had cause for concern. Seton Hall erased an early 3-0 deficit to beat the Tigers, 15-6.

The next day, *Huntsville Times* sports editor John Pruett, in a column headlined "The Pirates are Awesome," gave his endorsement. "Those guys from Seton Hall ought to be behind bars. They're armed and should be considered extremely dangerous. This isn't a college baseball team, it's a panzer division. In 52 games, Marteese Robinson had 122 hits in 226 at-bats for a .540 average. Come on, get real. This is roughly comparable to a tailback rushing for 2,500 yards in a single season, or a basketball player averaging 65 points per game. Marteese had a bad day against Auburn. He went only two-for-four, which was 40 points below his average. One of his hits was a 410-foot double that rattled off the green portion of the fence in straightaway center."

Frank Thomas was also impressed. "Those guys know how to swing the bat. I mean, they're good."

The Pirates met Clemson and its star shortstop, another

future major leaguer, Bill Spiers in game two. A three-run, eighth-inning homer gave Clemson a 6-3 lead heading to the ninth. The Pirates loaded the bases for Vaughn. Just as you would expect in the "feel good hit of the summer," Vaughn connected. High and far into the lights. It was headed towards the deepest part of the ballpark. The Pirates stormed out of the dugout to watch and hope. Did it have enough? No. Joe Davis Stadium was built six inches too long. The Pirates deflated.

The next day, the Pirates pitching woes finally surfaced when Auburn plastered four Seton Hall pitchers for eight runs in the sixth. It ended 22-1. The 1987 Pirates were eliminated, season over. They finished 45-10, the best record in school history, but the NCAA Tournament flameout dropped them to 22nd in the final *Collegiate Baseball* poll. Clark's Razorbacks went on to win the regional to advance to the College World Series.

"Auburn let the world in on a secret we've known all season," Sheppard told Barmakian. "We have problems with our pitching. The story for us this year has been our hitting, especially 'The Hit Men,' Marteese Robinson, Maurice Vaughn, and Craig Biggio. We got so many runs early that it made up for our lack of pitching. We just weren't able to do it down here."

Biggio, Vaughn, and Robinson went down as one of the most potent "hearts of the order" in college baseball history. Biggio hit .407 with 14 homers, 68 RBI, and 30 stolen bases. Vaughn set a school *career* record with 28 homers in just his *first* year. He added 90 RBI while hitting .429.

But it was Robinson who stole the show. He became the first Seton Hall player to lead the nation in hitting with a .529 clip, the second-highest average in NCAA history. He finished behind New Mexico's Keith Hagman, who hit .551 in 1980, but ahead of Dave Magadan, who hit .525 as a collegian at Alabama followed by 17 years in the major leagues. Robinson's 126 hits tied him for fourth all-time with Hubie Brooks who played 15 seasons in the big leagues after being drafted out of Arizona State. Robinson also finished second nationally with 90 RBI and third with 56 stolen bases. His .423 career batting average was the 10th best in college history.

GROWING UP

THE NEXT DOUG FLUTIE TURNS TO BASEBALL

Fifty miles east of New York City on the North Shore of Long Island, Craig Biggio took a lead from first. The speedy senior catcher had yet to be thrown out stealing in his career at Kings Park High School. The wind was blowing in from right field on a grey, spring day. Coach John Rottkamp, who was standing in the third base coach's box, gave Biggio the steal sign. Biggio took off with the pitch. Commack South was ready. As the ball approached homeplate, Kenny Manfree, the opposing coach, tapped an aluminum bat on the metal backstop. Biggio heard the "ping," bat hitting ball he thought, as he raced to second.

The Commack South catcher caught the pitch and threw a high pop up to his second baseman who screamed, "I got it. I got it." Biggio slid into second. "I see what is happening and I'm screaming, 'Stay there! Stay there!' But the wind was blowing in my face and Craig couldn't hear me," Rottkamp said. Biggio, thinking he was about to be doubled up on a pop up, sprinted back to first but did not beat the throw from the second baseman. He was tagged out.

"Craig would have been the first guy to ever steal second and first base in the same play," Rottkamp said. "That was the only time he got caught in his career. He wasn't out by much. The coach told him after the game that was the only way they would get him. It only worked because Craig knew baseball and didn't want to get caught in a double play."

Seton Hall assistant coach Ed Blankmeyer was at the game

recruiting Biggio even though the catcher was seriously considering playing football in college, a sport Seton Hall did not offer. Biggio's football career, having been completed no more than six months before, was legendary in Kings Park, a school that usually drew 300 for varsity football games but nearly 2,000 a game during the Biggio era.

Biggio spent his first two-and-a-half varsity seasons as the team's quarterback where the Boston College coaching staff compared him to Doug Flutie. Biggio usually rushed and passed for more than 100 yards each game, but football head coach Doc Holliday knew the youngster was out of position. "We knew Craig was a tailback," Holliday told *Newsday*, "but we didn't have anybody else to put in at quarterback. He was the best athlete on the team and he was willing to sacrifice himself."

Midway through his junior year, Biggio became a running back. In his first outing, he ran for 224 yards, including touchdown runs of 67, 62, and 21 yards. He also threw an 80-yard option pass and caught a 9-yard pass for a touchdown.

In another game, Biggio rushed for 200 yards in the first half before Holliday took him out of the backfield and only let him back in to play defense. "It is hard to tell kids to not score, so I left him in on defense because we had a shutout going," Holliday said. "Well, he intercepts a pass and runs in for a touchdown, then he runs another back off a punt return, then they did score, kicked off and he ran it back for another touchdown."

Once baseball season arrived, Biggio, a catcher/shortstop attracted attention from Major League Scouting Bureau officials Larry Izzo and Bryan Lambe. The two were in town to see Commack South shortstop Tony Pellegrino. They watched visiting Kings Park take infield practice and had a discussion that sounded like a Laurel and Hardy routine.

"Get a card in on that guy," Lambe, the northeast supervisor said.

"I have one," Izzo, an area scout, replied thinking his boss was talking about Pellegrino.

"No, not that guy! That guy!"

"Who are you talking about?"

"The catcher on Kings Park."

"Why? He's only a junior."

"Just look at him, he's an athlete. I don't know if he's gonna catch, I don't know where he's gonna play, but he's an athlete, so get a card on him."

Izzo did as told. Pellegrino, who advanced to the San Diego Padres AAA club after a solid career at St. John's, was Izzo's first report in his role with Major League Scouting. Biggio was his second.

Lambe later explained why he was the first scout to see Biggio's baseball potential. "Most of the time you can tell," he said. "When a scout goes to see a team play, without knowing who the kid is, you can tell when they get off the bus just by the way they carry themselves. He had 'that look.' I thought he could be a catcher like [Thurman] Munson at the time. He didn't have a really strong arm, but he had tremendous quickness, got rid of the ball quickly, and no ball was going to get by him behind home plate. I thought he would eventually shift to second base."

Lambe did not know it, but Biggio idolized Munson and enjoyed the late catcher's aggressive play. But even though Biggio was attracting attention on the diamond, he was still a football guy first. He went on to rush for 1,317 yards on only 154 carries in his senior season and led Suffolk County with 130 points — 14 touchdowns on runs, two on receptions, one each on kickoff and interception returns, 20 kicked extra points, and one two-point conversion. His numbers were so dominant that he won the Hansen Award, the county's version of the Heisman Trophy.

Boston College and Syracuse showed interest in the Long Island star, but Biggio's size hurt him on the recruiting front. "We went to an Awards Night for All-County and there were some recruiters there," Holliday said. "Craig and I walked in and we passed the line coach from Maryland. He said hi to me and then said, 'Nice boots' to Craig. I hadn't noticed, but Craig wore boots to make him taller and the guy noticed it. Craig was 5'10", 170, but he needed to be 6', 190."

His size did not stop him on the baseball diamond where national power Oklahoma State pursued him. Biggio, who had caught as a sophomore and played mostly shortstop as a junior, returned to catch as a senior largely because Rottkamp thought that was where his star would have the best chance for a scholarship.

Biggio, who switched from number 44 in football to number 1 in the spring, belted baseballs all over eastern Long Island. Many of the fields had no fences, so opposing outfielders routinely positioned themselves 350 feet away to track down some of his longer shots. Kings Park was losing a valuable offensive weapon. "I said to my AD that he's got to get me some temporary fencing," Rottkamp said. "The kid is hitting the ball 400 feet and it is an out. It's not fair. So we get one of those orange snow fences and called it 'Biggio's Fence.' Does Biggio hit a homer here? No. Hits them all on the road."

Biggio hit .417 his senior year in Suffolk County's League IV, an impressive stat in a league dominated by pitchers. So deep was the pitching depth that Biggio's future Houston Astros teammate Pete Harnisch, who called Biggio the best high school football player he has ever seen, was only the *third* pitcher for county champion Commack North. Biggio shared the league MVP award but missed out on the Carl Yastrzemski Award as Suffolk County's top player, losing in a narrow vote to East Islip first baseman Ron Witmeyer.

> "When a scout goes to see a team play, without knowing who the kid is, you can tell when they get off the bus just by the way they carry themselves."
> — Bryan Lambe, Major League Scouting Bureau

Pro ball, at this point, was not an option for Biggio. Detroit Tigers scout Ralph DiLullo, the same scout who Seton Hall coach Mike Sheppard turned down years earlier, had visited the Biggio family to determine if the youngster would sign out of high school if drafted. After a lengthy discussion, DiLullo advised Biggio to go to college largely because if he was drafted the signing dollars would never match the cost of college tuition.

Meanwhile, Biggio's football coaches worked feverishly to get him a scholarship to play college football. The campaign worked. Boston University offered Biggio a scholarship to play defensive back, and the two football coaches raced over to the Biggio house to share the news.

But when they got there, Biggio had some news of his own to tell. "We were so excited to tell him about BU, but when we did he said he wanted to go to Seton Hall and play baseball," Holliday said. "I wanted to kill him. I couldn't believe it. My reaction was, 'Are you stupid or something?' He had done a deal with Seton Hall before we did ours with BU. We didn't even have a chance to get him officially accepted."

Biggio's father Lee was thrilled his son would be a catcher at the next level. The elder Biggio caught at Butler [New Jersey] High School but dreams of a big league career were halted by a stint in the Air Force during the Korean War. "Craig liked to catch," Lee Biggio said. "He liked to be involved. I always told him catcher was the easiest route to the major leagues, but I never imagined he would do it."

"My dad is an awesome dad," Biggio said years later. "Whenever we wanted to play ball, or whenever we wanted to do anything, when he had the time in his schedule, he would do it. He was the bread winner. He'd work 7 AM-to-3 PM, 3-11 PM or the midnight shift. He would never say anything. If we said, 'Hey dad, you want to go hit some ground balls to us?' He would just say, 'Okay, let's do it.' He was a hard disciplinarian. His big thing in life was respect and values. That is one of the things that stays with me today. I'm who I am today because of the respect and values he made sure I had."

His dad also allowed him to compete against older competition. Lee Biggio, who worked at the Federal Aviation Association's ATC Center at Ronkonkoma, New York, approached colleague Marty Hasenfuss, who coached a successful Connie Mack League team, and asked if his 14-year-old son could try out for the 15-18 year-old's league. "At first, given his age and size — he was kind of small — I didn't know for sure. But his foot speed, quickness and agility really impressed me. I had coached since 1960 and had never had anyone that quick. I just loved everything about the kid. I told his dad that I would keep him as the 19th or 20th kid. It certainly paid off."

Biggio spent the summers playing for Hasenfuss, but in 1984 moved to another team while his coach took the summer off. Just days before he was set to leave for Seton Hall on a partial scholarship, Biggio, who normally caught or played shortstop, switched to second base for a makeup game because the regular second baseman could not attend. To Biggio's right stood 18-year-old Adriano Martinez. Clouds rolled in, and in a split second, the makeup game turned into a deadly tragedy. "It was like a nuclear bomb hit," Biggio remembered. "Boom! We were standing there and the next thing I knew I was on the ground. I said to myself, 'Wow, I was just hit by lightning.' I had a burning sensation in the back of my legs and in my back. It hit the field and knocked everybody down, all of us except the left fielder and he saw the whole thing. When I woke up, I was in a fetal position on the ground. I looked over and my buddy was hit. He was laid out at shortstop. We all ran over to him and…"

Kings Park High School assistant coach John Bogenshutz happened to be there. "The bolt came down and evidently hit the backstop and everyone was wearing rubber cleats because they had just started switching over to rubber cleats in high school, and the kid at short was the only kid wearing metal cleats. It went under the ground and got him. It killed him."

The tragedy shocked Biggio. "Craig was going more and more into himself," his mother Johnna said. "You could just see what it was doing to Craig. He had just run to this boy who had been hit by lightning. Smoke was coming out of his chest and his sneakers were burned off his feet. This is the picture Craig had in his mind. I knew it was bothering Craig."

"My mom was there all the time to give us support," Biggio said. "She was always there for us." But like any good mom, she knew when she needed help. After talking it over with her husband, she asked neighbor Charlie Alben if he might help them ease their son's pain over the lightning tragedy. Alben was happy to return a favor.

Long before Biggio became one of Major League Baseball's most community-minded players with a soft spot in his heart for children with cancer, he was a 14-year-old boy when leukemia claimed the life of his eight-year-old neighbor Chris Alben.

"Chris was six when he was diagnosed with leukemia and Craig was just starting high school and was arguably one of the best athletes on Long Island," Charlie Alben said. "At that age when you are in your early teens and you're first starting to get some notoriety, some success, you can become pretty self-centered, but Craig was over my house so many times to spend time with my son Chris. Craig was no more than a kid himself, which impressed my wife and me so much. He would just come over the house and spend time with Chris. We knew adults who didn't do this."

Chris died the day after his brother Chuck's sixth birthday. Biggio was determined to make certain Chuck did not grow up without an older brother.

"They are just a great family," Biggio said years later. "They are such a strong family. Charlie was awesome. He was the glue. His wife Pat is tremendous. Chuck is one of the greatest kids you are ever going to meet." When asked why at the young age of 14 he got heavily involved in Chuck's life, Biggio was a bit uncertain. "I didn't have to do anything," the Alben's former paper boy said. "We all make our choices. Friends are friends and you are there for them."

Even Biggio's own family was impressed by the efforts of their son. "He loved Chuck at an early age," Lee Biggio said. "He would take him over to the fields and play together, even before Chris died. That was a really awful moment. We were very close to the family. Craig really took care of Chuck after that. They lived right down the block from us and, for some reason, Craig just wanted to take care of him."

As time went on, the youngest Biggio wanted to do even more for the Albens, but he kept his idea to himself. It was the night of the Hansen Award banquet when Biggio approached the podium to accept the one of Long Island's top athletic prizes. He calmly took out a page of notes and announced he was happy to accept the award in the name of his friend, Chris Alben. "He was not a public speaker at all, but he wanted to do it," Charlie Alben said about Biggio. "He got up to the podium and accepted the award in Chris' name and said some really nice things about Chris and courage. It was obviously a very difficult thing for Craig to do, but he did it. His mom and dad told us that it was Craig's idea, he came up with at 18 years old."

"My proudest moment as Craig's dad was when he won the Hansen Award," Lee Biggio said prior to his son's 14th season in the major leagues. "That was a great thrill. He accepted it for Chris on his own. I didn't even know he had a speech prepared. He surprised me too."

The Biggio and Alben families, along with countless others, shared the emotional moment with a standing ovation for Craig Biggio. Ten-year-old Chuck Alben stood and watched in amazement. "I was too young to even realize anything. He was just an older guy that I could look up to. He was a great athlete and I loved sports. He was always over the house and I just looked up to him. He was my idol, but I was so blind to actually who he was. I always knew he was a special person, he was going to go somewhere, but even to this day watching him on TV, I don't see the dollar signs and Gold Gloves. I just see this guy who is an outstanding human being."

A Fire Sent Him to Baseball

America had not seen anything like it before. January 23-30, 1977. It was a made-for-TV miniseries like no other before it. The year before, ABC had televised, to moderate success, *Rich Man, Poor Man*, one of the first miniseries on network television. Alex Haley's *Roots* was next and it was a mega-hit. Running on eight consecutive nights, the adaptation of Haley's best-selling book attracted 130 million viewers, numbers unheard of for television movies.

Ten-year-old Marteese Robinson was one of those viewers. He was fascinated as he watched Haley's family tree grow on television from Kunta Kinte's hardships as a slave to Chicken George in the Civil War. The kid living in Newark, New Jersey, was mesmerized by the roots of a fellow African-American dating back to ancestors in Africa. He could not wait for the third installment and wanted the black and white television in his room to be closer to his bed. So he added an extension cord and moved the TV closer. He unknowingly made a mistake. The night before, his mother had noticed that same extension cord, attached to another appliance, was hot. She unplugged it and tossed it aside, never thinking her son would find it the following day.

Robinson decided *Roots* was too important to watch in black and white. He dragged his mattress off his bed and pulled it into his mother's room where the color TV was. "It was the only time I ever did that," Robinson said. "My mom was such a sound sleeper, so normally I just would lay down at the end of the bed and watch TV, but it was *Roots* so I wanted to be really comfortable." He fell asleep while watching. Next thing he knew his younger sister Shaquier was screaming for him to get up. The apartment at 19th Street and Springfield Avenue was filled with smoke. His room, luckily vacated for a better television experience, was on fire.

"I went and got my sister Shalonda and we got out," Robinson said. "I had to go back and get my mom because she was kind of overcome by the smoke and was trying to put out the fire, but I screamed at my mom, 'No, you can't put it out!' It was freezing outside. There was snow on the ground and all I had on was underwear, boxers, that was it. The saying, 'All we had was the shirts on our back,' that was us. There were three other families in the building. They suffered mostly water damage, but our house was destroyed."

A house destroyed? Yes. A life destroyed? No. "Even at that age I was not worried what my life would be like now that our house was gone. I just looked at it as another challenge to overcome." He had already overcome a big one, surviving the rugged streets of his neighborhood without the benefit of a two-parent home.

Born to 15 $^1/_2$-year-old Wayne Naylor and 15-year-old Betty Jean Robinson, Marteese was the oldest in a family that was not the All-American ideal. His mom gave birth to his sisters, each with a different father. Marteese's father sired four other children, two daughters and two sons, with different women before settling down with Deborah Love, whom he eventually married. The couple had two sons, Keith and Shawn.

Although Marteese's birth was the result of a spontaneous moment between teenagers, Wayne and Betty Jean made an adult decision. Marteese would be raised by his mother, with help from her mother, Katie Lee Campbell, and her grandmother, Bessie Mae Robinson. Naylor would not be shunned; he would be a part of his son's life. "It was a cordial relationship," Naylor said. "It had to be that way because of my son. I couldn't be there every day. I was trying to grow up; she was trying to grow up. We made a baby and we had to take responsibility. She was living one place, I was living in another. We were too young to not live with our own families."

Naylor, who also grew up in a one-parent home, was determined to be a part of Marteese's life. He visited twice a week, learning the father role on the fly. "When I would go by, I'd spend some time with him," Naylor said. "Any time I wanted to I could go by. I was basically a kid trying to understand the responsibility I had. Once I learned what was expected and what was needed, communicating with him was not a problem."

Still, it was the trio of women who guided young Marteese Robinson. His great-grandmother made certain the men in the family, Marteese's uncles, would watch over the young boy, take him places and play games with him. "Living in Newark there was always the possibility of Marteese getting in trouble," one of those uncles, Bobby Campbell, said. "But he was smart enough to know right from wrong. He just stayed ahead of it. We taught him to take care of himself. We were never really worried about him."

"I knew at a young age that I did have some athletic abilities and my Uncle Bobby got that athleticism out of me. I watched him play high school basketball and football. I watched him do those things and I wanted to do it. Because of him I got interested in sports." Campbell had role model written all over him. A gifted student, he was also a star football and basketball player at suburban Wardlaw Hartridge Prep in Edison, New Jersey.

Campbell often took his nephew to his family's home in Metuchen, New Jersey, a tree-lined, suburban town. "The standard of life was night and day," Campbell said of Newark vs. Metuchen. "Seeing the atmosphere at my school, seeing a different world, was an important part of his life. He would tell my friends that someday, you watch, they would see him be something special. You could see the light in his eyes. He got a glimpse of how things could be different."

The fire forced Robinson, along with his mom and sisters, to move in with his grandmother and great grandmother in the Ivy Hill Apartments in Vailsburg, a plusher section of Newark. The move put baseball in his life.

When the weather turned warmer, Robinson became curious about the group of kids his age, fifth and sixth graders, who gathered each day on the baseball field in nearby Ivy Hill Park. Never a shy kid, Robinson ventured to the field and said he wanted to play. "I told them I had played," Robinson said. "I lied. I didn't even have a glove. That first day I had to borrow a glove, but they didn't pay any attention to that because they figured I kind of wandered over to them."

"Marteese just showed up," said John Sheppard, one of the Ivy Hill "gang." "He walked down to the field. We were choosing teams and he said he played ball. We chose teams and obviously he was the last guy picked because nobody knew who the heck he was. He ended up on my team. That was the only time we didn't know him. From that point on, he was certainly one of the better players." Since Robinson had told the other kids he had played baseball before, he knew he could not return without a mitt. He made a call and ended up with his cousin Raymond's old one.

> "He would tell my friends that someday, you watch, they would see him be something special. You could see the light in his eyes. He got a glimpse of how things could be different."
> — Bobby Campbell, Marteese Robinson's uncle

Sheppard, a baseball junkie who happened to be the Seton Hall coach's second-youngest son, was impressed with the new kid's talent, but he needed more convincing. "He could play," John Sheppard said. "But I didn't know his dedication to the sport. He could just be a great player, but only play when he could. We went out the next day and he showed up. He became one of the gang. He and I got to be really good friends. I finally found somebody who loved the game as much as I did."

A friendship was born. A black kid and a white kid. Baseball was their bond. "I guess the trips to Metuchen I made with my uncle taught me that skin color did not matter," Robinson said. "My uncle had a lot of white friends and I got to know them, so I never paid any attention to John being white."

Eventually the two boys took the friendship home. "I guess five kids were not enough for the Sheppards, because they welcomed me with open arms," Robinson said. Open arms and an open refrigerator. "We would leave the side door open for him," John Sheppard said. "We had a front gate and no one would walk through the gate because our dog was out there. But Pepper knew Marteese. I would wake up in the morning at about 8 and go downstairs and Marteese would be sitting at the kitchen table eating breakfast."

As Robinson and Sheppard reached high school, it was time to part ways. Sheppard headed to Seton Hall Prep, a private school on the university's campus, and Robinson went to Vailsburg, the area's public high school. They both played baseball, but at different levels. Seton Hall Prep had a rich baseball tradition, while Vailsburg was part of Newark's City League, a hotbed of basketball and football talent. "He was one of the best players my age I had ever seen and he was in a league where no one would see him," Sheppard said. "And if they did see him, they would say, 'This is the City League, so of course he's good.'"

In the summer after their sophomore year, the boys began talking about Marteese going to Seton Hall Prep. "I knew he wanted to go there because he said it several times to me and he said it to my mother," John Sheppard said. "I always thought that would be a terrific place for him. He would be playing with better competition. I had a lot to gain from it. I would have my best friend at the school. I told my old man, 'Marteese shouldn't be going to Vailsburg. He should be going to this school. He wants to go.' I didn't know the financial aspect of it, but I pushed the old man a little bit and he realized overall it would be better for Marteese."

The Robinsons did not have the money for Marteese to attend the school, but Mike Sheppard had an idea. "I just felt sorry for him that he couldn't be with John," the Seton Hall coach said. "One night I was talking to [my wife] Phyllis and I said, 'We've got two kids [Michael Jr. and John] being taken care of with scholarships at the Prep, and we'll get help on another one. Let's see if we could work something out for Marteese. A bunch of us got together and came up with the money for him to go to the Prep."

Sheppard may have committed an NCAA violation because he was paying for a potential recruit to attend a private school. "Was it a violation for us to pay?" Sheppard asked himself years later. "I don't think so because Marteese was part of our family.

Who the hell was I? I was a teacher, the baseball coach at Seton Hall. I didn't have a lot of money. What I did for him was family. It had nothing to do with baseball."

When spring came, Sheppard and Robinson became a double play combination, John at shortstop and his buddy at second. By the time the two were seniors, Sheppard had the bigger reputation. He was named an All-American by *Baseball America* and was All-State in the Newark *Star-Ledger*. He signed with North Carolina where he would play with future big leaguers Walt Weiss and B.J. Surhoff. Meanwhile, Robinson was All-County and earned looks from Old Dominion and Kentucky. Seton Hall was interested but head coach Sheppard did not want to pressure him.

"I was interested in Marteese, but I wasn't that hot-to-trot on him," Sheppard said. "We were in the background and I think he wanted to go away. We would take him, but we didn't need a second baseman." Robinson then suffered a serious shoulder injury in an American Legion game and interest in him waned.

"The other schools kind of backed off him when he had the injury, so I told him, 'Why don't you come to Seton Hall,' " Mike Sheppard said. "You can hit, you can run, you can't throw, so we'll put you at first base and make you a first baseman. He wasn't sure. He said, 'How am I going to do that without throwing?' I said, 'Every time you get a ball, the pitcher would come over like he was covering first base and you would just hand him the ball and he would protect against other runners advancing.' " Without a choice, Robinson agreed. He accepted a partial scholarship and signed with Seton Hall.

Betty Robinson was thrilled her son was staying home, but even more excited he had the opportunity to go to college. "It would have been hard without the baseball for him to get to go to college," she said. "I was working two jobs trying to take care of him and his sisters. I was hoping he would get some sort of scholarship because I couldn't pay for college myself. I am so glad Mike Sheppard helped him out so much."

A Pull Hitter Because of the Right Field Dogs

Wrigley Field has its ivy. Yankee Stadium has its facade and monuments. Franco Field has its highway. The New Jersey Turnpike was an imposing structure. One of America's great toll roads stood high above, casting its shadow on the high school ballfield below. It would be a picturesque site if you were into huge slabs of concrete support beams, cars, trucks, horns, and traffic.

To John Valentin this was a picture-perfect setting. Jersey City was his home and Franco Field was the home of the St. Anthony High School Friars. He was small during his senior year, 5'10", 140 pounds, but his good glove gave him star power. Actually, he was a star with no power. The future major leaguer had yet to hit a high school home run and it was midway through his senior year.

The highway appeared closer than it was. The kids all thought they could jack one onto the eastbound lane and cause havoc up there. But the powerless Valentin could not even think of screwing up traffic as he settled into the batter's box.

He took a fastball; he only hit fastballs, and pulled it down the left field line. If it stayed fair, Valentin would call himself a power hitter. It did. Barely. "It is 260-270 feet down the line and it didn't make it over the fence by much," St. Anthony coach Mike Hogan remembered, laughing.

"I only hit one home run in high school," Valentin said. "It barely went over at Franco Field. When you hit your first home run as a kid it really stands out. It was a ball that I pulled. I connected one time. It was finally over. I didn't have to worry about it anymore. I was more of a defensive player. I wasn't an offensive player. I didn't strike out a lot. I batted first, second, eighth, or ninth. I pitched. I played short."

Playing sports was Valentin's passion ever since arriving in Jersey City from Mineola, New York, where he and older brother Arnold Jr. were born to Arnold Sr. and Davina Valentin. They moved to the housing project of Holland Gardens on 16th Street, just blocks from the Holland Tunnel. It was an environment only a kid could love.

"We had about eight to ten boys that we grew up with and we had a courtyard area in the back of the projects," Arnold said. "We had baseball games there all the time. Every day. At least two games a day. I think one of the reasons why we were all good athletes was because we played all the time."

Even though he was small, John carried the weight of an entire New York City borough on his tiny shoulders. "Being in New York I was a Yankees fan, even though my favorite player was Dave Concepcion on the Reds," John said. "My brother was a Mets fan and my family was a Mets family. I went with the team that was winning. The Yankees were always winning." So day in and day out, John battled Arnold in the Jersey City version of the Subway Series.

"We would go through the batting orders of each team, batting lefty and righty," Arnold said. "We had numerous games all day. Of course on the blacktop there were always cracks so we would learn how to anticipate groundballs from the hops. John was just very talented from the beginning."

The two boys also played in baseball games across the street from Holland Gardens on a field that would define John's hitting style. Right field was off limits. "There were houses in right field and they all had fences in the backyard," John said. "If we hit the ball in there it was three outs because there were dogs out there and you couldn't get the ball back. That's basically how I became a pull hitter. I never hit the ball there. Some of my friends, when they got tired of playing, they would hit it there, but I never did."

All of the sports action kept the Valentin boys from getting into trouble. Jersey City was rough. Crime was everywhere and, just like any inner city, trouble was always just around the corner.

"We had no choice but to go in a straight line," Arnold said. "With my parents it was school and sports and there was really nothing in between."

Arnold Valentin Sr. was a truck driver for Goya Foods. He worked long hours and the boys rarely saw him, but his goal was to provide for his family. "He made a lot of money for a truck driver," John said. Once the boys were older, his mother worked different jobs in Jersey City, including assembly line shifts and sewing dolls. Arnold Sr. and Davina demanded hard work in school and wanted the boys in the best schools possible. They enrolled Arnold, and then John, in St. Michael's High School, a couple of blocks away. Again they gravitated to sports and little brother began to gain recognition. The defensive wizard gained All-County mentions his first year.

"John came along two years after I got there and practically stole the show," Arnold said. "He was very small, but was a great, great shortstop. He had a good arm and a great, great glove. The fielding came naturally. The kid was born with it."

> "There were houses in right field and they all had fences in the backyard," John said. "If we hit the ball in there it was three outs because there were dogs out there and you couldn't get the ball back. That's basically how I became a pull hitter."
> — John Valentin

Had it not been for the almighty dollar, John may have become the greatest player in St. Michael's history. The financially-strapped Archdiocese was approached by developers midway through Arnold's senior year, John's sophomore year. They wanted the property to turn St. Michael's into condominiums. The offer was too good to refuse and St. Michael's closed. John headed to St. Anthony while his brother enrolled at Seton Hall University.

Before Coach Mike Hogan would get John on the baseball diamond, Bob Hurley Sr. had him on the hardwood where John joined the tradition-rich St. Anthony basketball program. St. Anthony had won two national titles and 20 state titles under Hurley Sr., while producing NBA players Bobby Hurley Jr., Terry Dehere, Roshown McLeod, and Roderick Rhodes. But before they took the mantle in the late '80s and '90s, it was the David Rivers and Kenny Wilson era. John Valentin was their backup at guard. He played sparingly while Rivers and Wilson earned scholarships to Notre Dame and Villanova, respectively, as the Friars finished 27-2 and won the 1984 state championship.

"John was always smaller than everyone else he played against, but he was tough as nails," Bob Hurley Sr. said. "I always thought that if he ever grew he would be a heck of a player because he knew how to play. He was just so small — 5' 8", 130."

After basketball, Valentin joined the baseball team where he played behind freshman pitching sensation Willie Banks, who also went on to play in the major leagues. After his junior season, Valentin joined Banks at Old Dominion's "Be The Best You Are" summer baseball camp run by Mark Newman, now an executive with the New York Yankees. James Madison University coach Brad Babcock saw Valentin at the camp and suggested he would recruit the skinny shortstop if he grew. That interest waned as Valentin knew it would. "I never thought going there was a possibility," he said.

Valentin returned for his senior year ready to compete for playing time in basketball, but a knee injury forced him to miss the season. Rather than hit the streets after school, Valentin rehabbed at basketball practice then went to baseball practice. Hogan credited that dedication to Valentin's parents. "His parents were always very supportive, very demanding as far as they didn't let him get away with anything. They saw other kids out there and saw what happened. Play baseball, fine. Play basketball, fine. But not hang out. His parents were tough, believe me. His father liked baseball and would give John anything he wanted, a glove, anything, but don't mess up in school. If he brought home bad grades, he wouldn't have played."

With a strengthened knee for baseball season, Valentin went on to became a productive hitter, shortstop, and part-time pitcher. Hogan's club finished 20-5 and advanced to the state tournament. Valentin's slick fielding and .325 average had Hogan's friend, Jersey City State College coach Larry Babich, intrigued.

"John was really a small kid, a good defensive shortstop," Babich said. "We were the only ones interested, but I knew he could field. John said, 'Thank you, but I want to go to Seton Hall. If I make the team, I make the team.' "

"My brother and I were very, very close. We were inseparable, we were best friends and the reason he came to Seton Hall University was because of me," Arnold said. "I had already completed two years at the university and it was majestic compared to where we had come from. The people were warm. The professors were great. It was a great atmosphere."

In the winter of his senior year, on a visit to see his brother, John Valentin staked claim to the Seton Hall shortstop position when the Valentin boys walked to Owen T. Carroll Field. John instinctively went to the left side of the infield and toed the frozen infield. "He wrote his name in the dirt," Arnold said. "And he said, 'This is going to be my home. This is mine. This is where I'm gonna be.' " But when spring came Seton Hall assistant coach Ed Blankmeyer was not so certain.

Blankmeyer was interested in a pitcher at Hudson Catholic and planned to see him throw against Banks and St. Anthony. White Sox scout Ed Ford convinced Blankmeyer to take a look at Valentin while he was there. "He was playing shortstop," Blankmeyer said, "and I looked at him and said, 'The kid needed to get stronger. Right now I project him as a second baseman, but if he gets stronger maybe he can play the left side of the infield.' John played with a lot of fire. He was more of a smooth and look-good type of guy."

Looking good and being good were two different things. Valentin was not All-State, was not even All-Parochial. He did make All-County, but big time schools like Seton Hall wanted players with more prestige. Blankmeyer said Valentin could come to Seton Hall, attend tryout camp, and see if he could make the team.

The youngster agreed, knowing it would be school first and baseball second. Arnold Valentin Sr. wanted his sons to be the first in the family to get college educations. "I had to worry about an education and getting a job," John said, realizing a baseball career was probably impossible.

Still, he wanted to make the team. "I was concerned," John said. "That was the year John Sheppard came back from North

Carolina and he was a shortstop in high school. Biggio was a catcher and I thought he wanted to go back to the infield. They had Joe Armeni who was the captain and the returning shortstop. How was I going to replace him?"

More than 50 kids attended the open tryouts in chilly weather before the fall baseball season began. They were divided into groups — hitting, fielding and throwing. During the fielding drills Valentin put on a show. He caught ball after ball. Made play after play. The balls kept coming, harder and harder. Further to the left, further to the right. Armeni noticed Valentin working wonders at his position and turned to volunteer assistant coach Fred Hopke. "Who is that kid at short?" Armeni asked. "He's gonna steal my job!"

Valentin made the Seton Hall Pirates. He was put on the JV team and performed well in a scrimmage against the varsity. After the game, Blankmeyer told Valentin that Armeni needed to rest a sore elbow, so Valentin would play for the varsity for the remainder of the fall season.

"I did really well," Valentin said. "They put me at shortstop and put John Sheppard at second base. That is when we became a tandem. We really played well together and they left us alone. They put Joe Armeni as DH and I hit ninth. That was the beginning of me playing every day."

BASEBALL WAS HIS FIRST LOVE

CHAPTER 6

He was just a 10-year-old kid. Of course, he was bigger than the other 10-year-old kids, but he was still just a kid. He was not Mo yet. He was still Maurice. But he could hit. He tore up Norwalk, Connecticut's, version of Little League to the tune of four singles and 32 home runs.

"I knew that Maurice could hit," Leroy Vaughn said about his only son. "He hit home runs all throughout Little League. I never realized his statistics until the end of the year at the banquet. They announced he had 36 hits and 32 of them were home runs. There was a little house, one of those portable houses in the school yard, and he would pepper the top of that house."

Leroy Vaughn liked baseball, but football was his first love. He had played quarterback collegiately at Virginia Union and then made the Baltimore Colts before a knee injury put him on the taxi-squad and effectively ended his chance at an NFL career. He later remained involved in the game as the head coach at Brien McMahon High School in Norwalk, the town where he and his wife Shirley were both teachers.

It was a common sight to see young Maurice wearing an oversized football jersey, marching up and down the sidelines with his father, the coach. "He always had to participate," oldest sister Catherine said about her brother. "He would try to tell the guys what to do. My dad let Maurice walk around with the whistle in his mouth when the kids were doing their exercises. Every time Maurice blew the whistle, they had to hit the ground and do a pushup. He was blowing, blowing, blowing. He didn't even give them time to get up. He was just blowing, blowing, blowing." The players got even with their taskmaster after practice. When Coach Vaughn visited his office, he heard tremendous laughter coming from the locker room and went to take a look at what his players thought was so funny. He too could not help but crack a smile as he saw his son, fully clothed, soaked, but still enjoying the shower treatment the team was giving him.

Following in his father's footsteps was something that Maurice enjoyed. Before he learned to do it at football practice, he learned it at church. The Vaughns were one of the first African-American families to attend The First Congregational Church on the Green in Norwalk and Reverend Henry Yourdon hoped to attract more. The Reverend watched kindergarten-aged Maurice attend Sunday service rather than Sunday school just so he could help his father, an usher, pass the donation plate. The father-son act was okay to the parish leader, but he started to worry when Leroy Vaughn was elected a Deacon. "In our church, the Deacons carry the eucharist elements to the people," Reverend Yourdon said. "Lo and behold, there was Maurice with his dad. Vaughn [Leroy's nickname] passes the bread to Maurice and Maurice passes it in. I saw an old Deacon sitting in the back and he just about busted three old ladies' legs storming out of the church. I said, 'Man oh man, here I am trying to get an integrated church and here comes Maurice messing the whole thing up.' "

To the older Deacons the holiest part of the service was no place for a child. It caused a minor controversy, but Leroy Vaughn solved the problem by removing himself from the pulpit. "Whew, saved the day right there!" Reverend Yourdon said. "He went on and became Chairman of the Board of Deacons."

His son also had aspirations to reach the top. "I remember one day he came home and asked me, 'What sport should I concentrate on?' " Catherine said. "He was trying to make a decision. He played all of the sports, but he really wanted to excel in one." Her brother kept going back-and-forth between football and baseball. Finally, Catherine said, 'Meece,' then you could do both.'

Shirley Vaughn, who had taught her son to hit lefty as a three-year-old despite his natural right-handedness, later realized baseball was her son's true passion. During high school summers, she watched him turn down job offers if they required afternoon hours. He wanted to work in the mornings and play baseball in the afternoons. Instead of all-day office work or jobs that required hammering nails or climbing ladders where he might get hurt, her son instead worked maintenance at a nearby grocery store, worked on a garbage truck, and the road-paving crew.

"People would tell me I should remind him that only a very few of those who play baseball would be chosen, so I should prepare him for something else," Shirley Vaughn said. "But I never even thought about it. I figured anyone who wanted to play ball could play ball. He loved public speaking, he loved debating, so I just assumed he would teach or do public relations. I never said, 'Don't play baseball' because we were making sure he was playing baseball. If Maurice was playing with a team and he needed to work on something, the next day we worked on it. Not because we wanted him in the major leagues, but because he just wanted to work on it."

"We are like a team," she said. "I assume that all families are like us." They liked to share their good fortune with others. Each Christmas morning the family would prepare meals and head to a Norwalk homeless shelter to serve them. Caring for others was a lesson Maurice Vaughn never forgot. There were more lessons.

Leroy Vaughn had caught eight-year-old Maurice and a cousin smoking cigarettes. Mom and Dad were furious, but rather than scream at their son, they decided to teach him a lesson. Leroy Vaughn headed to the store and bought two big cans of Colt 45 beer and two oversized cigars. He came home and took the beer and cigars to Maurice's room. He handed his young son one of each and told him, since Maurice was smoking now, they could have their first man-to-man talk.

"He said okay," Leroy Vaughn said of that night. "He lit up the cigar and was smoking and drinking. It didn't bother him. Those things always made me sick. So I'm getting sick and I decided to leave. I told my wife that I'm getting ready to be sick and she said, 'You get back in there and teach him a lesson.' I went back in there and told Maurice that the only way you are going to enjoy that cigar is that you have to inhale it, swallow it, and blow it out your nose. He did that, turned three colors, throwing up all over the place. He did it just before I did. As far as I know, he never smoked cigarettes after that."

Maurice Vaughn also learned about responsibility from his parents. After his parents brought home a new 10-speed bicycle for him, the youngster took it out for a test drive. An hour later the phone rang. It was Maurice calling to tell them the bike had been stolen after Maurice asked another kid to watch it while he went into a grocery store. "I picked him up and we drove him around looking for the bike," Leroy Vaughn said. "I saw people I knew, so I called them over. 'You get the word out that my son's bike' ... and I told them the story. Maurice said, upset that his father was blaming others, 'Daddy leave them alone, they didn't do it. It was my fault.' I said, 'Okay.' He knew it was his fault for trusting a kid he did not know. Two days later we bought him another one because he had learned a valuable lesson."

Maurice Vaughn attended New Canaan Country School during his middle school years and wanted to attend Brien McMahon High School where his father coached. But because he was not in the school's district and Norwalk High School was too large, the Vaughns felt private school would be a better option and settled on the Trinity-Pawling School in Pawling, New York, 50 miles west of Norwalk. "Maurice brought his Mickey Mouse sheets and lamp from home and the other students made fun of him," Shirley Vaughn said. "But Maurice told them, 'The man makes the sheets. The sheets don't make the man.' The next year, all the kids had Mickey Mouse sheets."

As a freshman, Vaughn was not able to practice with the football team until classes started. When they did, the coaches knew they had a prize. "He was very quiet in the beginning, the first couple of days, but he quickly got used to the school and was very vociferous after that," football coach Dave Coratti said.

The 6'1", 190-pound Vaughn was inserted as the starting tailback and strong safety for an awful team that scored just two touchdowns all year, one by the freshman on a 50-yard interception return against Avon Old Farms. "His first two years, we weren't very good, so he took his lumps," Coratti said. "I would say he was a better defensive player at strong safety, although he was basically an outside linebacker. He was very tough on defense."

In basketball, Trinity-Pawling Athletic Director and basketball coach Miles Hubbard Jr. had Vaughn at guard. It was during basketball that Maurice Vaughn became Mo Vaughn. "I gave him the name Mo," Hubbard said. "I talked pretty loud and pretty fast. One day I was after him for screwing up, so it kept coming up, 'Mo, Mo, Mo.' I could never get through the whole name Maurice. The kids picked it up and it stuck."

Once it was baseball season, Mo Vaughn played second base for Coratti. "He was quite good in baseball right away," the coach said. "He played very well. He could hit. He didn't hit for as much power his first year as he did when he was a sophomore, junior, and senior. But he was a contact hitter. Right away, he made an impact in baseball."

The three-sport star, who had once asked his sister which sport he should play as a pro, whittled his favorite to one. "The sport he always wanted to play, and he told me time and time again, was baseball," Hubbard said. "I said, 'That's great Mo, but you've still got to go to college and study.' His sophomore year he told me he was going to be a professional baseball player. I didn't think that much about it because a lot of kids tell that to you, but how often does it come true. Right from the beginning, baseball was the number-one sport. He never wavered."

And he got better and better at it. Coratti moved Vaughn to shortstop for his final three years of high school and watched him develop defensively. He also let the strong-armed kid pitch. "He would come in relief," Coratti said. "He could throw the ball really hard, but sometimes he got a little bit wild."

Offensively, Vaughn also scared Coratti, especially in pregame drills. "I pitched batting practice," the coach said. "In the beginning I was pitching basically naked with no screen. I was pretty nervous that he would hit one right back at me because he hit it so hard. But fortunately, when I complained enough to Miles that I didn't have the pitching screen, he went out and bought me one for next year."

Vaughn amazed his baseball coach with his dedication to the sport. Night after night, before or after study hall, Vaughn went to the tennis courts with an orange cone, his bat, and baseballs. Vaughn would place the ball on the top of the cone and hit hundreds of balls into the fence. He did this drill religiously, even during football and basketball season. If it were cold, he simply bundled up and went to work. "He told me we would see him in the major leagues and I didn't disagree with him either," Coratti said. "A lot of kids will say that, but he was very unusual. He was dedicated to furthering himself in baseball and preparing to play at the next level and the next level after that, yet still put everything he had into playing football and basketball."

As a senior, he was a leader in the school, on and off the field. He was one of six Prefects [school leaders], elected by the student body of 300, faculty and administration. "There was always more to Mo than being strictly an athlete," Hubbard said in summer 2000. "He liked to help the underdog kid."

Vaughn ended his high school baseball career with a .450 batting average and more than 24 home runs, although no one really kept accurate records. He would have hit even more home runs, but the fencing at Trinity-Pawling came a year too late. He made the All-Founders League team, the conference Trinity-Pawling played in, but prep school kids were routinely ignored on all-region and all-state teams. He even slipped under most college's radars.

Coratti tried to talk then-national champion South Carolina into taking a look at Vaughn, but coach June Raines was not interested. Thankfully, Vaughn played American Legion baseball during the summers and Rutgers and Seton Hall noticed him.

"The kid had enormous power," said Seton Hall Assistant Coach Ed Blankmeyer, who first watched Vaughn after getting a tip from fellow assistant coach Chris Buckley. "He was a big kid who played all the positions. He played all over the place, shortstop and catcher. He was a real good athlete. When you saw the kid hit a baseball you said, 'Oooh.' He crushed balls. The ball went off the bat like a golf ball. It just got out there fast. Some guys hit a baseball and hit a home run, but this guy ... it was just tremendous."

Vaughn and his father visited Seton Hall and liked what they saw. The Vaughns even told scouts from the Philadelphia Phillies that their son was going to college, not to pro baseball, so do not bother to draft him. "They pretty much left me out of it," Vaughn said years after his parents never even let him talk to the scout. "They convinced me that I would become more mature by going to college and working towards a degree. I always dreamed of getting the chance to play professional baseball, but I'm glad I didn't make that decision. I would have gotten swallowed up in the pros. The whole process, a guy 18 going in there facing guys 24 or 26, I think I would have competed, but I don't think my mind would have been ready."

Mike Sheppard Sr. was happy to hear that. The Seton Hall head coach headed to Trinity-Pawling as early as possible the day players could sign with a school. The Vaughns arranged for the signing to take place at Hubbard's house. After donuts, coffee, and some nervous chatter, Sheppard took out his pen. "Mo always wanted to sign a Division I baseball scholarship," Hubbard said, "and he did."

Sheppard looked at the signature. Was it "Mo" or "Maurice?" The kid had signed it "Maurice Vaughn."

> "They convinced me that I would become more mature by going to college and working towards a degree. I always dreamed of getting the chance to play professional baseball, but I'm glad I didn't make that decision. I would have gotten swallowed up in the pros."
> — Mo Vaughn

GOING PRO

DRAFT DAY TENSION

Ken Griffey Jr. was not a typical high school senior. Not many high schoolers can walk into the Atlanta Braves' locker room with their dad, a major leaguer, and joke with Dale Murphy and Ozzie Virgil about the type of car he would buy with his signing bonus.

"A Corvette," he said to Virgil. "A Porsche, maybe." Griffey Jr. had just hit .478 with seven homers and 26 RBI for Moeller High School in Cincinnati and had scouts drooling over him, even though he had only spent two years concentrating on baseball.

"I didn't like football, didn't like getting hit," the former wide receiver told the *Cincinnati Enquirer*. But the 6' 3", 17-year-old could hit on the baseball diamond. He also had a baseball pedigree. His dad, Ken Griffey Sr. was then in his 14th year in the big leagues as a career .301 hitter for the Cincinnati Reds, New York Yankees, and his current team, the Atlanta Braves.

Griffey Jr. was one reason why most baseball observers felt the 1987 Major League Baseball Amateur Draft would focus on high school seniors. Willie Banks was another. John Valentin's former St. Anthony High School teammate owned a 94 mile-per-hour fastball and was 11-1 with a 0.92 ERA.

Banks was pictured in a Peter Gammon's *Sports Illustrated* "Inside Baseball" column, which argued that while college baseball was on the rise, high schoolers would still dominate the draft. Gammons pointed out that 37 of the 56 players who participated in the 1986 Major League All-Star Game were drafted out of high school as were 59 of the 84 current major league pitchers with 10-plus wins or saves.

One National League scout told Gammons, "Teams prefer high school prospects. By the time you've professionalized a college player he's 24, and it's make-it-or-be-released time. What you see is what you get with a college kid, with little chance of improvement." Banks and Griffey Jr. were mentioned in the article. Craig Biggio and Marteese Robinson were not. But 35 pages later, Robinson got his due.

Page 107 of the June 1, 1987, issue, with Edmonton Oilers star Wayne Gretzky on the cover, had Robinson pictured as one of six "Faces in the Crowd." A 45-word paragraph describing Robinson's magical year, joined Dennis McDonald's color head shot of Robinson.

Robinson got a lot of recognition from the mention. Even Seton Hall grad and ESPN basketball broadcaster Dick Vitale framed the page and put it up in his Florida home, although, admittedly, not because of his love for SHU baseball. To the right of Robinson's mention, a pair of tennis-playing youngsters were pictured. Vitale's daughters, Sherri and Terri, had just led St. Stephen's [Bradenton, Florida] Episcopal School to the state's Class AA girls high school championship.

"Being in *Sports Illustrated* is really nice," Robinson said at the time, "but I'm definitely more concerned with the draft. I'm kind of nervous." He and Biggio both. They had talked about playing pro baseball many times during their three years of ups and downs at Seton Hall. Although they both earned star status, it was not until their junior years that they both were great together. As freshmen in 1985, Robinson earned Freshman All-American honors while Biggio, who was dealing with the divorce of his parents, struggled to learn the college game and hit .262 as the starting catcher.

Robinson and Biggio played in the Atlantic Collegiate Baseball League the summer after their rookie season, Biggio for the Long Island Nationals and Robinson for the Jersey Pilots. At that point Robinson seemed to be the established star, while Biggio was trying to figure out where he fit in.

Larry Babich, who had wanted Valentin to play for him at

Jersey City State College, coached the Pilots for 18 years. He had seen more than 100 of his summer players advance to professional baseball, 16 to the major leagues. Seton Hall's Rick Cerone was the first and Rutgers' Eric Young the last. "There were times where Marteese hit shots, rockets in the gap," Babich said. "Line shots that just took off. He looked like a pure hitter to me. When Cerone played for me in 1973, he hit long, high drives, but Marteese hit line shots. Marteese used the whole field."

Biggio, who had returned home to Long Island for the summer, moved to the infield with the Nationals. Scout Larry Izzo, who was still tracking the kid he first wrote up three years prior, now did so with a look to the future.

LARRY IZZO'S REPORT ON CRAIG BIGGIO — JUNE 21, 1985

Abilities: Overall quickness and running speed a plus. Playable hands with sufficient arm strength projected. Aggressive, hard-nosed player. Take-charge type. Solid contact hitter.

Weakness: Holds hands too high to body. Does not use his lower body when hitting. Must learn to open those hips. Needs more experience in the field, rhythm lacking. Boy is just making switch to infield from catcher, still shows arm action of a catcher.

Summation: Marginal prospect. Good athlete with a live body. Spent the entire spring catching for his college team and needs work and playing time to smooth out rough edges. His attitude and natural athletic ability are a plus. Best projected position: second base.

Biggio might not have been ready for pro baseball yet, but he was still good enough for the ACBL. He and Robinson both made the All-Star team that played in Fenway Park against the Cape Cod League All-Stars. "I hit a line drive off the Green Monster," Robinson said. "It was great just being there and seeing the Green Monster for the first time. We didn't change in the Red Sox locker room, but we did get to go in there. I saw Jim Rice's locker. It was a neat experience seeing that."

The two ACBL All-Stars saw their fortunes reversed as sophomores. Biggio earned All-Big East honors while leading Seton Hall with a .351 batting average, seven triples, nine home runs, 43 RBI and 42 stolen bases. He then caught 39 games in the Cape Cod League, considered by most to be the best college summer league in the nation, where he hit five homers for the Yarmouth-Dennis Red Sox and was third in the league with 21 stolen bases. Robinson suffered a sophomore slump, hitting just .287 in 39 games before breaking his arm. He did not play summer ball.

By the time Robinson, who returned from his injury, and Biggio got it going together as juniors in 1987, they became the talk of the town. Despite Izzo's earlier projections, Biggio was a catcher with rare speed and an arm that allowed only 29 stolen bases all year. He was told time and time again by scouts and know-it-alls that he would go in the first round. The same people projected Robinson would go by round two. "Obviously, they [Biggio and Robinson] are two of the best prospects in the area," evaluated Joe McIlvaine, New York Mets vice president of baseball operations.

Seton Hall head coach Mike Sheppard Sr. had been through the draft before. He had coached 50 players who got the draft call from major league clubs. But none had attracted the attention Biggio and Robinson were receiving. "It's unbelievable," the coach told *Newsday's* John Valenti on draft eve. "The phone in my office has been ringing like crazy. Scouts are calling to get last-minute information and statistics, agents are calling my players. It's really incredible. Based on what I hear, it is a real possibility that both will make it [in the first round]." He added prophetically, "But you can never tell what might happen on draft day."

The baseball draft was far different from the NFL and NBA meat markets. There was no ESPN or TNT coverage. There were no "mock drafts" on talk radio. There was limited public interest largely because only the first-round picks were announced publicly. The full list, which extended to 75 rounds and 1,263 picks in 1987, was not released until October.

It was Tuesday, June 2, 1987. The College World Series was still going on, but the pros did not wait. A conference call from the 17th floor at Major League Baseball's Park Avenue headquarters in New York City linked all 26 major league clubs, each listening on speaker phones. Each team's scouting officials were holed up in their respective war-room bunkers. It was 10 AM when the three-day ordeal began. Seattle picked first.

While sitting with his father at his family's West Chester, Ohio, home, Griffey Jr. learned quickly that he had been taken as the top pick. He signed 20 minutes later for a $160,000 bonus. He was off to Bellingham, Washington, in the Northwest League. Oviedo [FL] High School senior shortstop Mark Merchant went second to the Pittsburgh Pirates. The Minnesota Twins then touched off a celebration in Jersey City when they picked Banks.

An hour south, a nervous Biggio was with his Seton Hall girlfriend, Patty Egan, whom he eventually married, at her parents Jersey Shore vacation home. "I decided I didn't want to sit around my house waiting for a phone call that might come or might not come," Biggio said. "I kind of wanted to get away. If it happens, they will get in touch with me and if it doesn't, then they're not."

Although the sun and waves kept him at least partially distracted, he did not have to wait too long to learn his fate. A bit past 2 PM, the phone in Biggio's Kings Park, New York, home rang. Johnna Biggio answered. It was scout Clary Anderson. Her son had been taken by the Houston Astros in the first round, 22nd pick overall. He was the second catcher taken in the draft behind West Christian [Miami] High School's Bill Henderson, who went to the Detroit Tigers two picks earlier. She immediately called her son with the news and his toothpaste commercial smile went ear-to-ear. "When I found out, a lot of tension was released," Biggio said. He was the fourth first-round pick Sheppard had coached. Big leaguers Rick Cerone, John Morris, and Pat Pacillo were the others. He was Sheppard's 51st draft pick.

"I was so proud of him. He reached his goal," Craig's father Lee said. "I was working when Craig got the phone call, but when he called me, I was so happy for him. I was thrilled for him."

Craig's older brother, Terry, who was working in Minneapolis, did not get such a call. "I was watching the Cubs on TV, and the Cubs had announced who their draft pick was, and they were actually playing Houston at the time, and the announcer also said who Houston picked. I tried to make a couple phone calls, but it was a while before I got a hold of him."

Two hours later, after the initial excitement wore off, Biggio headed up the Garden State Parkway to Seton Hall where he turned his attention to Robinson, who had not yet heard anything. The catcher, who received plenty of pats on the back from school officials, sat down with the first baseman on the steps outside of Seton Hall's Stafford Hall under the warm, late spring sun. "Craig kept telling me what I already knew," Robinson said. "He did a great job trying to calm me down and kept telling me that they only announce the first round publicly. He said I would hear soon. Boy, I was hoping that would happen."

While Biggio later made the drive back to the Jersey Shore, Robinson stayed on campus, hoping he would hear something. At 6 PM Sheppard told him to go home and try to relax.

"I didn't know what to do with myself when I got home," Robinson said. "Every time the phone rang I jumped. But it was almost always someone asking if I had heard." It was 9 PM and Robinson was watching television on the couch when the phone rang. He thought it was just another well-wisher.

"I figured that if they didn't call by seven I wouldn't hear until the next day, if then, so I was really upset," Robinson said. "It was probably the lowest I'd ever felt in my life." His mood soon changed. Robinson got off the couch and answered the phone. It was Oakland Athletics scout J.P. Ricciardi. The nation's top-ranked hitter had been taken in the sixth round. "I got the call," Robinson said. "That is what I wanted. In my mind, that phone call was the start of my major league career. I had no doubts. It was an awesome feeling."

Robinson was thrilled and quickly called Sheppard. It was then that Robinson realized that he was not the hot commodity he thought he was. "Oakland did not have a pick in the fifth round, but I was still taken in the sixth," Robinson said. "Shep was really happy that I was drafted, but he was more disappointed than I was about being picked low. That is when I started to get mixed emotions about being picked, being that low." His disappointment became more evident the more he thought about it.

"Sixth round," he said that night to a member of the school's sports information staff. "What more could I have done this year?

I led the country in hitting. I hit for power and I played defense. I don't get it." Robinson knew in his heart the reasons why he had slipped, but it still hurt. There was a question about his arm. Would the two bones in his right arm, soldered together with 10 screws, hold up for season after season after season? Robinson did not buy that argument. He had a three-number answer for the critics, .529.

The scouts also worried about his power. Robinson understood that high-average contact hitters with speed were not the norm for first basemen. This was a position where the big guys dominated. Robinson had power, but not Mo Vaughn-power. Robinson's heir apparent at first base was the prototype. "I really thought my defense would carry me into the higher rounds," Robinson said. "Let's face it, there were not many guys going to full splits on stretches or had the range I did. But in the back of my mind, I knew power could be a problem."

Robinson's family, friends, and the Seton Hall community thought the sixth round was certainly good enough. As word leaked out around campus the next morning, Robinson received plenty of accolades. He heard over and over, "It doesn't matter what round, as long as you got drafted." He tried to believe it, but he knew it mattered. It mattered in the size of the signing bonus and it mattered that he would now be just another guy, not a really high draft pick the A's would push to get to the major leagues.

> "I got the call. That is what I wanted. In my mind, that phone call was the start of my major league career. I had no doubts. It was an awesome feeling."
> —Marteese Robinson

"I know the first, second-and third-round picks get treated differently by their organizations," Robinson said. "I've heard that a lot and it makes sense. They have invested a lot in that player and want him to make it. No one wants a draft where their top picks don't make it."

CHAPTER 8

BIGGIO AND ROBINSON JOIN THE PRO RANKS

Biggio was one of those first-round guys Robinson was talking about. And the Astros wanted him immediately. His negotiations moved swiftly and a week following the draft, Seton Hall called a press conference to announce Biggio's signing. The media, school dignitaries, and Biggio's friends filled the chairs in the Seton Hall Seminary dining room. But there was no Biggio. A floor below, Seton Hall coach Mike Sheppard Sr. and his star catcher were still working out the contract's final details with Astros scout Clary Anderson. Finally they reached a deal. Biggio signed the contract quietly and shook hands with Anderson.

"Coming from a little town like I did in Kings Park, Long Island, just signing was an unbelievable thing," Biggio said. "Nobody ever really signs from where I came from. I was really lucky because I had the opportunity to deal with so many great people when I was younger who pointed me in the right direction and gave me the proper guidance."

Wearing the same tan suit he wore in "The Hit Men" photo, Biggio walked upstairs and entered the press conference 45 minutes late. Biggio, Anderson, and Sheppard sat down as the notebooks came out and the television lights went on.

Sheppard, who had given Biggio a Seton Hall hat on the way in, announced it was time for the traditional "changing of the caps." As Anderson gave Biggio an Astros hat, the former Pirate star gave the Seton Hall cap back to Sheppard, smiled, put on the Astros hat and, for show, signed a copy of the contract to a rousing ovation. Although he did not want the amount of his actual signing bonus released to the media, Biggio did let on that it was in excess of $100,000.

"It is a great thrill to achieve another one of my baseball goals," Biggio said. "I will miss Seton Hall because of the people and all I have gained from the program and the school, but I feel I must move on in my baseball career. I've always wanted a shot at playing in the majors and now hopefully I'm on my way. I'll just try to give the Astros the best of my abilities. I'm going in with the attitude that I'm going to put out 110 percent and work as hard as I can to achieve my ultimate goal."

Sheppard, all smiles, brought up a familiar theme. "When he came to us as a freshman, he was one of the worst catchers we had and he leaves as a first-round draft choice. He worked very hard to better himself in all facets of the game and made a lot of people happy along the way."

"When I was 18, I was cocky," Biggio remembered as a 13-year major league veteran. "I thought I knew a lot about things in life, but you absolutely don't know anything about life. When you are a hard-nosed kid, you are going to need a hard-nosed coach and I couldn't have asked for a better person to be there and be the guy to follow than Mike Sheppard. I love him to death. He is a man who is a very, very strict disciplinarian and he doesn't care if you are the best player or the worst player on the team. If you step out of line, you will pay the consequences. When you are a young kid coming out of high school, you need someone there to treat you the right way and that is one of the main characteristics Shep brings. He's a great baseball coach, but he's always there and has the interests of the kids at heart, although they might not know it at the time."

Biggio's character, which included his loyalty to Sheppard, was one of the things that appealed to Anderson, a former catcher who became a legendary football and baseball coach at nearby Montclair High School before becoming a scout. "The Astros are fortunate to get Craig Biggio," he said at the press conference. "We felt he was the strongest available player at the time we drafted. He's an excellent athlete who runs particularly well, he is very quick in all of his actions, has a really good arm and hits well to all fields. He is not a typical big, slow-footed catcher. We have eight other catchers in the organization, but Craig has a chance to go ahead of all of them in a few years. His attitude is what is special. He never stops hustling."

Astros owner Dr. John McMullen was also happy to have Biggio as an employee. McMullen was forced to take a personal involvement in Biggio's signing because the beginning negotiations with Anderson were a bit rough. "McMullen called me up after Craig was drafted and said, 'What the hell is going on Shep? I put a ceiling of $80,000 on Craig Biggio. What are you and Clary doing?' " the Seton Hall coach remembered. "I said, 'John, I don't work for you, I work for the kid and that kid is worth more as far as I'm concerned.' We convinced Clary what Craig was worth, but then he called me back and wanted to back out of it. But I said I couldn't do that. I told him, 'You've got to go to McMullen and work it out.' " They did solve the problem. Biggio signed and was immediately assigned to the Astros' Class A Asheville Tourists of the South Atlantic League. They gave him until the weekend to report.

> "When he came to us as a freshman, he was one of the worst catchers we had and he leaves as a first-round draft choice. He worked very hard to better himself in all facets of the game and made a lot of people happy along the way."
> — Mike Sheppard, Seton Hall Coach

Standing in the back of the room by himself during Biggio's press conference and with a smile on his face was Marteese Robinson. Although still nursing his own disappointment with the draft, Robinson wanted to support Biggio. "We've been through a lot together and he was there for me last week," Robinson said. But, when pressed by reporters, the normally happy-go-lucky Robinson could not keep his disappointment hidden. "This is a great day for Craig," Robinson told the *Daily Record*'s Ed Mills. "I'm happy for him and I hope he is extremely successful with the Astros. But this day kind of brings mixed emotions for me. I'm not happy with the way the negotiations have gone with my parent club.

"I was disappointed that I was drafted that low; I thought I would go a lot higher. I think Craig has a lot of ability, but I think

I do too. I thought we both possibly could be taken in the first round." As Robinson knew it would, money became an issue. The A's were offering a $20,000 signing bonus, but he wanted $90,000. "I think those numbers [1987 stats] speak for themselves," Robinson told Mills. "I was expecting Oakland to offer something more, but so far they have not."

Oakland scout J.P. Ricciardi, now the General Manager of the Toronto Blue Jays, was battling more than dollar figures. He was battling Robinson's pride. "I didn't have him in as a first-round player, I didn't have him in as a second-round player," the scout said. "I had him in as a guy we'd be very comfortable getting in the third, fourth, fifth rounds. You are dealing with egos. I said, 'Marteese, I don't care where you went. I like you as a player, I think you have a chance to do some things. I think he trusted what I was saying, but I think his ego was bruised that he didn't go in the first or second round. I knew he wasn't going to be happy for a while."

Obviously Robinson and the A's had a long way to go. Robinson threatened to return to Seton Hall for his senior year with hopes of being drafted higher the next season. That would leave the A's with a wasted high draft pick. But it was not lost on all involved that Robinson's return to South Orange would be unlikely for a couple of reasons.

His stock was at an all-time high and drafted seniors were not normally offered extravagant signing bonuses, simply because they have no negotiating chips. Take it or leave it. Where else could they go? Sheppard had other thoughts. Robinson had been scheduled to play for Cotuit in the Cape Cod League and Sheppard thought it would be a good negotiating ploy to honor the commitment.

Sheppard knew summer baseball was an important part of a player's development. They needed games under their belt and 55 collegiate contests a year were not enough. Almost every one of his more accomplished performers played the game all summer long. With the 1987 collegiate season over, the current Pirates were already playing summer ball. John Valentin was in the Midwest's Jayhawk League. Mo Vaughn was on Cape Cod playing with Wareham. Dana Brown was there too, playing for eventual champion Harwich on a team which included future major leaguers Charles Nagy, Gary Disarcina, Bob Hamelin, John Flaherty, and Ron Witmeyer. Robinson joined them when he took his coach's advice and headed to the Cape while the negotiations with the A's continued.

"We didn't want to lose the kid," Ricciardi said about Robinson going to Cape Cod. "At that point we were into it for whatever we were into it. There was always the chance that he would go back to Seton Hall, but I told him, 'I think we have a good organization and I think you will prosper in our organization. We are fair to our kids. We are going to work with you. We are going to try to be the best that we can be for you. And history has proven that we are pretty good to all of our guys. If you talk to anybody in baseball, they will tell you we have one of the best farm systems in the game.' I thought he would prosper with us in that regard, but with a lot of kids it comes down to the money.

"At one point, I didn't give a shit if he went back to school or not. Sometimes the whole hassle of signing a player just gets to everybody. At some point you say, the kid is either gonna want to go out or he doesn't want to go out. If he doesn't want to go out, then you are better off going back to school and enjoying your last year. I wanted the kid to sign, but personally, if the kid wanted to go back to school, I'm not going to kiss his ass. I don't really care either way. After the kid said he was going to go to the Cape, I said to myself, 'If you want to go back to school, go back to school.' "

Even with his decision looming in the background, Robinson was determined to enjoy his time on Cape Cod, one of the nation's premier summer resorts. He was paired with Miami [OH] shortstop Tim Naehring at Cotuit where they roomed together in a sponsor's house. "Marteese came in as the leading hitter in the county. I think it was .540 or something, some crazy number," Naehring, a future big leaguer, said. "It was a nice experience. It was a new thing for me playing against that level of competition. It was a new experience rooming with someone in a small Cape Cod cottage-type home. Working and playing ball. All in all, it was a new experience, but it was a great experience. When you start seeing people like Marteese and some of the talent that's out there, at first it was a bit overwhelming. You could tell Marteese had the talent, ability, and makeup to be a major leaguer for a long time."

The disappointment over the draft and the ongoing negotiations never affected the newborn friendship between Robinson and Naehring. "He never came across to me that he was having a problem with the draft pick. Maybe, personally, he was a little upset about things. The guy was such a class act. He was so professional to me, to his teammates. When he stepped on the field, he had a presence about him."

Robinson's stature amongst his peers grew when he was named the first Northeast player in *Collegiate Baseball*'s 16-year history to be named National Player of the Year. Robinson shared the honor with Oklahoma State's Robin Ventura, who had a 58-game hitting streak which ended in the 11th game of the College World Series where his Cowboys lost to eventual national champion Stanford.

"It came down to Ventura and Robinson and we just couldn't make a choice," Pavlovich said. "We didn't want to pick one and slight the other. That's the first time we've picked co-winners." Both also earned similar honors from *The Sporting News*.

The honors allowed Sheppard to lobby for his star. "It is difficult for us to understand how the Player of the Year is picked in the sixth round," Sheppard told the *Star-Ledger*'s Ed Barmakian. "Marteese really came into his own and he'll just have to keep proving himself to the professional baseball people."

Playing on the Cape allowed Robinson to meet and impress Ventura who was playing for Hyannis. "You feel like you're having a pretty good year, then they say there is this guy hitting about .580," Ventura, now with the New York Yankees, remembered in 1999. "I didn't really know that much about him. He played in Cape Cod the year I was up there, Mo was there too, and I realized why Marteese was hitting that way. He just always hit the ball hard and everything was a hit."

George Greer, the Wake Forest University head baseball coach, managed Robinson in Cotuit. "I thought Marteese was every bit the player advertised," Greer said. "I've had two first basemen who made it to the big leagues, Terry Steinbach with the A's and Will Clark with the Giants, and he was as good a player as either of them. Marteese was bold on the bases and I thought he really needed to be with an organization that allows you to be that way. Some organizations are not concerned with that and would rather the runner protect the hitter.

"I was also concerned that Marteese was a first baseman who might get pigeon-holed. I didn't think he was the type of first baseman with the power of Mo Vaughn. I saw him as a tremendous table-setter, but most clubs don't want that. They want power." Greer was impressed with Robinson's attitude. "Some kids in the same situation as Marteese was in were so afraid their stock would drop if they played more. They would sit at home and not do a thing. They would quasi-work out, but when they worked up a sweat would stop and say, 'that is enough for today.' Marteese was not like that. He wanted to have fun. He wanted to win games. He wanted to play. He had no fear that he would do well. He knew he was going to do well."

Robinson, using a wooden bat for the first time after using aluminum models in college, continued to have success. He played in 14 games for Cotuit with 20 hits in 57 at-bats for a .351 average. He added three doubles, a homer, nine RBI, and six stolen bases. All this while he and Ricciardi continued to talk.

"I told Marteese at one point, 'Look Marteese, I can't apologize for taking you in the sixth round. We took the best player that we had on the board that we liked. I'm not going to apologize to you for that. I can't answer for you why you didn't go in the first or second round for all of these other clubs. I don't work for them. I'm just telling you what I represent. I like you as a player. Don't ever lose sight of how I feel about you as a player. I know your feelings are hurt because you didn't go in the first round, second round, I don't know what to tell you. Either you are going to get over it or you are going back to school and try to be a first or second rounder next year."

Cotuit's first baseman returned to New Jersey on July 2 to re-open negotiations with the A's. Naehring was disappointed his roommate left, largely because Robinson took his 1979 Thunderbird with him. "He was hauling me all over the Cape," Naehring said.

"Realistically, what more could he have done?" Ricciardi said, discounting Robinson's feeble negotiating ploy. "I said to him, 'Look, you had one of the best years of anybody in the history of college baseball. What more can you do going back to Seton Hall and what is going to stop someone from taking you in the second or third round and offering you $25,000 and letting you sit? At least we can get you some more money here, you are going with an organization that likes its players, that's good to its players, that believes in its farm system. Those are the things you got going for you. The thing you don't have going for you — I'm not going to walk in here with $100,000.' "

Five days later, Seton Hall called another press conference. Robinson was ready to sign. His signature smile was glowing again. While Ricciardi may have disagreed, the negotiating ploy had worked. The A's upped the ante and the two sides met almost halfway with a $55,000 signing bonus for Robinson. He would start his career in Medford, Oregon, in the Northwest League, the same league where Ken Griffey Jr. was sent.

Like Biggio, Robinson wore the same suit he wore in "The Hit Men" photo to his press conference. Sheppard and Ricciardi joined him in the Seton Hall Student Center. Before Sheppard was ready for the "changing of the hats" ceremony, he turned to his pupil, a guy to whom he felt like a father. His voice cracked. "You remember how everyone said that you played with a fire in your belly after you came back from your injury?" Sheppard said. "You have to go out there and be hungry again. This is professional baseball and you have to want to be the best." Robinson then removed his Seton Hall cap and placed a green and yellow cap with the A's logo on his head. He signed the contract to a round of applause.

Sheppard was excited when he spoke to Barmakian. "I think his chances of making it are great," Sheppard said. "He was the greatest first baseman to ever play here and, perhaps, the greatest player ever." Everyone was all smiles, but there were ominous signs that Robinson's road to the majors would be tougher than the coach thought. While Sheppard always spoke glowingly about Robinson's prowess at first base, the A's had different thoughts.

"Personally, I see him playing second base," Ricciardi told Barmakian. "We have Mark McGwire at first base and I don't see them moving him. Marteese really doesn't have the power to play first, but he's a good enough athlete to play second. He has the range and the arm, and I can see him hitting up to 15 home runs a year." Ricciardi thought his new signee could be like Frank White who was a five-time All-Star and eight-time Gold Glove second baseman with the Kansas City Royals.

Robinson did not mind the talk of making him a second baseman. "I've always wanted to play second base, anyway," he told Mike Moretti of the *Woodbridge News Tribune*. "They don't think I have enough pop in my bat to be a home run threat every time I come up like McGwire." Robinson was certainly not afraid of McGwire's presence even though the USC product was in the midst of hitting 49 homers in 1987 as the eventual unanimous Rookie of the Year.

"I am a more complete player than McGwire," Robinson told Theordore Gass of the *New Jersey Herald*. Sheppard agreed. "Marteese is a much better player than McGwire any day." They could only hope.

> "You remember how everyone said that you played with a fire in your belly after you came back from your injury? You have to go out there and be hungry again. This is professional baseball and you have to want to be the best."
>
> —Mike Sheppard, Seton Hall Coach

Former Walk-On Joins the Red Sox Chain

Fort Smith, Arkansas, is a long way away from the New Jersey Turnpike and Jersey City. The town of 75,000 on the Kansas-Oklahoma border is not a place John Valentin had ever heard of, let alone a place he ever thought of visiting.

"I knew going away would be good for me and I would be seen by a different group of scouts, but I didn't hit well my sophomore year, so the Cape Cod League did not want me," Valentin said. So instead of the local Atlantic Collegiate Baseball League's Jersey Pilots, Seton Hall assistant coach Ed Blankmeyer arranged for his shortstop to play in the Jayhawk League with the Fort Smith Red Sox.

Although Valentin struggled at the plate as a sophomore, hitting just .248 in the ninth spot, he opened a lot of eyes with his slick fielding. "Val was smooth," Mo Vaughn said. "We called him 'Johnny Glass' because he was so smooth. He was quiet and tough. Offensively, he was 150 pounds but wanted to hit 500-foot home runs."

Valentin and his offensive skills grew up that summer as he rode buses up to 14 hours for road games in Kansas and Oklahoma and earned money at a part-time job. "At times you want to get on a plane and go home, but I liked it after a while," Valentin said. "It was fun. You learn to grow up and you can't depend on your mom and dad. I had a job working on an assembly line for a company that bottled whiskey. I had to put the bottles into cartons, the cartons into small boxes, and the small boxes into bigger boxes.

"I worked from 7 in the morning to 3:30 in the afternoon. We had to be on the field at 4:30 and the games started at 6. Sometimes we had weekday doubleheaders and I wouldn't get home until 1:30 in the morning and then you have to wake up at 6:00 for work. You wouldn't get any rest until the weekends when we could sleep until one or two in the afternoon and play at night. I wanted to play well and get noticed." The plan worked perfectly. Valentin played every day and hit .346 with five homers, 18 doubles, and 26 stolen bases. He formed a potent double play combination with Southeastern State University second baseman Jeff Frye, his future teammate on the Boston Red Sox.

Even with a slick middle infield, the Fort Smith Red Sox were not a good team and failed to qualify for post season play. However, Valentin's job in the Midwest was not done. Jayhawk League rules allowed its members who were going to the playoffs to select two players off losing teams to join them for the rest of the summer. Liberal [Kansas] BeeJays coach Doug Clark, also the University of Arkansas coach, recognized Valentin's name from the NCAA Tournament in Huntsville and knew Valentin was a guy he wanted.

Valentin soon joined the nation's oldest, continuous semi-pro team. Liberal has fielded a team since 1955 and has seen more than 120 alumni play in the major leagues. Former Liberal general manager Don Carlile cites Duane Kuiper, Greg Swindell, Doug Drabeck, Phil Garner, Mike Hargrove, Ron Guidry, Rick Honeycutt, Craig McMurtry, Jack Morris, Tom Pagnozzi, and Calvin Schiraldi as some the finest to wear his uniform.

He now includes Valentin on his list of most successful products. "He could move defensively," Carlile said. "If the ball was hit in the hole, he got it. He was a nice kid, very quiet. We saw him bloom that summer. He was always cheerful. John never bitched or complained about anything. At least, I never heard it."

Valentin had nothing to complain about. He was playing baseball and having success away from home. More people noticed. He even hit. "John was *smooooth*," Clark said, accentuating the defining word. "He did things easily. He had great defensive skills with a good arm. He did it easy and had good instincts. He was always at the right place at the right time. He also had a very functional bat. He made contact, he got his hits." Valentin hit in the lower part of the lineup, but never ninth. "He hit ninth at Seton Hall? I never knew that," the surprised coach said years later.

Liberal, located in western Kansas, was hit each summer by swirling winds that dried up the BeeJays' infield, but Valentin was not affected. He reverted to his Jersey City days, where he once fielded balls with his brother on the blacktop at Holland Gardens. "He fielded like Ozzie Smith," Clark said. "He made two amazing plays. Two balls took bad hops and, boom, he caught them with his bare hands and he threw the guys out. Those two plays really got your attention."

Valentin spent a few weeks with Liberal before the team traveled to Wichita for the National Baseball Congress World Series, a tournament which brought together 30 summer league teams from around the nation. Valentin helped the BeeJays to a third-place finish. "I think what summer programs do for kids is when they go out, they realize they can play with these other guys." Clark said. "At Liberal, we had guys from all over the country from major schools and then you're playing against even more guys in the NBC Tournament. Guys from Wichita State, USC, Florida, Miami, Florida State. So I think it is a real confidence booster for a kid."

Blankmeyer noticed a different John Valentin when fall practice began at Seton Hall in September. "When he came back, you could see a difference," the assistant coach said. "He had a lot of confidence offensively. Defensively there was never a problem. It was his offense that had to come around and that summer catapulted him to being a prospect."

John Valentin, a prospect? That was a new one. He was used to being John Valentin, the skinny kid. John Valentin, the walk-on. John Valentin, the kid who batted ninth. Never before, John Valentin, a prospect. But he was, and Blankmeyer was not the only college coach to notice.

Stanford's Mark Marquess, LSU's Skip Bertman, and Mississippi State's Ron Polk were choosing the roster for the

United States National Team that would play in October's 10-nation Intercontinental Cup Tournament in Cuba. Marquess, the head coach, heard reports from pro scouts and college coaches about Valentin's play in the national summer tournament and recommended him as a possible middle infielder. The others agreed. "I saw him in Wichita," Marquess said. "I liked him and also had unbelievable reports about him. As we gathered information, the better players' names kept popping up and John was one of the them." Valentin got the call.

"It didn't have the impact and excitement until I saw the U.S. uniform in Miami," Valentin told the *Jersey Journal*'s Mike Rowan. "I got my number five and put on the shirt and uniform. My reaction was, 'I can't believe this is happening!' " Valentin had flown to Miami to meet the rest of the U.S. roster. Oklahoma State third baseman Robin Ventura and shortstop Monty Farris, Indiana infielder Mickey Morandini, Washington State first baseman John Olerud, and Creighton catcher Scott Servais were the big names on the team.

"I was there just to be a backup," Valentin said. "Morandini and Farris were the guys. I was just happy to be there. I was with these guys and considered one of the best in the country. I knew I wasn't going to play much, but during infield practice I knew I caught the ball better than most infielders there. I was confident about that, but I didn't know if I could hit the ball against Japan, Taiwan, let alone Cuba."

Off the field everyone thought Valentin would be a major factor for the young Americans. "I could speak a bit of Spanish, but I got ribbed a little bit because I couldn't translate when the guys needed it," Valentin said. "On the bus, travelling, they wanted me to translate. I could understand it perfectly, but the words just wouldn't come out."

He was still further along than any of the other U.S. players when it came to understanding the Cuban culture. "Everything about the trip to me was great," Valentin said. "I loved the food. My family is from Puerto Rico. Eating rice and chicken everyday, some of the guys couldn't believe it was rice and chicken again. I welcomed it. I was part of my heritage. It was a great experience for me, but it wasn't for most of the guys."

Morandini was one of the guys who struggled to enjoy the different culture. "The water, carbonated water," Morandini remembered while sitting at his Veterans Stadium locker as a member of the 2000 Philadelphia Phillies, "I couldn't stand it, but that is all we had down there. They didn't have wells, so we had to gut it out. It was a very depressed area where we were. I remember sleeping in a hotel with really small rooms and doubling up. They had a lot of security down there. I remember going through some tough neighborhoods that weren't really nice and seeing kids playing ball in the street. It was an experience, that's for sure."

"The heat was intense," Polk said. "It was the fall, the humidity and temperature were both in the 90s. Strange food, hotel. It is not a wealthy country. We are used to accommodations like air conditioning, hot water, seats in the bathroom stalls. Havana, back then, you had to experience it. It was different." Marquess made sure the trip was also educational. He took the team to see the Santiago jail where Castro was first imprisoned before rising to power, the U.S. Naval Base, and a museum which depicted the Cuban version of the Bay of Pigs invasion. The team also saw the Russian influence on the Cuban culture. "In Havana, you would see a '56 or '57 Chevy or you saw Russian vehicles," Marquess said. "The televisions were Russian, too."

The United States opened the tournament with losses to Japan and Taiwan in Santiago. Valentin, who had played second base only once at Seton Hall, got his first action in the tournament at second against Taiwan in the second game, but he was back on the bench when the U.S. rebounded with a 15-2 win over Aruba.

The United States rebounded with two wins over Nicaragua, the final win coming 90 minutes outside of Santiago. "It was hotter than blazes, but having this game in this little town was the biggest thing to ever happen to these people," Marquess said. "To us, it was a 1940s-like town in the middle of nowhere. It was amazing. We got there three hours before the game and this little wooden stadium that should only have held 2,000 was already filled with easily 4,000 people. They were falling on top of each other and didn't care about the heat. They came for the event."

Marquess' club fell behind 5-0 in the first, but rallied to win, 6-5. "At the start, they were rooting for Nicaragua, but by the end they were our fans," Marquess said. "The Cubans really respect good baseball and we had a hustling, good group."

The win advanced to the United States to the medal round in Havana with Canada, Cuba, Japan, South Korea, and Taiwan. The Americans opened with a win over Canada. Valentin then moved into the starting lineup against Taiwan, subbing for a struggling Farris, and celebrated by unexpectedly going deep. Valentin entered the tournament with only five home runs in six years of high school and college ball, but managed to hit a three-run homer in his first international start. Another win over South Korea put the collegians in a showdown against Cuba in front of 50,000 and a United States television audience.

"The people in Cuba really treated us well," Valentin said. "They were always trying to communicate even though it was tough for them because of the language barrier. They really did not show any hatred towards us. In fact, the only time they rooted against us was when we played Cuba. It was like a play-off game. It was somewhat intimidating. They were a lot older with a lot more experience." It showed. Cuba beat the Americans, 5-0, to clinch the gold medal. Morandini, who led the tournament with eight doubles, was picked to the All-Tournament team after the U.S. beat Japan the following day to wrap up the silver medal.

"We were a bunch of college kids," Morandini remembered. "We were juniors in college at the time. That was my first experience with travelling out of the country and being with a bunch of great players like that. It was a blast for me."

Valentin also enjoyed the trip, largely because he hit .304 with six RBI while playing in 10 of 13 games. He had shown earlier in the summer that he could compete against other college stars and now he knew he could play with some of the country's best. Valentin was living an American dream, but he refused to let success go to his head. "From my freshman year to my junior year, things happened really fast. I attribute that to the players I played with, the Biggios, the Robinsons, the older guys. Seton Hall is a player-oriented, blue collar team. I had to rise. If

I didn't, I would fall by the wayside. It was demanding. It fit my personality, though, because it was a challenge."

As spring approached, Seton Hall coach Mike Sheppard Sr. contemplated who would fill the offensive holes left by Biggio and Robinson's departure to the pros. He still had Vaughn, but desperately needed to find a number three hitter to hit ahead of the slugger. Valentin's progress and newfound confidence at the plate convinced the coach that the shortstop was his man.

Once the 1988 season began, Valentin made his coach look like a genius. Seton Hall started 15-5 and was ranked 30th in the nation. Through the first 20 games Valentin hit .412 with 19 RBI. "Val struggled his first two years," Blankmeyer said. "He went away that summer, played in Cuba and his stock went way up. I don't think the area scouts in New Jersey had John rated highly, but then they started getting reports from Midwest guys and John Valentin's name keeps coming up. John Valentin really stepped it up and got people to notice him."

Behind him, Vaughn, now the first baseman as Marteese Robinson's replacement, was also sailing along with a .508 average, 22 RBI, but just three homers as teams pitched around him to the tune of 22 walks. "Yeah, they're pitching around Mo," Sheppard said. "I don't like it. You walk a guy, you give a base away. I don't believe in giving anything away."

> "From my freshman year to my junior year, things happened really fast. I attribute that to the players I played with, the Biggios, the Robinsons, the older guys. Seton Hall is a player-oriented, blue collar team. I had to rise. If I didn't, I would fall by the wayside. It was demanding. It fit my personality, though, because it was a challenge."
> —John Valentin

By the time Seton Hall improved to 20-7, Vaughn was still at .500, but increased his home run total to eight. It was not just the home run totals that climbed, but also Vaughn's reputation. *The New York Times'* David Falkner came to Seton Hall to feature the sophomore slugger. Forget the homers in Vaughn's rookie year Sheppard told the writer. Instead, write about his power. He went on to tell Falkner about what happened against Monmouth in the current season's 15th game. "Mo hit a shot right at the first baseman that tore right through the first baseman's glove," Sheppard said. "Just blew it away and struck the guy's throwing hand which was behind it. You've never seen anything like it in your life."

Valentin certainly did not have Vaughn's explosiveness, but he too had a growing reputation. By mid-season he was up to .427 with 31 RBI and five home runs. He was named the New Jersey Player of the Week and credited his success to assistant coach Nick Bowness' weightlifting regiment. "I was the ninth hitter last year because I didn't have enough power and I had some trouble hitting the curve," Valentin said. "But I worked out during the off-season on a weight training program, hitting the weights. I feel stronger this year and I think that is the major reason I'm batting third."

The 1988 Pirates again made the four-team Big East Tournament. At 38-14, the defending champions wore the bullseye as they entered Muzzy Field for a pre-tournament workout. They could not help but remember what happened a year ago. "Yeah, I kind of looked over there," Vaughn admitted to reporters as he stared out at the trees in right field where his blast against Charles Nagy left the ballpark.

The year before Vaughn was the Big East's Freshman of the Year. Now, with a .487 regular-season average, he was the youngest-ever Big East Player of the Year. "I guess everyone is looking for a little extra from me," Vaughn said. "I have to make sure I set the tone and keep guys up."

It was a tournament filled with rain delay after rain delay and Seton Hall played just like the weather. Miserably. The Pirates won their first game over Providence, but then lost to Villanova and St. John's to end their season at 39-16.

Vaughn finished his sophomore year with a .463 average, the fourth best in the nation, 14 homers and 70 RBI. Good enough to repeat on the All-American team where Valentin joined him. The former walk-on finished his junior year with a .392 average, five homers, a Seton Hall-record 21 doubles, and 52 RBI. Valentin was eligible for the draft and, just like Biggio and Robinson had done a year ago, all he could do was wait.

"Draft day was stressful because I knew it was going to happen," Valentin said. "I had spoken to a lot of scouts and Coach Sheppard said I might go as high as the third round. That's pretty high. If you are taken within the first five rounds, you are almost set to go to the major leagues if you don't screw up. So I was pretty excited about it."

Valentin could not stand the tension on draft day and headed to the nearby mall. Taking the call, if it came, would be his brother Arnold's job. Soon the phone rang and it was Matt Sczesny from the Boston Red Sox. "Congratulations," he told Arnold, "John has been drafted in the fifth round of the major league baseball draft."

"We were screaming 'Boston! Boston!' " Valentin's mother Davina said.

Arnold ran to the mall to find his brother. "I looked all over the place until I found him," Arnold said. "I caught him in between stores and told him. He was ecstatic. He yelled, 'I've got to get out of here! I can't believe it! I can't believe it!' We came home and he returned the phone call to Mr. Sczesny. It was the happiest day of his life."

Valentin's family and friends were elated. Some even took credit. "To this day, Mo says he got me drafted because I hit in front of him," Valentin says with a smile.

Sczesny was a Red Sox lifer. He joined the organization in 1954 as a minor leaguer, but never advanced past Double-A. He stayed on as a coach and eventually managed the Red Sox minor league teams in Waterloo, Iowa, Winston-Salem, North Carolina, Wellsville, New York, Oneonta, New York, Greenville, South Carolina, and Pawtucket, Rhode Island. He had been scouting since 1971.

"I thought John could field in the big leagues," Sczesny said. "Any time he hit would be a bonus. I thought if he got stronger, he might have a little power, kind of like Alan Trammell. He wasn't strong as a sophomore, but he made good contact. It was just a matter of him getting bigger and stronger."

Sczesny did not know it, but Valentin also had to get healthy.

He had suffered a stress fracture on his left foot during the last few games of the college season. "Coach Sheppard said, 'Let's not sign right away,' " Valentin remembered. " 'Let's see how much money we can get out of them as a signing bonus and let your foot heal.' That was the plan. Money wasn't the issue. I was stalling so my foot would heal."

Sheppard also researched where Valentin would fit in the organization. He learned that Tim Naehring, Robinson's former roommate at Cotuit on Cape Cod, was also drafted by the Red Sox in the eighth round. "He was my competition going in so I wanted to get into a higher A league than him. But he signed really quickly and because of the stress fracture, they got to see him first and I got put on the back burner."

Valentin and Sheppard decided the shortstop should go to the Cape Cod League while negotiations with Sczesny continued. Valentin joined Hyannis but never played in any games.

> "To this day, Mo says he got me drafted because I hit in front of him,"
> — John Valentin

"John's negotiations were not easy," said Sczesny, who has sent eight players to the major leagues, including Valentin and Bob Stanley. "But I liked John. I liked the way he played."

It took from draft day on June 3, 1988, to June 27 for Valentin to become Sheppard's 53rd pro baseball product. He signed the standard Major League Baseball contract during a small press conference at Seton Hall. "John valued himself," Sheppard, who always fought hard for his players to receive the largest signing bonus possible, told the *Hudson Dispatch*'s Mike Neibart. "He held out a while. He'll get a real good look-see because they made a commitment to him. The valued him with a substantial contract."

Valentin wanted the media to know that he received a "substantial" signing bonus, one reported to be $40,000 by the *Jersey Journal*. "It was a deal good enough to leave school," Valentin said. In signing, Valentin gave up a chance to be invited to the Olympic Team tryouts. Instead he joined the Elmira Red Sox in the Class A New York-Penn League.

As Valentin left campus he had a smile on his face. "Can you believe it?" the shortstop asked himself. He had come from nowhere, from walk-on to pro baseball. He was now John Valentin, property of the Boston Red Sox.

NORWALK PAIR GOES IN THE FIRST ROUND

Mo Vaughn finished his second season at Seton Hall with incredible numbers. The two-time All-American had hit .444 with 42 home runs and 160 RBI in just 110 collegiate games. But he still was not convinced pro baseball was a certainty. That is why the summer of 1988 was so important to him.

"People were watching me more now because of the numbers I put up at Seton Hall," Vaughn said about playing in the Cape Cod League. "If I was going to be considered as a top draft pick, I had to show I could do it against the best players in the country. I also had to show that my power was not because of the aluminum bats. With wood, it is an entirely different game."

Following the college season, Vaughn, along with Seton Hall teammate Dana Brown, were welcomed by Wareham Gatemen General Manager John Wylde. Vaughn was assigned to room with Texas A&M infielder Chuck Knoblauch.

Memories of the Summer of 1988 came rolling back to Knoblauch as he momentarily removed himself from the problems he was having throwing to first base as the New York Yankees second baseman during the 2000 season.

"The guy we lived with was into hang gliding," Knoblauch said. "He was a widower and lived by himself. He was into hang gliding where the plane would tow you up and release you. He used to talk to Mo and me about it. The guy told us one night, 'If you want to go I'll wake you and you can come with me.' I'm thinking I'll go, whatever. We are both dead asleep and all of a sudden I hear Mo whisper, 'Act like you're asleep, Charlie, act like you're asleep. Here he comes, here he comes. You don't want to go up there, you don't want to go up there.' So the guy comes, knocks on the door, and we both pretend to be knocked out because Mo doesn't want any part of the hang glider. He didn't want me to go with him in this two-seat hang glider. We laughed so hard about it when the guy left.

"It was a good summer," Knoblauch continued. "So many great players. We definitely had a good time. We were roommates, living in the same room. He wasn't as big as he is now, but he was still bigger than everybody. It was a fun summer, both on and off the field. When you look at him, he looks mean. A 'don't-come-near-me' type of guy, but when you get to know him, he's one of the best people you can talk to for advice, about life. That's a reflection of his parents. I got a chance to get to spend some time with his parents. They were around a lot because they lived pretty close. They are great people."

While the elder Vaughns helped Knoblauch feel comfortable in New England, their son helped the Texas native enjoy a winning season. "Dana, Mike Weimerskirch from Iowa State, and I all stole more than 20 bases and we had Mo for power," Knoblauch said. "We had a great team and won the league."

Knoblauch made his trip east worthwhile. He led the league with a .361 average and won the Top Pro Prospect Award. Vaughn, who hit .271 with five homers and 35 RBI during the regular season, got hot in the playoffs with game-winning RBI in all four post season games as Wareham won the title. Vaughn earned playoff co-MVP honors with teammate John Thoden, a North Carolina pitcher.

Vaughn also earned a spot on the league's All-Star team, which traveled to Boardwalk and Baseball in Orlando to meet the best from the ACBL, Jayhawk League, Great Lakes League, and the Shenandoah Valley League.

The Cape Cod League team was loaded with future big leaguers. Vaughn and Knoblauch played first and second, respectively. Hartford third baseman Jeff Bagwell, North Carolina catcher Jesse Levis, Grand Canyon outfielder Tim Salmon, and Wichita State catcher Eric Wedge were also on the team. The team, which won the tournament, had so much talent that several other potential major leaguers were left behind, including Auburn first baseman Frank Thomas, Villanova third baseman Gary Scott, Oklahoma State outfielder Jeromy Burnitz, and Wichita State second baseman Mike Lansing. "I knew I had a chance to play professional baseball when I played well in the Cape Cod League," Vaughn said.

As September approached, Vaughn and the rest of his college teammates returned to Seton Hall and readied for their fall practice season. On one occasion, the Pirates assembled for batting practice in preparation for a game. But their opponent failed to show because of a scheduling mistake. Instead, Mike Sheppard Sr. had his troops scrimmage. It turned out to be an important day for Vaughn. Boston Red Sox scout Matt Sczesny, who had signed John Valentin just four months before, was there anticipating a game. Instead, he watched the scrimmage and saw Vaughn hit a home run onto the roof of a house about 500 feet away. "Aluminum bat or no aluminum bat, that convinced me he had great power," Sczesny said.

Vaughn continued to work on his game. He often locked himself in a racquetball court for hours and threw against the wall, fielding ball after ball. Just as he did in high school, Vaughn knew he had to put in extra work to make his dream of playing pro baseball a reality. He knew his power was not enough. "Mo has obviously had a tremendous two seasons at Seton Hall," Sheppard said. "I still feel he has a lot more work ahead of him. He must improve at first base and work very hard on his defense."

Vaughn, like Valentin the year before, got the opportunity to play for the United States National Team. Miami Dade South coach Charlie Greene invited him to play first base for him on the USA squad in the 1988 International Harbor Baseball Tournament in Kaohsiung, Taiwan.

Andy Baylock, the UConn coach, was one of the United States assistant coaches. It was his second time going overseas with a collegiate all-star team and both times a Seton Hall player made the roster. Right-hander Rich Scheid was part of the 1985 United States National Team which spent 10 summer weeks touring Korea, Japan, and Canada. Although Scheid eventually pitched in the major leagues, he was not one of the team's stars. Those roles were reserved for Kevin Brown, Matt Williams, Jack McDowell, Joe Girardi, and Jeff King. "That was quite a team," Baylock said. "But we still couldn't beat Cuba."

This time around, Baylock knew the Seton Hall player would be the star. He had known the Vaughn family for a long time, having played football against Leroy Vaughn in the semi-pro Atlantic Coast Football League. Baylock was a linebacker for Springfield, Massachusetts, while the elder Vaughn was a running back for Stamford, Connecticut.

Mo Vaughn was reunited on the United States team with Knoblauch and Levis, a fellow Cape Cod League All-Star. Several other future big leaguers were on the team. Miami's Alex Fernandez and Joe Grahe, Fresno State's Erik Schullstrom, Arizona's Lance Dickson, and North Carolina-Charlotte's Chris Haney led the pitching staff. Minnesota's Dan Wilson, Montevallo's Rusty Greer, and Western Michigan's Matt Mieske were position players. "It was a lot of pressure to coach that team," Baylock said. "We had to take care of those guys because we knew they were going to be worth millions and millions of dollars someday."

The players were comfortable on the baseball field, but off the field it was a different story. "We were at a banquet and they put chicken on the table," Baylock said. "But it still had its head and legs. The guys could barely look at it, let alone eat it. Mo took the table cloth and put it over the chicken's head so we didn't have to look at it. Some of the guys from the other teams looked over and started to laugh with us. Then, after the chicken, they brought out the fish. The heads were still on and their eyes looked at you. The players didn't touch it. They couldn't get out of there fast enough. They ran right away to find fast food. McDonald's, Wendy's, whatever was there."

While eyes were on Vaughn in the dining room, even more were focused on him on the diamond where he became a crowd favorite. The Taiwanese were well versed in American baseball, largely because of two-sport star and Nike commercial icon Bo Jackson. "Mo hit a bomb out of Taipei Stadium," Baylock said, "and they were yelling 'Bo, Bo, Bo' as he rounded the bases. Mo loved it. He gave them a big wave and they cheered even more."

"They called him Bo," Greene said. "I called him 'Sir.' I had never seen anyone else like him." Just like Bo, Mo knew baseball. Vaughn led the United States to a second-place finish and was the only American named to the All-Tournament team. He hit .400 in eight games, with 12 hits, two homers, and 10 RBI.

Back on American soil, Vaughn and Seton Hall opened the 1989 season with a 5-2 win over the second-ranked Miami Hurricanes. Junior left-hander Kevin Morton, another Norwalk, Connecticut native, allowed only four hits, struck out 12 and walked one to begin a brilliant season. He set Big East regular season records with a 6-0 mark and 0.92 ERA to earn the league's Pitcher of the Year. Sheppard was named the conference's Coach of the Year for a third time, while Brown and Vaughn, for the third year in a row, were all-conference picks. Seton Hall was the Big East Southern Division champion with a 32-17-1 record, the ninth straight year the Pirates had won more than 30 games.

> "It was a lot of pressure to coach that team. We had to take care of those guys because we knew they were going to be worth millions and millions of dollars someday."
> —Andy Baylock, UConn Coach

Big things had been expected of Vaughn as a junior. Amazingly, a .348 average, 12 homers, and 51 RBI were called "below par" by many observers. He had been frustrated all year by the lack of good pitches he saw. "The most important thing for me is to get a pitch that I can hit hard. Then I can do some damage up there," he said about the Big East Tournament.

Morton took the hill against Connecticut in the opener, fell behind early, but settled down to retire 16 of the final 17 batters.

Morton's 11-strikeout outing proved to be the final one of his Seton Hall career and also the final win of the 1989 season for the Pirates. They were eliminated the next day with losses to Villanova and Providence.

Vaughn was not the problem for the Pirates. He hit a Big East Tournament-record three home runs in his final day wearing the Seton Hall uniform and added seven RBI. Fittingly, in what would be his final collegiate at-bat, Vaughn came up in the eighth with his friend Brown and outfielder Mike Randazzo, who grew up with Vaughn on Norwalk's St. Mary's Lane, on board and hit a three-run homer to deep center field. Vaughn wrapped up his career as the greatest offensive weapon in Seton Hall history. The three-time All-American had school records of 57 home runs and 218 RBI, while hitting .417 over his three years.

Draft day was 17 days away on June 5, so a long wait ensued. Vaughn thought he could go in the first round. Morton thought he would go high. "There were always scouts at our games," said Morton, who finished his career as a 1989 All-American, along with Vaughn, with a career record of 27-5 and a 2.45 ERA. "They all wanted to talk to us. It took a lot of concentration to stay focused all season long and not get caught up in that game."

As expected, Vaughn heard first on draft day. He was taken by the Red Sox in the first round, the 23rd player taken, and the second by the Red Sox after Sarasota High School outfielder Greg Blosser was chosen with the 16th pick. "I was kind of surprised because I didn't see them around too much," Vaughn said about the Red Sox. What he did not know was that Sczesny had been tracking him all along.

"The fall of his freshman year, I was with some other scouts at a game at New York Tech," Sczesny said. "We saw him walking in and I said, 'Who the hell is that?' He was huge. Another guy asked if he could dunk a basketball and Mo said he could and laughed. He had a great personality. A lot of people were off him because they didn't think he could field his position. But I knew that if he could reach it, he could field it. His hands were not that bad. I don't know why the other teams let him go. I was really happy when he was still there when we picked. He had a quick stroke and quick hands and I told the Red Sox in his report that if you want someone to hit home runs, then take him."

The Red Sox listened and Sczesny got to make the congratulatory call. Vaughn picked up the phone when it rang. "I was there when he got the phone call," Vaughn's sister Donna said.

"We were just sitting at the table waiting and then the phone rang and we were so excited. I said, 'I want to be the first to get your autograph.' I had a piece of paper and I had him autograph it after he got the call!"

Vaughn immediately called his parents, who both were at work. "That was the most exciting day of my life," Shirley Vaughn said. "I told my principal that I might get a call, and he called me and said, 'Shirley, I think this is the call.' It was Maurice. When I got home, it was so exciting. The telephone was just ringing. Donna was on one phone, Maurice was on another and they just kept switching phones. The newspaper reporters were all calling. That phone rang so much. It was so unbelievable, so exciting."

Vaughn overshadowed Morton on draft day. The headline on the front page of the Newark *Star-Ledger*'s sports section screamed: **Vaughn picked 23rd by Bosox**. And yes, reporter Thomas Bergeron mentioned in passing in the second paragraph that the Red Sox also took Vaughn's teammate, Kevin Morton, with the 29th overall pick.

When Valentin heard the news that Vaughn and Morton would be joining him in the Red Sox organization, he was elated. "Before the draft, Eddie Haas, who was a Red Sox scout, asked my opinion of Mo and Kevin," Valentin said. "I said, 'If you are looking, you've got to get those guys because they are East Coast players. They are tough. They know how to play.' Bam, they took them both in the first round. I thought I had something to do with it, but I probably didn't. I was really excited that I would get a chance to play with my teammates."

Vaughn and Morton wanted Leroy Vaughn to handle their negotiations with the Red Sox. The elder Vaughn was well prepared when he sat down with Sczesny to talk money. "Mo and Kevin were the second easiest to sign out of all of them," Sczesny said of his stable of signees over the years. "Bob Stanley was the easiest and he would have gone for nothing. Mo and Kevin were a close second. After I gave him the proposal, 'Mr. Mo' asked for an additional $5,000 each to cover school costs. Without calling the office, I said, 'Okay.' There was no point dickering around over $5,000."

Sczesny thought his guys had what it took to get to the major leagues when he joined Vaughn and Morton for their signing press conference just four days after the draft. The two players wore ties. They participated in the traditional "changing of the caps" when the scout handed them Red Sox caps. Royal blue and white of Seton Hall to Red Sox navy blue and red. The players signed their contracts to a round of applause. Neither revealed their signing bonus, but they were each over $100,000. Both were assigned to begin their careers with Boston's rookie league team in Winter Haven, Florida.

Vaughn, who had spent every Thanksgiving with his family at his aunt and uncle's house just blocks from Fenway Park, was confident about his chances and did not think it would be long before his relatives could walk to see him play. "From what I know about their minor league organization and with me from this area, I think this is the best situation for me. I'm hitting with the best of them right now. I just need some time to smooth out the rough edges in my game. If I work hard, I think I'll be up there in two years." He was not far off.

> "I said, 'If you are looking, you've got to get those guys because they are East Coast players. They are tough. They know how to play.' Bam, they took them both in the first round. I thought I had something to do with it, but I probably didn't. I was really excited that I would get a chance to play with my teammates."
> —John Valentin

THE MINOR LEAGUES

Mom, Can You Keep a Secret?

CHAPTER 11

Craig Biggio flew to Asheville, North Carolina, in June 1987 for his first full-time job, catching for the Asheville Tourists in the South Atlantic League, not knowing much about what he was getting into. The Tourists were in the first inning of an important game that night at McCormick Field when the first-round pick arrived with little fanfare and took a seat in the stands.

He had no idea that Asheville, the Houston Astros' A-ball club, had to win against Charleston [West Virginia] to clinch the league's first half title. "Because of the tough time we had, it was that much sweeter when we won and the champagne was flowing in the clubhouse," Asheville manager Keith Bodie said. "The team was going nuts and here comes Craig Biggio walking into the clubhouse. I welcomed him to the Houston Astros organization and his first response was, 'Do you guys do this every time you win?'"

Bodie, who explained the circumstances to his new recruit, had heard a lot about his new catcher. Baseball people, including Detroit Tigers General Manager Joe McDonald who had signed Bodie as a third-round pick in the 1974 draft for the Mets, had called Bodie with reports. "Joe told me he had scouted Craig Biggio at Seton Hall and that I was getting an outstanding player and a great kid," Bodie said.

Their first meeting convinced the manager that McDonald was right. "I told Craig, 'You are going to play every day and you should expect to hit third in the lineup and if you need a day off, just come and tell me. Otherwise you are in there everyday,'"

Bodie remembered while managing the 2000 Double-A Wichita Wranglers.

"I don't need any days off, I'm here to play. But there is one thing you can do for me," Biggio said.

"Anything. What is it?" the manager replied.

"You don't need to pat me on the back. You can kick me in the ass if you have to so I can get better, but don't worry about patting me on the back," the player said sounding like a true believer of Mike Sheppard's Seton Hall system.

Biggio made his pro debut the next day to kick off the second half. Rain showers forced the Tourists to cancel batting practice. But once the game started, Biggio immediately excelled. His pro career began with a pair of doubles and an RBI. "The first hit he got was on a hanging breaking ball that was up in the zone, probably a ball, but he jumped all over it and hit a double in the gap," Bodie said. "I'm thinking to myself, 'There are not many players that would swing at that.' Young players don't know that is a good pitch to swing at. They will take it for a ball. Craig had great hitting instincts, baseball instincts." Biggio even threw out a runner trying to steal second.

Five days later, Biggio hit his first professional home run. The catcher was not overly impressed with the momentous feat. "We had a short porch in right field," he said in October 2000, barely remembering the personal milestone. "I mean really short. Fenway Park short. It had a big wall like that. It was basically a flyball that went out."

"It didn't take long to know he was going to the major leagues," Bodie said. "A couple of days of watching him play. You knew he was special, he was heads and shoulders above everybody else. Not only his performance, but in his approach to the game."

Even though Biggio was earning rave reviews, he had not been around long enough to play in the South Atlantic League All-Star game. Bodie was announced as the North Division manager. He was joined by six of his players, including future big leaguers — first baseman Mike Simms, shortstop Lou Frazier, third baseman Ed Whited, and pitcher Ryan Bowen. His North Division All-Star squad also included another future major leaguer who would become a household name — Gastonia outfielder Sammy Sosa.

The All-Star game in Charleston, South Carolina, came with the Tourists red-hot at 17-6 in the second half, but the three-day All-Star break did not slow them down. With Biggio on board, the Tourists won 11 straight after the break, lost and followed by winning 9-of-10 to build a 10 $^1/_2$ game lead over Fayetteville in the Northern Division.

The hot streak was lit by Biggio. He toyed with South Atlantic League pitching, hitting .378 with eight homers and 32 RBI in 40 games. He scored 30 runs and added 18 stolen bases. His speed fit in perfectly with the rest of the Tourists, who had earned the nickname "Bodie's Bandits" on their way to setting a league record with 324 stolen bases.

It was not only the offense and speed Biggio offered that had Bodie so excited. "There are people who play this game that elevate the performance of the people around them," the manager said. "Craig Biggio was one of those people. He is an example of how this game is played on and off the field. He is a quality person and a quality player. He's got a domineering personality and is a very confident kid, not cocky or brash, but very confident. He had no insecurity."

Bodie was learning what they already knew about Biggio back home in Kings Park. But now Biggio was more than a high school or collegiate star, he was a pro. Lee Biggio went down to visit his son in Asheville and had Craig sign a bunch of photos of him in an Asheville uniform for people back home. "It was a bit weird asking my own son for an autograph." Lee Biggio said.

Chuck Alben, who had become close to Biggio after Alben's brother Chris had died of leukemia, got one of those signed photos, but he was not overly impressed. Instead he wanted a letter from his idol. Every day, young Alben ran to the mailbox to see if Biggio had written. The two were now pen pals and Biggio's notes seeped of Sheppard's teachings.

"He'd write the same thing every time," Alben said. "He would always tell me how he was doing, but he never, ever bragged about how things were going. When he was in the minors, he ended every letter with, 'I have to go to work.' I can remember the things he would stress. Always give 110%, not a 100% on and off the field. He'd tell me to respect my elders and play the game hard. Respect the game."

Astros owner Dr. John McMullen wondered if the always-hustling Biggio might be ready for the major leagues, even though he was just a few months out of college. "McMullen called me up when Craig was in Asheville and he was wondering if Craig could play in the major leagues," Seton Hall coach Mike Sheppard said. "He was worried about it psychologically. I told him, 'I don't know a lot about pro baseball and what goes on there, but are you asking me what will happen if the kid fails? Will he go into the cooler? No.' So many guys have a bad experience and never recover. I told him that Craig Biggio is not like that. He could go 6-for-6 or 0-for-6 and his demeanor doesn't change. He'll handle that."

But the discussion never went further and Biggio stayed in A ball. The Tourists completed a 54-16 second half to finish 91-48 overall and won home field advantage in the playoffs. Leading 5-2 in the ninth inning of game four, the Tourists needed one more strike to clinch the crown. Instead, they made two errors and Myrtle Beach came back to win 6-5. The Jays then won game five to end the Tourists' magical season.

"It was a negative moment not being able to win," Biggio said. "But we had a great team. It was a great bunch of guys who wanted to win and have fun. Asheville was probably the best place I ever could have ever asked for because they had a good team already and I was just able to play and help them out a little bit. It was a great city and I had a great manager."

"I had a bunch of good ones," Bodie said. "It was a fun time. Those kids would run through walls for you. You tell them the sky is blue and they always think it is blue. It is a very refreshing level of baseball."

Biggio finished hitting .375 in 64 games with 17 doubles, nine homers, 49 RBI, and 31 stolen bases. "This player came into half a season after coming out of college and put up numbers that people don't put up in an entire season," Bodie said. *Baseball America*, the bible of minor league coverage, put

Biggio on its list of the top 10 major league prospects in the South Atlantic League.

But it was not yet time to savor the success of his initial campaign. Biggio was one of 34 of the Astros' top prospects invited to play in the Instructional League in Arizona from mid-September to early October. Each major league team invited its top, young minor league prospects to a postseason camp that featured a grueling routine of practices and games.

Bodie, who managed that Astros' Instructional League team, believed Biggio was ready to make the jump directly from the South Atlantic League to the National League and made his thoughts known at the Astros' organizational meetings held in conjunction with the camp.

Astros Farm Director Bill Wood ran the three-day meeting and allowed each manager in the Houston system the chance to talk about their players. "I said how good a player Craig was," Bodie remembered. "They looked at me a little cross-eyed. They said, 'Keith, don't get too excited.' But that is what I felt." Bodie got a partial victory when the Astros invited Biggio to attend spring training with the big club.

> 'I have to go to work.' I can remember the things he would stress. Always give 110%, not a 100% on and off the field. He'd tell me to respect my elders and play the game hard. Respect the game."
> —Chuck Alben about Craig Biggio's letters

After the Astros finished the 1987 season, Houston coaches Matt Galante and Yogi Berra returned to their winter homes in Staten Island, New York, and Montclair, New Jersey, respectively, and made plans to visit with Biggio, who had also returned home. One afternoon, as Biggio prepared to hit with his old Seton Hall teammates in their underground batting cages, he told Sheppard that Galante and Berra were coming over.

"Yogi and I were friendly over the years," Sheppard said. "We used to do clinics together with Elston Howard. Yogi used to love when I showed up at clinics because I was younger. I would do all the talking and he wouldn't have to use his energy." The Seton Hall coach wanted to play a joke on Berra and convinced Biggio it would be okay to have fun at the Hall of Famer's expense. Sheppard knew Berra had never met the catcher, so he had his 5'7", 250-plus pound student manager Mike Cocco dress in an Astros shirt and cap.

In came Galante and Berra. "I met them and we were talking for a while," Sheppard said. "We walked into the gym and Cocco was doing some drills with the catchers and Craig is over on the side laughing his ass off."

With the Houston coaches at his side wanting to see Biggio, Sheppard pointed at Cocco. Galante had seen photos of the catcher and knew something was amiss, but Berra was ripe for the prank.

"When he first got a gander of the size of this so-called number one draft pick, Yogi was aghast," Galante said. "But you know Yogi. He said, 'We'll make a player out of him! We'll make a player out of him!'" Berra took a couple more steps towards Cocco and said to Sheppard, "You're putting me on! You're putting me on!" Sheppard and the two Houston coaches moved even closer.

"When Yogi came in, Shep introduced Yogi to 'Craig Biggio,' but it was me," Cocco laughed, 13 years later. "Yogi looked at me, looked at Matt Galante, and, as only Yogi could say, 'He must be some phenom!'"

"I loved it," Galante said. "It was a great joke. Yogi was great. He was one of the guys. To treat him any differently would be disrespectful to him. He wanted to be treated like one of the players, like one of the coaches. He is always into that type of stuff."

Berra's son Dale, who finished the 1987 season as a shortstop with the Astros, had arrived to work out with former Seton Hall star and then Yankee catcher Rick Cerone. Biggio and his friend and former college teammate Bobby Gallitelli, who was playing professionally in Italy, joined the two in the batting cages as the elder Berra and Galante watched.

"Yogi was sitting there while the four of us took batting practice," Gallitelli said. "We each took turns hitting and throwing the ball. Craig was really pumped that Yogi was here looking at him and taking an interest in him. Craig wasn't in awe of him. He was staying focused. From day one, those two were tight. He's almost like a father figure for Craig."

"I saw him hitting the ball, working in the cage," Yogi Berra said. "Craig was a good worker, he worked hard to get where he's at."

When spring training arrived, the *Houston Chronicle*'s Neil Hohlfeld made comparisons between Berra and Biggio. "If the Astros need reassurance that a man Biggio's size can catch, they need only look at coach Yogi Berra, who muddled through to the Hall of Fame despite being 5'8"."

Biggio got his first exhibition game action with the Astros on March 8, 1988, with a seventh-inning single to score their only run in a 2-1, 11-inning loss to the Milwaukee Brewers. His defense also drew attention from the Astros' pitching staff. "He handles the glove well and I like his attitude," reliever Dan Smith said. "He's going to be a major league catcher." Larry Andersen also chimed in. "He learns quickly. He caught me once before and knew today exactly what I wanted."

Soon it was all-time great Nolan Ryan who hopped on the Biggio bandwagon. "He catches the ball well and seems to be a good receiver. I like his attitude and his enthusiasm. He seems like the type of kid who's not going to be overwhelmed by things. My attitude is that if they're going to take him, they've got to play him. What I'd do is platoon him with Ash [Alan Ashby], let him start against left-handed pitchers."

It had not even been a year since Biggio had left Seton Hall, and Houston manager Hal Lanier was already considering keeping Biggio to back up 36-year-old Ashby. Biggio hit .385 through the first two weeks in Kissimmee, Florida, and was clearly ahead of the competition for the backup role.

"I would love to follow in Alan's footsteps and I think I can," Biggio told the *Houston Chronicle*. "Alan is a great person. I've always had a positive attitude. Like I've always said, 'Baseball is 70 percent mental and 30 percent physical.'" Biggio had the percentages right, unlike his mentor Berra who once uttered the famous phrase, "Baseball is 90 percent mental and the other half physical."

Berra and Biggio continued to bond. The Hall-of-Famer liked what he saw in the new kid. "I like small guys," the renowned wordsmith explained. "Small guys are better targets for the pitchers. A small guy doesn't have to stand up as far. Big guys really have to work to get up and down. A small guy just stands there." Berra liked Biggio's size, while Lanier liked the kid's attitude. "He shows so much enthusiasm," the manager said. "When he walks on the field, you notice him. He makes you notice him." Biggio thought it was his speed that was getting him attention. "My father always told me that when I get to this level, speed will be of the essence," the 22-year-old said. "It definitely has been an asset."

Whatever it was, Biggio had played himself into a serious candidate to make the club. He made it through the first round of cuts, but even though he was hitting .333, the dream ended on March 26 when Biggio was assigned to Triple-A Tucson in the Pacific Coast League. He was not upset with the decision.

"I picked up a lot of things this spring," he told the media. "Whatever anybody had to say I listened to it. I'm real happy to be in the position I'm in right now. When I came to camp, I thought I'd spend this year in Osceola [A ball]. I'm sure I made a good impression, but I knew this was going to happen. All I can do now is play hard and try to incorporate everything I learned here into my game. I got my feet wet down here and stayed a lot longer than I thought I would. Now my job is to keep getting better."

But he started his Triple-A career in the opposite direction of his start in Asheville. Instead of .395 [17-for-43], he was hitting just .167 [6-for-36] with no homers and just one RBI. "When I went to Triple-A, the difference was everyone was trying to get to the big leagues," Biggio said in September 2000. "I went from a team in Asheville with 20-to-22-year-old kids to Tucson with a bunch of guys who were older, 29-to-30-year-olds trying to get back to the big leagues. It was a different feeling. Triple-A was an eye-opener. The year before it was a bunch of young guys going out to have fun and now it was a bunch of older guys who wanted to win, but really wanted to get to the big leagues or get back to the big leagues."

But soon the hits started to fall again. Two one night, two another, four against Tacoma. Biggio went on a .400 tear for two weeks and upped his marks to .309, 13 RBI, 17 runs scored with seven stolen bases.

"When he played for me in Tucson, he ran really well. He could hit and he was a good catcher," Biggio's Triple-A manager Bob Didier said. "We got out and worked on his release, although it is hard during the season because you're playing every day. And throwing is something you can't do too much because you will hurt a kid's arm, but he was very coachable. He was a good receiver. He didn't have a really strong arm, but we were working on a quicker release. That was one of the knocks, he didn't have a really strong arm. There are guys like that. Craig learned how to get rid of the ball. You make adjustments. And when you hit well…"

Good things will happen. Offensively, once on track, Biggio made Triple-A look easy. On a trip to Phoenix to play the San Francisco Giants Triple-A affiliate, Biggio came out of the dugout before the game to talk with a visiting friend from Seton Hall. Biggio invited him to sit by the first base dugout so they could talk again when Biggio came to the on-deck circle. His third time up, Biggio turned to his friend and said, "Let me hit one for you." Less than a minute later, Biggio roped a drive off the left field advertising and stood on third with a standup triple. The two friends shared a laugh.

Those happy times continued when his family came to visit. His mother came to Tucson on her way home from an Oregon vacation. Older brother Terry came to visit with his wife Carole. Biggio's father, who was now divorced from Biggio's mother, also made plans to see his son, but was scheduled to arrive a few days later. But Lee Biggio never got to see his son in a Triple-A uniform.

Didier was in his office when the phone rang at 3 PM on June 25. It was Wood, then Houston's general manager. Ashby was going on the 15-day disabled list with back spasms, leaving Alex Trevino as the only available catcher. The Astros needed a rested receiver the next day in Houston. Wood told Didier to play Biggio in the outfield that night and tell him after the game to get to the airport. After only 141 minor league games, Biggio was going to Houston.

"Craig's mom had been sitting by the dugout for three or four days in a row," Didier, a former big-league catcher, said in the New York Yankees' clubhouse where he served as the team's bullpen coach in 2000. "I came out right before the game and I asked her if she could keep a secret. She looked at me. I said, 'Craig is being called up to the major leagues, but I can't tell him until after the game.' It was one of the big thrills for me as a manager. Any time you get to tell a player he is going to the major leagues, but to be able to tell his mom first, even before he knew, was pretty special."

Johnna Biggio remembered the moment well. "I was sitting in the stands and his coach came over to me and said, 'This is the first time I have ever been able to tell a parent this first.' That was a proud moment."

"You have to have that fire burning inside you," Biggio said, again showing he had learned something from his college coach. "You have to always scratch and work to get there. It was a great feeling. I spent just one full year in the minor leagues and now I was going to the big leagues. I knew I had a lot to learn and a long way to go. I knew there were a lot of tremendous people up there I could learn from. It was probably one of the most exciting times of my life."

> "You have to have that fire burning inside you. You have to always scratch and work to get there. It was a great feeling. I spent just one full year in the minor leagues and now I was going to the big leagues. I knew I had a lot to learn and a long way to go. I knew there were a lot of tremendous people up there I could learn from. It was probably one of the most exciting times of my life."
> —Craig Biggio

Johnna Biggio was starting a new job back home, so she could not go to Houston. But at least she knew Craig was a major leaguer, something his father had yet to learn.

Craig had wanted his white Saab, the car he bought with his signing bonus, with him in Arizona, so he asked if his dad would be willing to drive it out from the East Coast. His dad agreed and made plans to visit friends in Phoenix after the long drive was over. "He drove the whole way without air conditioning because the freon was out and he didn't know the car had heated seats and they were on the whole time," Craig Biggio said with a laugh. "It couldn't have been a very pleasant drive. He complained to me later that the seats were so damn hot."

Hot seats and all, Lee Biggio drove west. "I got a little west of Oklahoma City and read in *USA Today* that the Astros might call him up," the elder Biggio said. "I couldn't get him so I just kept going to Phoenix. But Craig was gone. By the time I got to talk to him, he was already in Houston. We then drove the car to Tucson and the team made arrangements to send it up to him. It was OK that I didn't see him. I was really proud of him."

CHAPTER 12

NOT ONE OF THE CHOSEN FEW

Boston Red Sox center fielder Darren Lewis had finished eating a bowl of cereal at a table smack in the middle of the spacious visitors locker room in Philadelphia's Veterans Stadium. Batting practice for the day's game with the Philadelphia Phillies was still hours away. As Lewis changed into his uniform, he realized how lucky he was to be a major leaguer.

"If you make it to this level, you make it for a reason and that is why everyone in this room is so special, because it is that difficult to get here," Lewis said during the 2000 season. "The odds of making it are extremely slim. It is talent, a combination of work ethic, staying healthy, desire and those are the only reasons why you're here. Baseball players are a dime a dozen and that is why very few make it."

He reflected on his fortunes this day because he was asked to comment about his former minor league roommate Marteese Robinson. It was Robinson, then a year out of Seton Hall, who welcomed Lewis, an 18th-round draft pick out of the University of California in 1988, to professional baseball. The two shared a baseball bond. "You always think everyone is going to make it," Lewis said of Robinson. "He was a good player who could swing the bat pretty good."

Lewis knew how Robinson's baseball story ended. But when Marteese Robinson set out for professional baseball, he had no idea how many ups and downs he would endure over a four-year career which began in Medford, Oregon.

Once Robinson arrived to the Northwest League, Medford

manager Dave Hudgens immediately put him at first base and had him hit third. "Ordinarily, I'd give him a couple of days to get acclimated," Hudgens, who briefly played for Oakland in 1983, told John Lowry of the *Mail Tribune*. "But he's been playing in the Cape Cod League and you kind of hope that maybe he can come in and get something going." He did not. Robinson went 0-for-4 in a 5-0 loss to the Everett Giants.

The rookie ball A's needed some punch in the lineup. They had dropped four of the last five games before Robinson came west and expected big things from the NCAA batting champion. "They knew I was the Player of the Year, but I really tried to downplay it," Robinson said. "If I was going to succeed, I had to put that behind me. This was different. This was pro ball."

But the players knew all about his .529 average. "I kept track of him because I finished 12th in the country that year," said outfielder Bob Parry, now a California high school teacher, who had signed with Oakland out of San Diego State. "I hit .418. When I met him, I said, 'You're the guy who led the nation in hitting. How did you hit over .500?' It was amazing that a guy could get a base hit every other at bat."

Robinson also impressed his new teammates with his defense at first base. He took a throw from third baseman Scott Brosius, and, knowing it would be a bang-bang play, went to a full-split stretch. The extra inches made the difference and the runner was called out. Brosius' jaw dropped. "'Wow, look at this guy,'" the Linfield College product said. "He had that stretch. Most guys did not have that."

The Oakland brass liked what they saw of Robinson. He went 2-for-4 with two RBI in his sixth game in Medford to lift his average to .292, three RBI and two stolen bases. That was good enough and Robinson was promoted after the game to the Modesto A's, Oakland's A ball affiliate in the California League.

Robinson flew to Palm Springs to meet the team and was met by Modesto manager Tommy Reynolds. Reynolds had never met Robinson, had not even seen pictures of him, so he was shocked when the smiling, young man got off the plane and approached him.

"I found out later that the players wondered if I was going to be black or white," Robinson said. "They had heard about me, how I had speed, could hit and had some power. Some of the guys thought I was a white first baseman who could run. Some others thought I was going to be this huge black guy because I could hit home runs. When I met the team, they were kind of disappointed because they expected me to be larger than life. I was only 6'1", 175 pounds."

Though not what they expected, the players were thrilled when Robinson arrived. They needed a first baseman. Dann Howitt, a big-armed, future major league outfielder, currently had the spot and was more than happy to move out of the infield. Mike Bordick was another guy who grew to appreciate Robinson. The two had a lot in common. Both were signed by the same scout, J.P Ricciardi. Both had been Northeastern college stars, Bordick at national power Maine and Robinson at Seton Hall. "We had a lot of fun," Bordick said. "He had a great sense of humor. The minor leagues are pretty tough and having a guy like Marteese around makes it that much easier."

The Maine product also learned why Brosius had been impressed with Robinson. "He was amazing at first base," said Bordick, while playing shortstop for the Baltimore Orioles before a mid-season trade to the New York Mets took him to the 2000 Subway Series. "He was a great athlete. Athletically, he was one of the best first baseman I'd played with. He certainly made me look good. It is certainly comfortable, especially for a young minor league infielder, knowing that the guy over there is going to do the best he can to catch the ball. Marteese was a very talented player. He enjoyed the game. He had the attitude. He was willing to put the time in to work at it. With his athleticism, he certainly helped a lot of guys out."

Initially, he also helped the team with his bat. Through his first eight games in A ball, Robinson had seven hits, four for extra bases. He also added six RBI. Unfortunately, he still had the rest of the year to go. "My junior year at Seton Hall took so much out of me that I had nothing else to give," Robinson said. "I was so mentally and physically drained that I was done for." Over the final 40 games in Modesto, Robinson struggled to hit just .215 with only five more extra bases and 16 RBI.

Still, Robinson, Bordick, Brosius, and nearly 40 other players spent September and October at Oakland's instructional complex in Scottsdale, Arizona. Besides being fatigued, Robinson also had the pressure of learning a new position.

The Oakland minor league player personnel staff allowed Robinson to play first base at Medford and Modesto so he could get comfortable with pro baseball. Now it was time for the expected transition to second base, where Robinson took hundreds of groundballs.

Robinson finally completed his whirlwind year. It started with doubts and ended with more doubts. Could he come back from a broken wrist and still compete at the college level? He proved he could. But now he returned to New Jersey and wondered if he could turn himself into a second baseman? "I spent a lot of time thinking about it that winter," Robinson said. "Once I rested, the doubts went away because I realized that I had run out of gas." Once Robinson relaxed, he began workouts with his former college teammates.

"In hindsight, I probably should have asked Blanky to help me," Robinson said about his former college assistant coach, Ed Blankmeyer. "He had been a second baseman and played in the Orioles chain. He could have helped me, but I thought I had enough ability and since that was my position in high school, I would be OK." Robinson went to spring training and was assigned to Madison, Wisconsin, in the Midwest League, a second Oakland A ball team.

Robinson lived with Darren Lewis, a future major leaguer, and was now part of a double-play combination with another, third baseman-turned-shortstop, Scott Brosius. The two were not exactly Whitaker-to-Trammell-like. "I spent a lot of that year playing shortstop for the first time, so we had two guys up the middle playing different positions," Brosius said while wearing pinstripes in 2000 as the New York Yankees third baseman. "I know on my end, I made a lot of mistakes on that side. I had 61 errors that year. Before that year I played mostly third base and the outfield. I had never seen shortstop before and Marteese had never really seen second base before. Second base is a whole new position with the pivot and all of those things. He had a whole new set of things to think about. He was asked to do a pretty difficult thing to switch from a corner position to play a middle infield position."

Robinson added 21 errors and struggled to make the switch from first to second. "He wasn't a guy they thought at the time was going to hit a lot of home runs and that is why he changed positions, but everybody doesn't make those types of adjustments," Lewis said. "It would be like me leaving college and all of sudden becoming a shortstop. I'm not a shortstop; I had been an outfielder since I was a little kid. You have to understand what happens once you get to this level. They were looking for a stereotypical first baseman, somebody who is going to hit 20-plus home runs and that was not Marteese. He had a little pop. They probably figured at the major league level he was probably better off being a second baseman since he wasn't going to hit 30, 40 home runs."

Lewis was right. Robinson had only eight homers while hitting .251 in Madison, but he did add 21 doubles and 49 RBI in 125 games. One of his better hot streaks came when Biggio was called up to the Astros. "When Craig made the Astros, I was so pumped up," Robinson said. "We always knew the guy was going to make it, but it was shocking how quickly it happened. Since my former teammate had made it, I figured my time was coming too."

For that to happen, Robinson needed to improve. "I had a couple of multi-hit games, but my stats weren't that good," he said. "I thought I went out there and held my own. The doubles showed that I did have some power. I took a lot of concentration to play second and maybe that hurt me offensively." Robinson, who was now hitting .245 in his two-year minor league career, was struggling for the first time in his life on the baseball field.

"Marteese never played relaxed," Oakland's sports psychologist Harvey Dorfman said. "You never saw the same Marteese Robinson in an A's uniform you saw at Seton Hall. He just wasn't the same guy. We once had McGwire at third base and he hated it. He wasn't that good in the field. They gave him the first-base glove at the major league level because Robbie Nelson couldn't get it done, and the waters parted for him. But that never happened for Marteese. I'm not comparing Marteese to Mark McGwire, but I'm showing you how important that comfort zone is."

Robinson agreed. "I knew I could do better, but what was happening is I was getting advice from everyone and I tried to do everything everyone was telling me. I was screwed up. I had so much success for so long that I forgot how tough baseball was."

Robinson also never let on that he was uncomfortable at second base. "Part of being mentally tough is being up front with us and discussing with us the concerns you have," explained Karl Kuehl, then Oakland's director of player development. "That is part of the process. Marteese had the attitude that he was going to play second and work hard because that is what we wanted him to do. He never got to the point where he said, 'I'm doing this because I want to.' Marteese certainly had the potential, but the best guys don't always make it. There is something inside the guys who make it. They make adjustments. Scott Brosius was tough. He wouldn't quit. He would fight and wouldn't give up."

Robinson admitted to giving in a bit. "I wasn't hungry because what good is going after something when you know you're never going to make it?" Robinson said. "Karl and his guys wanted me to be a home run hitter, but that was not me. I tried, but you can't try to hit home runs. That's what I tried to do and my hitting suffered because of it. They also wanted me to play second base a certain way. They were always on me to do it this way, do it that way. Getting the job done was not that important. How I got the job done mattered more to them. But in the end, it was my fault. I let them take away my concentration. I definitely lost my hustle.

"I forgot everything Shep taught me about mental toughness," Robinson continued. "Everything he did was designed to teach us how to handle adversity. He was so tough on us in college that I really should have been able to better handle this."

Even after struggling for a second season in A ball, Robinson was again invited to instructional ball where he met former major league second baseman Lenn Sakata, who would be his manager the next season back in Modesto. "It was really the first time that somebody who knew how to play the position was able to help me," Robinson said. "I started to work on my footwork and my arm action from second." The two also talked about Robinson's struggles. "Guys like Marteese had it hard," Sakata said. "It was hard to conform to standards. They had the perfect player syndrome. Every at-bat, every swing, every play, they wanted perfection in a game that is not about perfection. I would say to my coaches that this is unfair to the players. Every day was a different guy critiquing them. It is impossible to play that way."

When Robinson returned for a visit to Seton Hall, Mike Sheppard blasted him for feeling sorry for himself and making excuses. He thought Robinson was not utilizing all of his tools. "I told him he should be stealing bases," Sheppard said. "I always saw him as a late-inning replacement for McGwire. Marteese would come in and run for him in the eighth inning, steal a base and score. He would then stay in the game for defense. Marteese told me that they didn't let him run. I really thought he was bullshitting me. I didn't buy it. I told him to get on base and read the pitchers. Learn if he was slow to the plate. If you steal the base, they are not going to yell at you. If you get thrown out that is something else. If that keeps happening then you can back it off."

> "Part of being mentally tough is being up front with us and discussing with us the concerns you have. Marteese certainly had the potential, but the best guys don't always make it. There is something inside the guys who make it."
> —Karl Kuehl, Oakland A's

Sheppard did not understand Robinson's role as well as Sakata did. "Lenn wanted me to make it," Robinson said. "I don't think he was happy with the situation with me and how they dealt with it. I could see that he knew something he couldn't tell me." Robinson was right.

"Karl Kuehl was impatient," Sakata said. "He put too much pressure to perform right away. Given time, Marteese might have been able to make the transition, maybe could have made it. They didn't like him at first; they didn't like him as an outfielder because he didn't steal enough bases. He was pretty good at a lot of things, but not great at one thing. He wasn't a skilled position player — shortstop, second base. At the time Oakland was power conscious. Players like Marteese weren't appreciated. He could run. He could bunt. But they weren't interested in small ball. He was not considered a turd! He was drafted pretty high and was a prospect, but not a front line guy."

The second base experiment lasted only 16 more games in Modesto. Kuehl told Sakata that Robinson was finished as a middle infielder. "Defense is not what stopped him," Kuehl insisted. "He just didn't put up the numbers."

Through 16 games, Robinson was hitting just .162 and had nine errors. But Parry, who watched Robinson play second base from the outfield did not agree with the decision. "He was a pretty good second baseman. Half the things they did, I couldn't figure out. Maybe there was a player somewhere else in the organization who they thought was better than him at second. If Marteese could have made it at second base, it would have been helpful. He would not have had to hit for the same power as he would have at first. The organization at that time had these powerful guys in the major leagues. José Canseco, Rickey Henderson, Dave Henderson, Mark McGwire. Marteese did not have that power that they were looking for at that time. I think with another team he would have had a better shot, but with the A's, that was their big thing at that time."

> "I forgot everything Shep taught me about mental toughness. Everything he did was designed to teach us how to handle adversity.
> He was so tough on us in college, that I really should have been able to better handle this."
>
> — Marteese Robinson

Sakata, who soon after was fired from his manager position and reassigned to a roving instructor role, was forced to tell Robinson he was being sent to Madison. "He just shook my hand and said, 'Prove 'em wrong,' " Robinson remembered. "I was pissed off. On the plane ride from Modesto to Madison, I said, 'Screw it! I'm not doing what they told me to do. I'm gonna play the game the way I was taught to play the game. I'm gonna go back to doing that and that's it.' I knew I changed my game, my style of play, and I said, 'I'm gonna stop and I'm gonna go back to doing what I did to get me there.' I totally got away from what made me successful in college."

Former major leaguer Jim Nettles welcomed Robinson back to Wisconsin. "Marteese, you know what you need to do," the Madison manager told him. "Just prove 'em wrong. Go out there and show 'em that you can do it."

"They had given up on me. But now I was hungry to do well for myself." Robinson said with the fire that Sheppard would have loved. With second base not an option, Nettles had Robinson play first and third, another new position. But this time, Robinson handled the position change well. "I knew third base was not going to last," Robinson said. "I didn't have the arm strength to make the long throw." But he started to hit again. A week after rejoining the Madison Muskies, Robinson was hitting .391.

Robinson was back to his old ways. Through 36 games he had 40 hits, including a team-leading eight doubles, and 24 RBI. "When I was in A ball with Marteese, he was very talented. He had a great body and was a great athlete," Ozzie Canseco, who eventually played 24 games in the major leagues, said. "He could run. He could hit. He could do it all. He was a very good hitter, a very good player. I always thought Marteese was one of those guys that was going to make it to the big leagues."

But Ozzie Canseco was worried that his twin brother Jose's success as one of Oakland's Bash Brothers with McGwire might hold Robinson back. "I'm sure there would have been more opportunity to move up more quickly in the organization, or even get a chance at the big league level, if guys like Mark McGwire and Rob Nelson, Dann Howitt weren't in front of him," Canseco said during the 2000 season when he hit 40 homers for the independent Newark Bears. "They had some great power at first base. At that position it would have been virtually impossible for him to make it to the big leagues with the Oakland Athletics."

Robinson agreed that the move back to first base would hurt him in the long run with Oakland. "Deep down I knew I wasn't going to the major leagues because they had McGwire there," Robinson said. "No one was moving. They were winning and if it ain't broke, don't fix it. But I still wanted to do it for myself. I was hoping I could become a defensive guy who could pinch hit."

Robinson, back to running, hitting, and playing "rubber band man" at first, was named the Midwest League's June Player of the Month and then made the league's All-Star team. Oakland officials noticed Robinson's .342 average through 70 games with nine homers and 44 RBI and promoted him to AA Huntsville, Alabama, less than a month after the All-Star game.

"We wanted to find out if he could hit in Double-A," Kuehl said. "What kind of numbers would he put up?"

"Jim Nettles told me I was promoted to Double-A," Robinson said. "Of course I was excited. It was my first time going to Double-A. I earned it. I thought I was back on track." He was. Robinson feasted on Double-A pitching like it was the Big East. He went on a 16-game tear, all but one as a first baseman, where he hit .338 with six doubles and nine RBI. "When I got there I was swinging the bat well. I was still getting my hits. I was still driving the ball. I was doing what got me there."

The hot streak ended when the Stars traveled to Knoxville. Robinson opened the day with a single off future big leaguer Juan Guzman, but disaster struck later against a reliever. Robinson topped a pitch to the right side and was in a foot race with the pitcher. "He stepped in the middle of the base as I was getting ready to hit the bag," Robinson said. "I had to go to the outside of the bag and I rolled my ankle. I could see the bottom of my ankle and that was it. I knew it was messed up. I went to the hospital, they put me in a cast, and I went home to New Jersey."

Robinson stayed in the cast for six weeks, did physical therapy for two more, and, as a prospect again, headed to Arizona

> "I was pissed off. On the plane ride from Modesto to Madison, I said, 'Screw it! I'm not doing what they told me to do. I'm gonna play the game the way I was taught to play the game. I'm gonna go back to doing that and that's it.' I knew I changed my game, my style of play, and I said, 'I'm gonna stop and I'm gonna go back to doing what I did to get me there.' I totally got away from what made me successful in college."
> — Marteese Robinson

for the instructional league. His ankle, however, had not had enough time to heal, and Robinson had a poor September and October. "I would be walking and if I stepped on a crack or a rock, my ankle would just turn over and I would fall," Robinson said. "They taped my ankle, but it just wasn't right. I ran with a limp and in hitting, I couldn't use my back leg. Everything collapsed because I couldn't drive off my back leg to get everything going. I thought it was important to play so I continued to play. It never healed properly."

Robinson was penciled in as the starting first baseman at Double-A Huntsville when he returned to spring training in Arizona four months later. His sore ankle became an afterthought when Robinson complained to his roommates that he was not feeling well. "I had had chicken pox before my junior year at San Diego State. I was 20 or 21 at the time, and I knew exactly what they were," said Parry, who roomed with Robinson and Darren Lewis for a third straight spring training. "Marteese was itching his head and complaining he didn't feel good. Darren and I realized it was chicken pox. We turned into two mothers taking care of him because he shut everything down. When you are sick, you want someone to take care of you. The doctors quarantined him. I had had them and so did Darren, so we were not scared to get them again. Marteese was a very needy patient. He needed his food and everything taken care of while he sat and watched television."

> "He could run. He could hit. He could do it all. He was a very good hitter, a very good player. I always thought Marteese was one of those guys that was going to make it to the big leagues."
> —Ozzie Canseco

Not only did doctors quarantine Robinson, but they quarantined the entire Oakland farm system for the final 10 days of spring training. "We had to play against ourselves for all of spring training and that got pretty old playing the same guys over and over again," Brosius said. "We didn't get a chance to go and play different teams. It was one of those spring trainings you go through once, but you don't want to do it again."

Once Robinson was cleared by doctors he rejoined the Double-A Huntsville Stars along with Brosius, Lewis, and Ozzie Canseco, while Parry headed back to Modesto. Robinson, when hitting well, was a line drive hitter who would pepper balls all over the place. But his ankle, which continued to bother him, prevented him from doing that. "I wish I had broken it because had I broken it, it would have healed much better. Everything was just totally stretched out around it. Just like in instructional ball, I had no power coming from my back side because my ankle had no strength."

Midway through the season, Ron Witmeyer, who had been drafted out of Stanford, was called up to Huntsville. Witmeyer had been an East Islip [New York] High School junior in 1984 when he hit .442 and beat out Craig Biggio for the Carl Yastrzemski Award as the best player in Suffolk County. Now he was sharing time with Robinson at first base in Huntsville. "Can you believe it?" Robinson said. "The same guy who beat Craig out beat me out," Robinson said. "What are the odds of that happening?"

Robinson finished the 1990 season hitting .265 with six homers and 50 RBI in 104 games. He did not return to Seton Hall that winter, largely because he did not want people to see him as a struggling minor leaguer. "By this time Craig was in the majors, Mo was being considered the next great Boston superstar and Kevin Morton and Val were in Double-A and they had a shot to make it. I was the only one struggling."

Robinson is an admittedly stubborn man. By keeping away from his friends, he lost a chance to get frequent confidence boosts. "I saw Craig after he got to the big leagues one time at Seton Hall and he knew I was struggling a bit," Robinson said. "He wanted to keep me going. He said, 'I've seen a lot of players now and I've haven't seen too many first baseman who can play like you.' That's the type of stuff I didn't hear enough of because I stupidly kept myself from hearing it. Looking back, I wish I did it differently. I tended to do things alone." Years later, he realized he also missed Sheppard's tough love. "There is no way Shep would have tolerated the attitude I had."

When 1991 spring training opened in Scottsdale, Robinson

was in the minor league camp when he and Parry got word that Keith Lieppman, Oakland's assistant director of player development, wanted to see them. "We said, 'Uh-oh, that's either really good news or really bad news.' " Parry said. Parry went first and got the news that his .252 average in Modesto was not enough for Oakland to keep him. When Robinson went in, Parry thought his friend was going to be told what team he would play for in 1991.

"When we went to Huntsville in college it was a new place and it seemed nice, but we were only there for few days," Robinson said. "I never thought I would ever be back in Huntsville, let alone end my career there."

"Marteese was a good first baseman with good hands," Lieppman, now the A's director of player development, said. "He never hit for the power that you need, like a McGwire, a Frank Thomas, those type of guys. He reached the point in his professional career that you have to make the adjustment in order to advance, but Marteese just didn't have the power to do it. As for second base, where we also tried him, he didn't have the speed and quickness for that spot. He kind of fell in between. We couldn't project him at second because he didn't have the range. I remember telling Marteese that we were going to try and find another organization that was interested in him because it did not look like things would work out with us."

"What Keith told me was that there were some younger guys behind me with more power, and I said, 'I understand, I'm a big boy,' " Robinson said. "Keith said to me that there are some clubs interested in me and the White Sox were one of them. I never heard the words, 'We are releasing you.' But I imagine he said it. I tried to be upbeat, so I focused on a trade. I told Keith, 'Okay. When you trade me let me know.' Then I left to go back to the Days Inn."

His friends Parry and Canseco rushed to his side as the reality set in that he was no longer wanted by the A's. "We drove back to the hotel together," Parry said. "I don't think he knew it was coming. I think he was shocked. I couldn't understand how a guy like Marteese could get cut. I could see why I did, but Marteese...?"

Canseco was just as stunned when he visited his friend at the hotel. "I could not believe a player of that caliber and that kind of talent got released. They basically just thew him away. It was sad to see that happen. There were other players who honestly didn't deserve to be there, and here you did have a guy who did deserve to be there, or even at a higher level, and this guy gets the ax.

"At that point, it really opened my eyes as to how unfair baseball can be. That was when it really hit home, when I saw that happen. I was very distraught and upset as to how the decision making process was handled. I said to him, 'Wow, that is really not fair. You are a good player and I can't believe this is happening.'"

Robinson did not think his baseball career was over. He waited three days in the hotel to be told about a trade, never heard anything, and headed to share an apartment with another friend, Freddy Hill, who had also been released. Robinson, who did not have an agent and was too naïve to understand the baseball business, made no job-seeking calls to other team's minor league scouting directors. Robinson incorrectly believed they would call him.

> "There is no way Shep would have tolerated the attitude I had."
> — Marteese Robinson

Lieppman liked Robinson personally, but thought the decision to release him was in the player's best interest. "The fatality rate is incredible in baseball," Lieppman said. "Considering only five to six percent of those in the minor leagues ever get to the big leagues and only one to two percent become everyday players, it's a lottery-type chance that a player is going to make it. I always have trouble releasing a player, but having done it for so long, I've come to realize that for the most part it is for the good of the player when the time comes. Guys go on to do far better things in their lives than they would if they just hung on in baseball."

Marteese Robinson would never play another professional game again. The 1987 collegiate national batting champion was now just another sad statistic, tossed aside by the game he loved. It took many years for Robinson to truly get over the hurt. Finally he did. "I really should be proud of what I accomplished as a player," he said by phone in 2001. "When you think about it, a lot of guys who made it to the big leagues I had played with or against and I had held my own. Guys like my teammates Scott Brosius, Darren Lewis, Ozzie Canseco, and Mike Bordick. How many guys can really say that?"

> "The fatality rate is incredible in baseball. Considering only five to six percent of those in the minor leagues ever get to the big leagues and only one to two percent become everyday players, it's a lottery-type chance that a player is going to make it. I always have trouble releasing a player, but having done it for so long, I've come to realize that for the most part it is for the good of the player when the time comes. Guys go on to do far better things in their lives than they would if they just hung on in baseball."
> —Keith Lieppman, Oakland A's

Three Teammates Play Their Way to Pawtucket

CHAPTER 13

Marteese Robinson had roomed with Tim Neahring in the Cape Cod League and liked the guy immensely. When he got the news that Neahring had been drafted by the Red Sox in the eighth round of the 1988 draft he was delighted, but also petrified. Who would he pull for to become the eventual shortstop for the Red Sox? Neahring or his former Seton Hall teammate John Valentin who was the club's fifth-round draft pick. "Thank God Val didn't sign right away and they didn't put them together on the same team," Robinson said. "That would have been tough on me."

Robinson was relieved when the Red Sox put Neahring ahead of Valentin in the minor league chain, a decision made easier because Neahring left Miami [Ohio] almost immediately after the draft, while Valentin stalled his way to July before inking his contract. "The reason I was playing on different teams than Val was they thought we were both prospects and they never wanted us to play together on the same team," Neahring said. "That probably hurt our friendship early on in our careers because we never really got a chance to know each other."

Valentin and Neahring eventually became friends and shared the left side of the infield for four years in Boston. But prior to 1991, Naehring was a thorn in Valentin's side.

When Valentin arrived in Elmira to begin his pro career, Naehring was immediately promoted to Winter Haven, Florida, the Red Sox' long-season A ball team. "From that point on Timmy was always ahead of me, which was very difficult,"

Valentin said. "When I was in the minors, my goal was not to make it to the major leagues, but to play well wherever I was. Everywhere I've been, if I played well, good things happened. I was very patient with myself. Where I got that from I don't know."

It was a good thing that Valentin was not concerned with the major leagues because after the first season in Elmira, he was likely as far away as a minor league player could be. "I thought it was difficult," Valentin said. "It was hard. I was playing against better players than college. Strength was a factor and I wasn't that strong. Playing every day, I got tired, the next day I was tired. It was more like a job. That was where baseball life began." He struggled to hit .217 in the 60 games with only eight extra base hits in 207 at-bats.

The next season, after playing together in instructional ball, Valentin was assigned to Winter Haven and Neahring to Lynchburg, a higher A ball team. The HaveSox, as the Winter Haven club was known, were not a good team. A 9-33 start in 1989 had Valentin in a funk when his family arrived for a Florida visit. "It was the worst thing in the world to see John struggling in the minors," Arnold Valentin Jr. said. "He was homesick and he was wondering if it was all worth it. I sat down with him before we left. He was a little choked up seeing us leave, and I told him someday this will all be worth it."

The journey became more worthwhile when John was moved out of Florida within a month. Boston's shortstop position was in disarray when Marty Barrett, a converted second baseman who was filling in for Jody Reed, went down with an injury. Luis Rivera was brought up from Triple-A Pawtucket and Naehring and Valentin got caught in the wake. Naehring went to Pawtucket and Valentin, who hit .270, with 13 doubles and three home runs in 55 games in the pitcher-friendly Florida State League, took Neahring's place in Lynchburg. The move north agreed with Valentin and he suddenly had a power surge with five quick home runs. He also had the Seton Hall cavalry coming right behind him. "I was so excited when Mo and Kevin were drafted and signed with Boston and that I might get a chance to play with my teammates," he said.

Mo Vaughn (l) and Marteese Robinson flanked Craig Biggio for a 1987 on-campus promotional campaign. Robinson's first name was misspelled by teammate John Brogan.

Seton Hall head coach Mike Sheppard
graduated from the school in 1958.
(photo by S.R. Smith)

The 1987 Seton Hall Pirates

John Valentin (middle row, fifth from left); Craig Biggio (middle row, second from right); Mike Sheppard (top row, left); Marteese Robinson (top row, fifth from left); Mo Vaughn (top row, second from right) (courtesy Mike Sheppard)

The Hit Men: Craig Biggio (44) and Mo Vaughn (33) greet Marteese Robinson after one of his 16 homers in 1987. (courtesy Seton Hall Sports Information)

John Valentin hit ninth for the 1987 Seton Hall Pirates.
(photo by S.R. Smith)

Team USA star John Valentin (r) posed with Mo Vaughn
for the cover of the 1988 Seton Hall baseball media guide.
(photo by S.R. Smith)

"Wow! Look at this guy!" former Yankees third baseman Scott Brosius said when he first saw Marteese Robinson go into his stretch.
(photo by L. Morris/NYT Pictures)

Mo Vaughn (l) played on a 1988 U.S. National Team with Nebraska's Bob Benjamin and Maine's Mike LeBlanc (r).
(courtesy of the Vaughn family)

First-round pick Craig Biggio starred in Asheville.
(courtesy Mike Sheppard)

"If someone would say the three of you would be together in Triple-A," said Kevin Morton, "you would say you would have a better shot of getting hit by a truck." But John Valentin (l), Mo Vaughn and Morton (r) ended up playing together on the Pawtucket Red Sox.
(photo by Louriann Mardo-Zayat)

Marteese Robinson was a Midwest League All-Star in 1989.
(courtesy of the Robinson family)

Yogi Berra (l) posed with Craig Biggio
on the cover of an Astros gameday magazine.
(courtesy Yogi Berra Museum)

Marteese Robinson advanced to Oakland's Double-A affiliate in Huntsville, Alabama.
(courtesy of the Robinson family)

Three Seton Hall catchers—Craig Biggio (l), Mike Sheppard and Rick Cerone (r). (courtesy Mike Sheppard)

Chuck Alben (l) accepted his friend Craig Biggio's invitation to serve as a batboy for the Astros.
(courtesy of the Alben family)

Jason Leader wore a Seton Hall cap the day he met Mo Vaughn at Fenway Park.
(photo by Louriann Mardo-Zayat)

Craig Biggio (r) and former Houston Rockets guard
Scott Brooks joined Julian Zagars at his high school graduation.
(courtesy of the Zagars family)

John Valentin with his nieces Francesca (l)
and Alexandria (r) who has recovered from a brain tumor.
(courtesy of the Valentin family)

Marteese Robinson spent eight years in law enforcement, including a stint with the Scottsdale Police Department, before getting back in baseball. Charlene Robinson noticed her husband never smiled in photos of him as a police officer.
(courtesy of the Robinson family)

Montreal Expos Director of Amateur Scouting Dana Brown (r) urged his former college teammate Marteese Robinson to get back into baseball.
(photo by Dave Schofield)

Seton Hall head coach Mike Sheppard (seated) with four of his greatest stars. (photo by S.R. Smith)

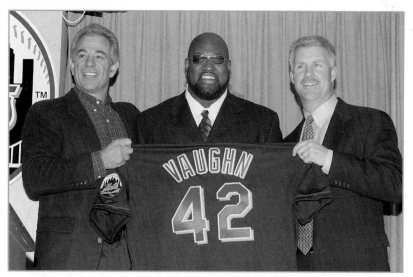

Mets Manager Bobby Valentine (l) and General Manager
Steve Phillips welcome Mo Vaughn to New York.
(courtesy of the New York Mets)

Marteese Robinson (l) was inducted into Seton Hall's Athletic
Hall of Fame in 2002 by Mike Sheppard.
(photo by S.R. Smith)

While Valentin had a year in pro baseball under his belt, Vaughn and Morton were just starting out. The two arrived in Winter Haven just after Valentin had left for Lynchburg and roomed together in the Gulf Coast League for a month. "I was shocked at what minor league baseball was like," Vaughn said. "You got dressed for practice everyday, and it was so hot in Winter Haven. It was just on fire and we were practicing at one in the afternoon. I remember saying to myself, 'This is what professional baseball is all about.' You had to change your mind from what you thought it was. Once you got down there and got to it, you realized why it was work. We did drills. We went over every facet of the game to understand it and to get good at this game. I realized how much repetition it was gonna take to have success."

After the brief Winter Haven introductory lesson, Morton was sent to Elmira, while Vaughn went to Double-A New Britain to begin his journey to the major leagues. "Mo was always one step ahead of us," Morton said. "Val and I started calling him 'Step-Ahead Mo.' "

> "When I was in the minors, my goal was not to make it to the major leagues, but to play well wherever I was. Everywhere I've been, if I played well, good things happened."
> — John Valentin

Morton got a quick initiation to the New York-Penn League, which he called "real minor league ball," when eventual major league All-Star Kenny Lofton singled off him in Elmira. "He had played basketball at Arizona and I heard he was so fast. I found out I had to work on my pickoff move because he was on first and 10 seconds later he was on third. He stole second and third like that. Holy Cow!" Morton said with an emphatic snap of his fingers. Morton got only three starts in New York, including a no-hitter through eight in his final outing, before he was promoted to Lynchburg where he moved in with Valentin.

"Val really took care of me when I got to Lynchburg. There were five guys in the apartment. I would sleep on the floor. Sometimes he'd say, 'Come on, you can share the bed.' But don't get the wrong idea. We both had serious girlfriends," Morton said, laughing.

Living arrangements aside, Morton had a successful first month in the Carolina League and earned the league's Pitcher of the Week honors. By season's end, *The Sporting News* had him as the seventh-best pitching prospect in all of baseball. Valentin also earned postseason praise when *Baseball America* voted him the league's best defensive shortstop. He finished the 1989 season in Lynchburg with a .246 average, eight homers, and 34 RBI, the same number he produced in 115 games in Elmira and Winter Haven combined.

> "I had Big Mo in his first professional game out of the Gulf Coast League and his britches were hanging down to his ankles. They were a little too big for him if you can imagine that. He drove in his first RBI when he got hit in the ass with a pitch with the bases loaded."
>
> —Butch Hobson, former Red Sox third baseman

While Valentin and Morton did their thing down south, Vaughn was in the spotlight in New Britain. The BritSox were happy to have the local slugger because he was a gate attraction, playing just 45 minutes from Norwalk. But if fans were coming to see the local kid hit homers, they should have saved their money. Vaughn joined a team that had finished last in the Eastern League in home runs each of the previous seven years, largely because BeeHive Field featured a 16-foot high fence in the power alleys 386 feet from homeplate. "That place was Death Valley," Leroy Vaughn said.

Butch Hobson, who eventually coached all three of the Seton Hall products in the Red Sox chain, remembered Vaughn's first Double-A outing. "I had Big Mo in his first professional game out of the Gulf Coast League and his britches were hanging down to his ankles," the former Red Sox third baseman said. "They were a little too big for him if you can imagine that. He drove in his first RBI when he got hit in the ass with a pitch with the bases loaded."

Vaughn started slowly, but finished with a .278 average, a team-high eight homers and 38 RBI, one behind team leader Scott Cooper. "Being sent out of college to here [Double-A], he wasn't ready for this level," New Britain pitching coach Rich

Gale, a former Boston hurler, said at season's end. "But he's certainly ready now."

Vaughn was less than a year out of Seton Hall when the Big East Conference named him its Baseball Player of the Decade. Vaughn, who hit .417 with 56 homers and 218 RBI at Seton Hall, joined the New York Knicks Patrick Ewing [basketball], Olympians Vicki Huber [women's track], and Roger Kingdom [men's track], along with 10 other conference stars, at Madison Square Garden's center court during the 1990 men's basketball tournament to receive his award. "I never got to play basketball at the Garden, so that was fun for me to be on the court," Vaughn said.

Once Vaughn got to Winter Haven for spring training in February 1990, he showed why he was the Big East's best and impressed Red Sox manager Joe Morgan. "He works his butt off," the manager told the Boston media. "He can hit. He doesn't cheat himself at the plate."

Vaughn was practicing a lesson his college coach, Mike Sheppard Sr., had taught him. "I tried to teach them to never be satisfied," Sheppard said. "Don't cheat yourself at the plate. Get two hits and you think that's great. You think, 'The worst I can do today is go 2-for-4, .500, today. You get that happy feeling.' But I tried to convince them that that was bullshit. Go out and swing the bat."

Morton and Valentin were promoted to Double-A New Britain and "Step-Ahead Mo" earned a ticket to Triple-A Pawtucket. He started with a .161 April before Tidewater Tides pitcher Shawn Barton, an eventual big leaguer, lost control of a pitch and shelved the slugger for two months with a broken right wrist.

Morton also started poorly, beginning 2-2 with a 5.61 ERA. He thought something was wrong with his pitching, but later found it was his karma that was flawed. On Opening Night, Morton, the starter, was welcomed to the mound by the BritSox' Bumble Bee mascot. "I told him to get the fuck out of here," Morton, who was all business between the lines, said. "He went buzzing away, but the Bumble Bee was mad and he told his wife what I did. She put a curse on me. Apparently she was into voodoo. I didn't know she had a curse on me, but some really weird things happened early in the season. Twice on flyballs, our outfielders stumbled and fell and guys got extra-base hits on outs. Then another guy, who hadn't had a home run in something like 1,300 at-bats, hits one against me. I didn't know what the hell was going on."

But catcher Eric Wedge, who was friendly with one of the sorcerer's friends, found out about the evil spell. "Wedgey came up to me and said, 'Morty, I don't know how to tell you this, but the Bumble Bee's wife put a curse on you.' I told him to get lost, but he said he was serious and said that she would take it off if I apologized to the Bumble Bee. By this point, I would have done anything to straighten myself out, so I ran and found him. He was in full uniform, but without his head and I told him how sorry I was. I begged him to ask his wife to take the curse off. I guess she did because after that I did a lot better."

> "Don't cheat yourself at the plate. Get two hits and you think that's great. You think, 'The worst I can do today is go 2-for-4, .500, today. You get that happy feeling.' But I tried to convince them that that was bullshit. Go out and swing the bat."
> —Mike Sheppard, Seton Hall Coach

Valentin also suffered from what might have been called the "Seton Hall Curse." He made it only a couple of weeks into the season before succumbing to a sore knee. In mid-April, Valentin visited Boston Red Sox team physician Dr. Arthur Pappas who discovered possible cartilage damage and the shortstop was put on the disabled list. He underwent surgery on May 3, three days after Vaughn suffered his broken wrist.

Morton emerged from the voodoo hex and won Eastern League Pitcher of the Week honors. He then went winless for 40 days, largely because of his teammates' poor hitting, but turned his season around by getting clocked in the mouth by Reading Phillies infielder Kim Batiste during a 15-minute brawl at Reading.

"Batiste kind of snuck around Morty and pretty much suckerpunched him in the face and then ran away," Jeff Bagwell, who had played third base that year in New Britain, said in August 2000. "It was a pretty bad fight and we all chased after Batiste, but he ran into the dugout and into the clubhouse, so we never really got a hold of him. Morty was our boy. It was an unfortunate incident. You never like to see someone get sucker-punched, especially one of your good friends."

Morton, who somehow pitched the third perfect game in Eastern League history five days later, ended up with a couple of teeth knocked out and needed an emergency root canal at midnight. Wedge called Morton's soon-to-be-wife Dana Santrella to tell her the upsetting news. "I had to calm her down and tell her everything was all right," Wedge said. "He got messed up pretty good."

Vaughn had also rebounded in Pawtucket. He returned in June, started 1-for-12, and then went on a tear that had him hitting .292 with 16 homers and 50 RBI in 73 games after the injury. "There were some people who came up to me in April and said there was talk of me going back to New Britain," Vaughn told the *Boston Globe*'s Nick Cafardo. "I'd like to see those people now. I had the game taken away from me for six weeks and I had a lot of time to analyze myself. If you have a passive attitude, you're going to play that way. If it's dog-like, you can do some damage. I play every game like it is my last."

> "He went buzzing away, but the Bumble Bee was mad and he told his wife what I did. She put a curse on me. Apparently she was into voodoo. I didn't know she had a curse on me, but some really weird things happened early in the season."
>
> — Kevin Morton

That was another lesson Sheppard instilled in his Seton Hall players each and every day of their college careers. "The game is a passion for me," Sheppard said. "I know I love the game and I hope I pass it on. When guys come here, I say to them, 'We will test your love for baseball. You say you love the game. We will give you so much baseball it will come out of your ears.'"

Vaughn, who loved baseball that much, almost played himself straight to Boston. Boston general manager Lou

Gorman was hunting for a power hitter and was set to call up "The Hit Dog," a nickname Vaughn got in Seton Hall's Omega Psi Phi fraternity [Vaughn honored fraternity tradition by having its horseshoe logo branded on his right bicep]. But the GM was able to get veteran Mike Marshall from the New York Mets instead. "I'm not disappointed," Vaughn said. "I'm going to have my day up there and I don't think it's going to be too long."

The media, fans, and even the Pawtucket coaches told him he would be called up to Boston in September when the roster expanded to 40 players. The *Boston Globe* reported Red Sox manager Joe Morgan was going to bring up six players with Vaughn, who was on his way to hitting .295 with 22 homers, and 75 RBI for the season, as a strong possibility. It was just talk. Vaughn never got the call.

Valentin, who eventually returned to the lineup after surgery, was also unsure of his status. "Offensively I was an out," Valentin said about his 1990 season. "I just wasn't strong enough and I was really struggling. They were knocking the bat out of my hands." On a late-season trip to Hagerstown, Maryland, Valentin was moping when Hobson exploded at him. "I remember going 0-for-3 and I was sulking before the fourth at-bat," Valentin said. "I had also made a couple of errors and Butch aired me out in front of the entire dugout. He got all over me, worse then Shep could ever do. He yelled, 'Get your head out of your ass. You're sulking in front of everyone. You should be ashamed of yourself.' I retaliated. I said, 'Go fuck yourself. I don't need someone to put fire under my ass. I know I suck.'"

"Johnny Val went out and made five of the dangest plays I'd ever seen that game and I saw right then that not only can he take and accept constructive criticism, but he learned how to light a fire under his own butt," Hobson said. "A lot of times players who have a lot of ability don't know how to light that fire

> "The game is a passion for me. I know I love the game and I hope I pass it on. When guys come here, I say to them, 'We will test your love for baseball. You say you love the game. We will give you so much baseball it will come out of your ears.'"
> —Mike Sheppard, Seton Hall Coach

by themselves; they have to have someone do it for them. I saw right then that he was going places."

Valentin, who grew up at Seton Hall with Sheppard's in-your-face coaching style, learned in college to recognize the message and discount the way it was delivered. "I thought Butch was going to put me in the doghouse, but he didn't. He was Butch Hobson, major leaguer, big guy, strong. He was a motivator. He was really good for me. He was the manager I needed to give me that push. I started to play well and I started to mature. I started to fight back."

Soon after, Valentin got a phone call from Sheppard, who could also tell his former star was destined for stardom. "He sounded so confident," Sheppard said, not knowing that Hobson had gotten loud with the shortstop. "John knew he was going to get there. John was one of the most special for me. It was exciting for me watching a walk-on, a guy who had nothing handed to him, gain confidence in college and gain even more confidence in the minors."

When the season ended, Valentin went back to Jersey City convinced he had to get stronger, and visited his former high school coach, Mike Hogan, each day to lift weights at St. Anthony. While the added 10 pounds helped his confidence going into the 1991 season, the biggest boost came during a winter breakfast. "I was looking in the *Star-Ledger* every day with my brother to see if I was protected," Valentin said. "Then, there it was. That was another turning point." Valentin avoided the Rule 5 Draft, which allows third-year players to be selected by other clubs unless they are protected on their parent organization's 40-man roster.

Morton and Vaughn also faced insecurity when the Atlanta Braves, Houston Astros, and Toronto Blue Jays all inquired about their availability, only to be turned down by Gorman. The two were pegged as the future of the Red Sox and the general manager was not ready to lose them.

In his weekly column in the *Boston Globe*, Peter Gammons went so far as to pick Vaughn as the likely Rookie of the Year. He led his January 6, 1991, article with an unattributed scouting report on the first baseman. "There are three words to describe

Mo Vaughn: impact, intelligence and character. This is an impact hitter, especially in Fenway Park. He'll crush The Wall, like Fred Lynn. Then when they come in, he'll pull the trigger and show unbelievable power. This year I can see him hitting 20 homers and knocking in 90-100 runs. Two years from now, I see a .320-.325 hitter with 25 homers, 70 extra-base hits, 110-120 RBIs. He's a great athlete, which some people don't understand, with great work habits from a great family ... As far as I'm concerned he's the best prospect in the International League in the last three years."

With a buildup like that, Vaughn did not need to introduce himself to many people. On opening day of his first spring training with the varsity Red Sox, Vaughn dressed in a back room next to coach Al Bumbry. The *Boston Globe*'s Dan Shaughnessy asked the 1973 American League Rookie of the Year if he had the same hype as Vaughn. "I crept up on 'em," the coach told the writer. "I didn't have no buildup." Hearing this, Vaughn interjected. "I guess I won't be creeping up on anybody."

Vaughn, who was locked in a battle with steady first baseman Carlos Quintana for the starting job, opened 0-for-7 in the exhibition season before singling up the middle against the White Sox' Jack McDowell. "All the guys have tried to relax me, from Roger Clemens to Wade Boggs," Vaughn said. "I talk to [Jack Clark] every morning. I ask him questions. He likes it because he says it keeps his head tuned to the game. The big thing is that they've accepted me. Jack tells me that my skills are there, I just have to get my timing down. I'd be a fool not to use the resources around me." The *Boston Globe*, which ran plenty of articles building up the 23-year-old, ran a story with the headline: **MOMENTUM. MO VAUGHN IS THE MOST ANTICIPATED ROOKIE SINCE CARL YASTRZEMSKI ARRIVED 30 YEARS AGO. ARE WE EXPECTING TOO MUCH FROM A SLUGGER WHO HAS NEVER EVEN SET FOOT IN FENWAY PARK?**

In the lengthiest article to date about Vaughn, former Sox great Johnny Pesky, who managed Vaughn in Pawtucket, declared, "If he don't make it, I'm gonna get out of the game." But author Nathan Cobb also pointed out that Vaughn, who had never even been to a Red Sox game in Fenway, was facing more than just baseball pressure. "Mo Vaughn is black," Cobb wrote. "He is, assuming he makes the club, about to play for a team that has had a sorrowful racial history, stretching from its rejection of Jackie Robinson after a tryout in 1945, through the ignominy 14 years later of being the last major league team to field a black player, to the 1985 firing of minor league batting instructor Tommy Harper after he publicly revealed that Red Sox management regularly gave white players and other white personnel passes to a segregated Florida Elks club."

Vaughn was not concerned with the race issue, having learned about black heroes from his parents as a youngster. His former Seton Hall assistant coach, Nick Bowness, urged him to ask for Robinson's number 42 in a tribute to the first African-American to play in the major leagues. "Mo was not big into numbers," Bowness said in 2000. "He was not even aware that the number 39 he wore in Pawtucket was Roy Campanella's number. Johnny Pesky and I were talking with Mo about what number he would wear when Mo eventually got to Boston. I said he should be 42 to honor what Jackie Robinson did. Mo thought it was a good idea and Johnny Pesky did too."

Boston was waiting for Vaughn to save the Red Sox and bring racial equality to the town, but they would have to wait because the savior, who hit .265 in the spring, was sent back to Pawtucket for more seasoning.

Vaughn's college teammate John Valentin, who had what he called his greatest spring while working out with the Triple-A PawSox, also got bad news from Butch Hobson, now the Pawtucket manager. The skipper told Valentin that the Red Sox kept his rival Naehring and sent major league veteran utilityman Mike Brumley to Triple-A, forcing Valentin back to New Britain. "Butch said, 'You played great,'" Valentin remembered. "'We want you here. You will be here soon. Don't worry about it, just go down there and play.' I was pissed."

Hobson was true to his word and placed a call to Valentin on May 8, 1991, because his Pawtucket shortstop, Luis Aguayo, suffered a hamstring injury. Hobson wanted to use "his" guy and promptly sat Brumley for Valentin, who responded in his first game with a homer, a double and several good fielding plays. "I played for 10 days in a row," said Valentin, having hit just .198 in 23 Double-A games. "I did really well and Butch said, 'You are not going back.' I was like, 'Yes.' It was amazing!"

Valentin's call-up to Pawtucket allowed the Seton Hall trio — Vaughn, Valentin, and Morton — to play together in pro ball. "Think of college," Morton said. "If someone would say the three of you would be together in Triple-A, you would say you would have a better shot of getting hit by a truck. But it happened. We were back to the old days."

Hobson knew quickly that Vaughn was ready to move on. On Opening Day at Scranton, Pennsylvania, the PawSox and the Triple-A Phillies lined up on the opposite foul lines for the pre-game ceremonies. Bad blood remained from the previous year's brawl between New Britain and Reading with many of the participants now standing just feet away from each other.

Rick Lancellotti, who Morton called a "real-life Crash Davis" because of his 15 years in professional ball with just 36 big league appearances, began jawing at Morton's nemesis Kim Batiste. "I'm thinking, 'Oh my God, this is right out of *Bull Durham*,'" the lefty said. 'I got Crash Davis standing next to me, Batiste looking over at me.' Once the game started, guys started throwing at each other."

The head-hunting ended when Vaughn took matters into his own hands on a late-inning trip to the plate. After he was dusted by eventual big league reliever Tim Mauser, Vaughn slowly got up and silently glared back at the mound. "They threw at me and I kind of looked back at him — like you gotta be crazy or something," Vaughn said.

"The next pitch," Morton remembered, "Mo hit a shot so far, it was just like, 'Boom!' It was like the UConn shot but with a wooden bat. Everything in Scranton is dark so all you saw was this little white ball going forever. It looked like it went over the damn mountains into the Poconos! It was unbelievable!"

"That shot really impressed me," Hobson said. Vaughn, who had 14 homers, 50 RBI, and was walked an International League-leading 60 times by summer's arrival, had heard from his parents that the *Boston Globe* was calling for his promotion, but

Red Sox manager Joe Morgan quieted the rumblings by saying, "Not yet. I'd like to see him continue to go the way he's going for a while."

Vaughn answered all doubters when he hit a *broken bat* home run in Pawtucket and finally the call came after a late June game in Scranton. It was after midnight when the PawSox returned to their hotel. Hobson asked Vaughn to come to his room. "I thought he was going to chew me out for something," Vaughn remembered while sitting in the visiting team's clubhouse in Camden Yards during the 2000 season, "but instead he wanted to tell me that I was going to Boston." Hobson reminded his star that the game was the same in the major leagues and it was important to stay the same. "Butch told me not to change," Vaughn said of the meeting. "He said I would be in the big leagues for 10 or 12 years and that when I was done, I would be the same person I went up as. It was good advice."

"Mo got called up first," Morton said. "We were happy for the guy. Everyone knew he was going; it was just a matter of time." Once Vaughn said goodbye and boarded his flight, he was not so sure he really wanted to go to Boston after all. "It was a prop plane all the way to Boston," Vaughn remembered. "It was unbelievable. It was rocky. I hate flying. When I retire, if we can't get there by car, then we ain't getting there." By the next week, Vaughn's stomach had settled and his Boston arrival was made even sweeter when Morton also got the call to the big leagues.

> "Think of college. If someone would say the three of you would be together in Triple-A, you would say you would have a better shot of getting hit by a truck. But it happened. We were back to the old days."
>
> — Kevin Morton

Valentin was left in Pawtucket, but things were looking up for him too. He was hitting over .300, while his rival Naehring was struggling through back problems and an 0-for-39 slump as Boston's shortstop. "I was getting close," Valentin said. "I started to pay attention to what was going on at the major league level. Timmy was having problems with his back. He went on the DL, but they still had a veteran shortstop up there. I still didn't think

I would get a chance, so all I was concerned about was playing well at Triple-A right now. Finish the year."

With Naehring out, the Red Sox made Luis Rivera the starter and recalled veteran Mike Brumley, who played second in Pawtucket because of Valentin's steady play. The BoSox considered Valentin as a possible September call-up, but he was not one of the six Triple-A players to join Boston after the PawSox season ended.

Instead Valentin headed back to New Jersey and lifted weights each day. He also learned that Hobson, his manager in New Britain and Pawtucket, had been hired on October 8 to replace the fired Joe Morgan in Boston. Hobson made sure Valentin was invited to join the Red Sox in late February for his first spring session with the big club.

Valentin wore linebacker number 56 in spring training and was considered a long-shot to make the club, but Hobson did not care. The manager, who had played football for Paul "Bear" Bryant at the University of Alabama, knew what Valentin could do. "He's just a good shortstop," Hobson told the Boston media. "He's gonna surprise. You're gonna look up and be impressed."

Although he was nervous, it did not take Valentin long to show his defensive ability. In his first spring training game against the Toronto Blue Jays, he robbed John Olerud, his former USA teammate, of a certain up-the-middle base hit with a diving stop and strong throw.

"To be invited to spring training was great," Valentin said. "It was somewhat intimidating. I had the confidence that no one was fielding like I was, but I still thought I was a ways away. Sure, I was thinking that I am playing behind Roger Clemens. When he's pitching, anything hit to me I've got to catch. But I was always confident about my fielding. I had to prove to Wade Boggs, playing next to him in spring training, that he could depend on me. I knew if I took care of what I had to do, I would be OK."

It was like Seton Hall all over again. Valentin had a good glove and was back in the ninth spot in the order. Vaughn and Morton were with him in the dugout. The three even showed their Pirate Pride when they got into a verbal battle with new

Red Sox ace Frank Viola about who was better, Seton Hall or Viola's school, St. John's.

Valentin hit .344 in the spring and Hobson wanted him as his shortstop. But General Manager Lou Gorman overruled him and sent Valentin back to Pawtucket. "Butch told me I did really well and he said I eventually would be a major leaguer," the Red Sox final spring cut said. "He said, 'Go down to Pawtucket and do well. Don't let them see you not play well.' " He did that immediately, hitting over .300 to impress his new manager, Rico Petrocelli.

Petrocelli, who spent 13 seasons as the Red Sox starting shortstop from 1963-76, enjoyed sharing his experiences with Valentin and also liked testing him. A string of early-season rainouts forced Pawtucket to play seven-straight doubleheaders and Petrocelli had Valentin play every inning of every game.

"I said, 'This kid is tough,' " Petrocelli said in 2001 from his New Hampshire-based sports marketing agency. 'This kid is tremendous.' He's kind of quiet, but very aggressive. He made some great plays. Jeez, you knew he was going to be a big leaguer." Valentin settled into the .250 range, but showed some power with five early-season homers.

Hobson benched Luis Rivera in July for not running out a groundball, and made it known that he wanted Valentin in Boston after the All-Star break. Ironically, even with Hobson seething at his starting shortstop, it took a wrist injury to his longtime nemesis, Tim Naehring, to finally get Valentin invited to Boston on July 26. With Naehring headed to the disabled list, Hobson called Petrocelli and let the Pawtucket manager give his shortstop the good news after a game in Scranton.

"He had a great game that day," Arnold Valentin Jr. remembered. "My wife Liz, John, and I were in the hotel room talking about the game and all of a sudden the phone rings. John answered it and he got this look in his eye. He turned pale, white as a ghost. I thought something had happened. He hung up and started yelling, 'I'm going to The Show! I'm going to The Show!' He was so friggin' happy. He was flyin'. They wanted him to play the next night." John grabbed the phone and called his wife Marie in Pawtucket.

"Rico just called me in the room," he told her. "We're going to Boston!" Then he dialed a familiar number in Jersey City. "Mom! Get Dad!" he yelled into the phone. "Get ready! We're going to Boston!"

THE MAJOR LEAGUES

BIGGIO GETS THERE FIRST

CHAPTER 14

Bobby Gallitelli got plenty of letters from Craig Biggio while he played professionally in Italy. He learned about his friend's success in the minor leagues at Asheville and then Tucson. In one of the last letters he received from Biggio, the catcher wrote about how excited he was that he was on the cusp of getting to the major leagues.

Like most others, Gallitelli figured his buddy would be in Triple-A until the 1988 September call-ups when the Houston Astros expanded their roster. Still, he checked the delayed editions of *USA Today* each day at a newsstand in Padova to see if maybe, just maybe, something might have happened. While looking at the same issue Lee Biggio saw while driving his son's hot-seated Saab to Arizona, Gallitelli skimmed the sports section and was stunned to see the news. Biggio was going to the major leagues. But by then, Biggio was actually already catching for the Astros. "I called my mom," the former Seton Hall center fielder said, "and my mom did the legwork for me and got me Craig's phone number. I was so excited and finally got to talk to him."

Biggio told him of the whirlwind ride from the minors to the majors. It all started when Alan Ashby suffered serious back spasms and was put on the disabled list. Houston manager Hal Lanier could not take a chance having Alex Trevino as his only catcher, so he made the long-distance call for Biggio on June 26. The team arranged for Biggio to catch a 2 AM flight for Houston, which arrived at 8:30 AM. "It was too cramped and I was too nervous to sleep on the plane; so when I got to the

Dome, they stuck me in a back room, where I tried to sleep for a few hours," Biggio said.

Soon his teammates started to roll in for the Sunday matinee against the San Francisco Giants. "I probably never even slept, and the manager, Hal Lanier, asked me if I wanted to go out and play," Biggio remembered. "He said, 'I know you weren't able to get much sleep, but are you able to play?' I said, 'Heck yeah, I can play. I want to play!' "

Biggio, with Jim Deshaies on the mound, got the start and the Giants were eager to test him. José Uribe, standing on second in the second, took off with a pitch, but Biggio gunned him down for his first major league assist. Offensively, Biggio, who became the fourth member of the 1987 major league draft class to make it to the big leagues, went hitless but stole his first base after walking in the fourth. "This is the busiest day I've spent," Biggio told the media after the game, "but probably the best 24 hours I've spent in my lifetime. I was pretty ecstatic when I got the call."

Deshaies and Lanier praised the young catcher. "It was Biggio's first big league game and he caught a shutout," the pitcher said. "That ought to tell you something." The manager agreed. "We didn't bring him up to sit on the bench, that's for sure. I'm very satisfied with the job he did today. He has to feel good about catching a win in his first big league game, scoring a run and getting a stolen base. He handled himself real well."

Biggio's brother Terry and his wife Carole thought so too. They also flew all night to get the game, and the adrenaline kept them wide awake. "It was just amazing," Terry Biggio said. "It was kind of funny to hear the different fans around us asking about where did Craig come from, and all this other stuff. We just kind of sat there and took it all in. I was probably more nervous than him. It was nerve wracking."

Even though his mom and dad could not get the time off to see their son perform on the grand stage for the first time, childhood neighbor Charlie Alben hopped a plane as quickly as he could. "When I walked into the Dome, I'll never forget it, he was stretching behind first base," Alben remembered in 2000. "Just to see him in that environment, not having spoken to him yet or seen him, was pretty emotional. He meant a lot to me. It was just incredible."

Friend, brother, and sister-in-law, sitting together, saw Biggio's first major league hit, which came during one of the season's best pitching match-ups: the Dodgers' Orel Hershiser against Nolan Ryan. Hershiser won the dual and improved to 12-3 with a two-hitter, one coming to Biggio on a single to center field. "It was a bullet," Biggio jokingly argued after learning a close friend had called his first base hit a "flair." "It was a legitimate line drive. It was a rocket."

A trip to New York was next for the Astros, and Kings Park was ready for Biggio's arrival to Shea Stadium. Biggio's smile was ear-to-ear when he walked onto the field, looked into the stands and saw a huge banner, "Kings Park Loves Craig Biggio." It was a fairy tale moment and Chuck Alben, then a high school underclassman, took it all in. "All of Kings Park was there. It was incredible. Every time that he came to the plate, I forgot that it was the Mets, that it was [Darryl] Strawberry, [Howard] Johnson, Lenny Dykstra, that it was the Astros, that it was Major League Baseball. It was just Craig."

Biggio's former high school coaches were in the same section, but they were a bit more animated. "We were having a few beers and [Ron] Darling got an 0-2 count against Craig in the second inning," Kings Park assistant coach John Bogenshutz said. "One of our guys, Peter Thompson, who was a football coach with us, was betting these guys that Craig would get a hit. $10 this guy, $10 that guy. We were telling Peter he was out of his mind. 0-2 to Darling, but Craig doubles down the line. Peter collected and we drank beers the rest of the night on Craig."

After leaving New York, Biggio got his first major league RBI two weeks later on a bases-loaded walk while catching Ryan's 100th win with the Astros. The win was historic as Ryan, who also had 138 wins with the Angels, joined Cy Young as the only pitcher to win 100 games for two teams in two different leagues.

Midway through the summer, Lee Biggio finally made it to Houston to see his son. "Craig took me to the Astrodome, the field and the locker room," he said. "It was amazing. I'm a quiet guy, laid back in that way, and I saw Nolan Ryan. He walked right by me. I saw Yogi Berra, who was my favorite growing up, but I did not approach him. I'm not like that. I wouldn't want to impose myself on them. I remember watching the game and fantasizing about things from when Craig was growing up. All those hours we spent playing baseball together."

But the youngest Biggio was a long way from the fields of Kings Park and was starting to get used to the National League. Although he was hitting just .190 a month into his career, Biggio felt that he only had to get to know the pitchers a bit better before he started to hit. Berra was equally optimistic. "He's a baby," the former catcher said. "But I like everything I see in him. You tell him something and he learns it."

August of Biggio's first year was not a busy month for him. With Trevino getting more action, Biggio had only six at-bats all month long when he pinch hit on August 22 in the 10th inning against Goose Gossage. With the score tied at six on a misty night at Wrigley Field, Biggio hit his first major league homer, a shot to left, to help lift the Astros to a 9-7 win over the Chicago Cubs. "Well, this sure is strange," Biggio said after the game. "You [media] guys are coming over to talk to me with your note pads open. I can't tell you how much this does for my confidence." That confidence suffered a jolt on the 30th when the Astros made room on the roster for the recalled Ashby by sending Biggio back to Tucson with his .202 average in 36 games.

Before Joaquin Andujar took the mound that evening in the Astrodome, Biggio packed his travel bag and began searching in vain for his girlfriend Patty. "That was the first time I met Patty," Charlie Alben, who was again in town, said. "Craig brought me into the Dome at 3 in the afternoon. I met Yogi and Nolan Ryan. The game was at 7:30, so Patty and I went out to get a bite to eat. We knew we would be back in time for the game. Three bottles of wine later, it was about 7:15 and we were a half hour away from the Dome. We were late. We figured he'd hit a home run in the first inning and we'll miss it and he'd be furious. So we get to the player's parking lot and the guard told us that Craig had just gotten sent down. We thought he was kidding, but we turned around and there was Craig sitting on the hood of the car in the parking lot waiting for us."

Biggio went back to the Toros and went 8-for-13 before going back to Houston on September 6, where he finished his first season in the majors hitting .211 with three homers and five RBIs. "I didn't play much," Biggio said by phone from his Houston home in October 2000. "But I learned more by not playing than if I would have been playing. The reason why I say that is because I got to sit in the bullpen, and sit on the bench a lot, and listen to the older guys that were around. Buddy Bell, Billy Doran, Mike Scott, Nolan Ryan, the list goes on. I had the opportunity to listen to these guys and talk about certain things. That was an education in itself. I benefited a lot by sitting, watching and listening than by actually playing."

CRAIG BIGGIO: MAJOR LEAGUE MOMENTS HE'LL REMEMBER (Listed Chronologically)

Becoming the Astros Starting Catcher: Biggio started the 1989 season, his second in Houston, platooning with Alan Ashby. But new manager Art Howe soon installed Biggio as the starter in early May and released the veteran on May 11. Biggio got two hits against David Cone in his first game as the starter. "I can't really honestly answer why they decided to start me because I don't know," Biggio told the media after his competition was let go. "All I know is they like what they see, and they want me to be out there every day. That gives me a lot of confidence. I just want to take advantage of it."

Meeting Dr. John McMullen: Astros owner Dr. John McMullen first saw Biggio play at Seton Hall. He saw him again in 1988 in spring training and in Triple-A and liked what he saw. "I was in the habit of going on vacation in Tucson, so I saw him play there," McMullen, who owned the Astros until 1993, said. "His personality, his demeanor, his playing style were terrific. He's an outstanding young man."

McMullen, now nine years removed from the Astros, will talk at length about his love for Biggio. "As a person, what more could you want. He's just outstanding. Outstanding. He epitomizes everything you would want to see in a young man. He's one of a very few that still stays in contact with me. He's one of my very fine young friends."

Although the two met because of baseball, their passion for golf is what made them close. "Craig was one of the guys that I would take to go on a golfing trip after each season," said McMullen, who also owned the NHL's New Jersey Devils until the summer of 2000. "I will say I helped their golf games because they were all so competitive. They wanted to get better and better. Jeff Bagwell, Joe Morgan, Mike Scott, Yogi always came, Alan Ashby. We had guys begging to go on the trips. Every year we went to a different place."

While Biggio loves golf, Berra and Bagwell are not too complimentary about his game. "Craig's a good golfer...sometimes," Berra said, laughing. Bagwell was a bit less kind in his evaluation. "He stinks," the former National League MVP said. "He hits balls where people don't hit balls, but he'll go get it, keep hitting it until he gets it in a good place. I'm like, 'Just pick it up and let's go.' But he's persistent. This is part of Craig's personality. He loves the game and he could be better, but he just doesn't play enough."

Current Astros owner Drayton McLane joined McMullen in praising Biggio. "Craig is the image of what the Houston Astros are all about, and that's what the public loves about him," the owner said. "They love the image of Craig. As I tell people, 'The pitcher is going to throw about 130 to 150 pitches a game and you watch Craig and he is into every pitch. He's rolling up over his toes, and he is ready for whatever is going to happen.' That just shows what kind of intensity he has. He's as intense as anybody I have ever seen."

McMullen believes that intensity and the second baseman's ability will make him immortal. "He'll be there in the Hall of Fame," the former owner said. "He's had longevity and he's played well."

Longtime baseball observer Bill James in his *2001 Historical Baseball Abstract* supported McMullen's belief. James listed Biggio as the fifth best second baseman of all-time behind Joe Morgon, Eddie Collins, Rogers Hornsby and Jackie Robinson. Of James' top 10, only Ryne Sandberg and Roberto Alomar, at seventh and tenth, respectively, are not yet in the Hall of Fame.

First All-Star Game: Biggio, who finished the first half hitting .315 with 11 stolen bases, finished second to San Diego's Benito Santiago in the fan's voting to start the 1991 All-Star Game in Toronto, but Cincinnati Reds manager Lou Piniella selected him and teammate Pete Harnisch as reserves. "I'm one of the happiest people in the world right now," Biggio told the media after learning he was the first Houston catcher to ever be selected. "You hope to have a long, productive career and make a couple of All-Star teams along the way. It probably won't hit me until I'm there." Once in the game, Biggio immediately made All-Star game history. As he reached for a pitch from John Smiley of the Pittsburgh Pirates, Biggio was called for catcher's interference on Paul Molitor. "I thought the ball was in my glove and all of a sudden the bat hits it," Biggio said of the first catcher's interference ever called in the All-Star Game. "That happens about once in a blue moon." Biggio also grounded out against Dennis Eckersley.

Moving to Second Base: "He was an All-Star catcher, so why move him out from behind the dish?" Astros coach Matt Galante asked rhetorically. "He's a guy who could run pretty well. He's got really good hands and really good feet. We wanted a guy like that to be around for 14, 15 years and we didn't know with him as a catcher, with all the strenuous work back there, if we would be able to take advantage of the assets he had. We thought that if he could play infield it would prolong his career. He could steal bases and be an offensive force. We approached him with that and he was totally against it. We tried to explain the benefits to him, but his heart had his ears."

But Biggio finally relented and agreed to try. In a meaningless series at San Francisco near the end of the 1991 season, Biggio moved to the middle infield. "We put him at second base and he made an error," Galante continued. "The ball went right through his legs, and that didn't help the cause."

Galante visited often with Biggio during the off-season and started to wear him down. In spring training, Biggio tossed away his catcher's mitt and grabbed a couple of foam gloves, which Galante had him use to learn how to catch the ball with two hands. Galante hit thousands of balls to Biggio and, along with shortstop Andujar Cedeno, taught him how to turn a double play. "We would go out early every day and stay late every day," Galante said. "I'm talking hours and hours. I'm telling you he put in a lot of work. We were not out to become a good second baseman. We were out to become an All-Star second baseman. We were out to become a Gold Glove second baseman."

Just like he told Keith Bodie upon his arrival in Asheville, Biggio repeated a familiar, Mike Sheppard-inspired line to Galante. "Don't tell me the good things I'm doing," Biggio said. "I know them. Tell me what I'm doing wrong." Galante liked hearing this. "He didn't mind being knocked down a peg or two. He wanted to change the bad. This did not happen overnight or in a week, two weeks. When we left spring training that year, I was not confident that we had a great second baseman. But I was confident that because of the progress we made, this was going to work." Biggio began the 1992 season leading off and playing second base.

Sheppard was amazed at how quickly Biggio made the adjustment to second base. He was also shocked that Biggio, even though he was a catcher at Seton Hall, remembered a trick Sheppard had taught his infielders. "I went down to see Craig in Philadelphia and I noticed him tossing a little rock in the field so he knew where he wanted to be when the pitch got to the plate. You start one place and as the pitch comes in, you are moving to the rock. I had to smile because that was something that we taught them here."

Second All-Star Game – At Second Base: Biggio made the All-Star team for the second straight season in 1992, this time at second base. He became the first player in major league history to make the All-Star team as a catcher and second baseman. Biggio struck out and lined out in the game.

Japanese Tour: Biggio joined 24 other major leaguers on a team that traveled to Japan to face a Japanese All-Star team in November 1992. Roger Clemens, Ozzie Smith, Cecil Fielder, Ken Griffey Jr., Wade Boggs, and Larry Walker were the big stars on the team, who visited Tokyo, Osaka, and Fukuoka. "At the

All-Star game, which I've been fortunate to play in, it is just one game," Biggio said eight years later. "But on the trip we played a bunch of games and we traveled all over together. I met a lot of different guys and got to see the culture of a different country. It was a great opportunity. It was a long trip going over there. Patty was pregnant so it was a long trip for her, but it was a great experience seeing a different culture and the way they lived. Japan was really, really clean. It was something I wouldn't have done on my own, with Patty and the kids, but to do it the way we did it with a group was really cool."

Gold Glove: The Gold Glove, a baseball tradition since Rawlings first awarded it in 1957 for defensive excellence, is a prized possession. Biggio, when he made the switch from catcher to second base, had it as a goal. On November 16, 1994, he got one. "The proudest I've ever been of Craig was winning the first Gold Glove," Galante said. "That was my job to help him become a defensive player. To see a Gold Glove come to him was a great moment." Biggio, who went on to win three more Gold Gloves in 1995, 1996, and 1997, wanted Galante to share in the award.

Towards the end of the 1996 season, Biggio called Galante into a back room in the clubhouse where the two often talked. The second baseman had asked equipment manager Dennis Liborio to drape his second Gold Glove on a table before the coach came in.

"I want to give you something," Biggio told the coach when he got to the room.

"Fine, what do you want to give me?" Galante asked as Biggio pointed to the draping and had the coach pull it off.

"If it wasn't for you, I wouldn't have had it," Biggio said as the Gold Glove glistened back at Galante.

"Craig, it's yours," the coach said.

"Yeah it's mine, but you've done a lot to get me this," Biggio said, insisting that the coach take it with him.

Several years later, Galante remembered the moment vividly. "I was ready to break down, but I didn't want to in front of everybody else," he said. "That was a very touching moment. I have it in my house. My son thinks it's his, but it's not."

All-Star Starter: In his fourth All-Star Game, Biggio started at second base. "Getting voted in by the fans is a great honor," Biggio told the Houston media. "I'm tickled to death to be voted in." He became the first Astros player to be voted as a starter since Cesar Cedeno in 1973.

Biggio played in four more All-Star Games — 1995, 1996, 1997, and 1998 — and included his friend Gallitelli in the 1997 contest in Cleveland. "When I got to the hotel, he told me it was time for the breakfast where the players get their All-Star rings," Gallitelli said. "He asked if I wanted to go and of course I said yes. We went down to the buffet and everyone is there. [Mark] McGwire, Randy Johnson. I'm sitting with Nomar Garciaparra, Craig and Ken Griffey Jr. At the end of the breakfast, we were the last ones in the place. Me, Craig, Patty, his kids, Ken Griffey Jr. and his wife and children. We just sat around and talked."

The two sets of parents talked about their kids, something Craig Biggio did not mind doing at all. "I became a better baseball player when I started having a family. After Patty and I got married, I would take the game home, be angry, go over everything. Then I had kids and I said to my wife, 'Listen Pat, I think I'm starting to understand this thing a little bit. If I'm a little bit late coming up after a game, don't be upset. At least now when we go home, I'll be fine.' The kids don't care whether you have a good game or a bad game. They just care that you are Dad and they just want to be with you. The three of them [sons Conor and Cavan and daughter Quinn] are the greatest kids in the world."

Terry Biggio, Craig's older brother, believes that early impressions of a major league catcher shaped his brother's family life. "Craig loved Thurman Munson," Terry Biggio said. "He's got a Thurman Munson bat downstairs in his house. I know that Thurman Munson played a role in his thought of what a player should be and Thurman was always a family guy. The reason why he died in his Citation crash was because he went from a prop to a jet because he wanted to get home to see his family. Thurman Munson died because he was trying to move up to an airplane that was faster and that would get him home and closer to his family quicker, and that's a lot of the way that Craig is."

50-50: Biggio already had 51 doubles when he singled to start the sixth inning at St. Louis on September 23, 1998. As he inched off first with his lead, Biggio neared baseball immortality. Seconds later he joined Hall-of-Famer Tris Speaker as the only player in major league history to have 50 doubles and 50 stolen bases in a single season. Speaker had 53 doubles and 52 stolen bases with the Boston Red Sox in 1912.

The following year, Biggio hit a club-record 56 doubles and became only the sixth player since 1900 to have 50-plus doubles in back-to-back seasons. It was the most two-baggers in the major leagues since George Kell hit 56 for the Detroit Tigers in 1950 and the most in the National League since Joe Medwick had the same number for the 1937 St. Louis Cardinals. Both of them are in the Hall of Fame.

200 Hits: Biggio became the first player in Astros history to reach the 200-hit plateau for a season on September 15, 1998 with a ninth inning single off Turk Wendell in the second game of a doubleheader against the Mets. He finished the season with 210 hits. Even with this success, Biggio still took advice from Yogi Berra, the Hall-of-Famer and former Astros coach. "I talk to Craig when I talk to Dennis [equipment manager Liborio] over there," Berra said. "I tell Dennis to put Craig on the phone. I get on him every once in a while to tell him to stop jumping at the ball. Does he listen? I don't know. I'm not there to find out. I watch TV and I can see what he does. He gets too antsy sometimes. 'Stay back, stay back,' I would tell him."

Making the Playoffs: Mike Scott pitched the most memorable game in Astros history on September 25, 1986, with a no-hitter against the Giants to clinch the National League West Division crown. Eleven years later to the exact day, the Biggio-led Astros clinched the National League Central Division title with a 9-1 win over Chicago in the Astrodome. "After we won the first championship, Craig came up to me and gave me a big hug," former Astros manager Larry Dierker, who had been with the team as a pitcher, sales rep, broadcaster and manager since 1964, said. "He thinks of himself as an Astro first, last, and always and he knows that it has been that way for me even longer. He is the kind of player who appreciates longevity and also loyalty, so there is a kinship there in our desire to make this franchise better and our desire to accomplish something for the Astros, for Houston and the community and obviously, for ourselves as well."

Postseason baseball has not been kind to Biggio and the Astros. Biggio has hit just .130 in the 1997, 1998, 1999 and 2001 playoffs where Houston has won only two games.

Knee Injury in 2000: For most of Cal Ripken's consecutive game streak of 2,632, the guy behind him on that active list was Craig Biggio until Dierker gave him a rest after 494 straight games. "He is like Pete Rose with more ability," Dierker said about Biggio in 2000. "He'll play everyday. He'll play different positions. He'll bring a certain intensity to the field every day that is rare. Most guys have a few days during the course of the year when it looks like they are going to work and going home. They are not putting everything they've got into it. The ability to put everything you've got into it for 162 games in 175 days, we hardly have any days off, and he never wants any days off even when he is hurt. He's got to summon some sort of inner desire, inner fire, to play like a maniac every day, to fight to the last out every day. I emphasize every day, not just most days."

But Biggio, who Sheppard would say plays with "fire in his belly," was not in uniform for most of the second half of the 2000 season. Instead, he was on the disabled list for the first time in his 13-year career, exactly 1,800 games, after suffering a season-ending knee injury in an August 1 win at the Florida Marlins. With Florida's Preston Wilson on first base, Mike Lowell hit a grounder to third. Chris Truby grabbed it and threw to second base thinking a double play was in the works. As Biggio caught the ball and pivoted, Wilson came in hard and took out the second baseman.

Biggio collapsed to the ground and remained there while Houston trainer Dave Labossiere came out to help. Eventually, Biggio limped off the field and headed to the hospital where he was diagnosed with torn anterior cruciate and medial collateral ligaments. "He's the emotional centerpiece of our team,"

Dierker told the media after the game. "He plays with such energy, and with a rage to win. It rubs off on the others. He makes every pitch and every at-bat seem so important because of how he plays the game."

The day after the injury, Biggio, who finished 2000 with a sub-par .265 average, eight homers, and 35 RBI was looking ahead to 2001. "I will be the same player again," he told the *Houston Chronicle*'s Carlton Thompson. "In fact, I'll be better. I'll be stronger, and I'll be faster. I'm looking forward to the challenge. I'll be ready. You have to be confident." Dierker agreed. "This will probably have him even more motivated next year. I would be surprised if he didn't come back next year and have a much better year than this year."

Biggio made his manager proud. The second baseman put an exclamation point on his return on May 4, 2001, when he became the first Astro and the 216th player in major league history to reach the 2,000 hit mark.

"It's 2,000 more hits than I ever thought I'd ever have in my life," Biggio told the *Houston Chronicle*'s Jose De Jesus Ortiz after he reached the milestone in Montreal. "I came from a small town. To be able to play with some of the players I've had the opportunity to play with and the organizational people that I've been around with, it's a nice feeling." Biggio went on to hit .292 with 20 homers in 2001.

"The guy is just amazing," Biggio's former college teammate Marteese Robinson said. "Nothing he does surprises me. He's just Biggio being Biggio."

> "He is like Pete Rose with more ability. He'll play everyday. He'll play different positions. He'll bring a certain intensity to the field every day that is rare ... He's got to summon some sort of inner desire, inner fire, to play like a maniac every day, to fight to the last out every day. I emphasize every day, not just most days."
>
> —Larry Dierker, former Astros manager

CHAPTER 15

NORWALK BOYS MAKE IT TO BOSTON

A late-night phone call sends chills down the spines of parents. Leroy and Shirley Vaughn were sound asleep when the phone rang around 12:30 AM on June 27, 1991. "Something must be wrong," thought Shirley Vaughn as she looked over at her husband while he reached for the phone. But it took only a split second for her panic to turn to joy as Leroy Vaughn broke into a huge smile and yelled out, "Maurice is going to Boston!"

Sixteen hours later Vaughn and his parents were reunited at Fenway. They went into the Red Sox dugout to look at the legendary stadium from the inside. They had never been there before. The Vaughns looked out towards left field. There it was, Fenway's icon, the Green Monster, in all its 37-foot high glory. "Dad, remember how we used to come by Fenway during Thanksgiving at Auntie Loretta's and Uncle Paul's and I would tell you guys that someday I would play here?" With that, Maurice gave his dad a hug as he realized that he really *was* in the major leagues.

It was already mid-season, June 27, when Mo Vaughn came out of the Red Sox dugout for batting practice. It should have been just another pregame routine, but Mo Vaughn's much-hyped arrival made it a special day. When Vaughn, then 23 years old, entered the cage for his first hitting session in Boston, everyone stopped. With cameras clicking, reporters, players, and coaches moved in closer to watch. Manager Joe Morgan yelled, "It's like Seton Hall, Mo. Just like Seton Hall, Mo."

Two hours after batting practice, Vaughn, hitting sixth in the

Red Sox lineup, again came out of the home dugout, this time for real, and went to the on-deck circle. The energy level in Fenway lifted immediately. "I was so nervous," Vaughn said, "just so nervous. No doubt about it. I was playing against Don Mattingly and the Yankees in Fenway Park. Yeah, I was nervous." What was there to be nervous about? After all, how many guys get a 25-second standing ovation for their *first* major league at-bat?

"So much is expected of The Rook," Michael Madden wrote about Vaughn in the *Boston Globe*. "He is expected to knock in runs, he is expected to hit home runs, he is expected to perform mouth-to-mouth on the Red Sox, lifeless for so long, he is expected to light a fuse in Boston, send off a rocket over Fenway and fire a flare or two over New England."

Vaughn went hitless in that first game, but his family did not care. "When he got to the major leagues, it was weird," said his sister Donna, who was joined at her brother's Fenway debut by her husband, Willie, and daughter, Courtney, along with an oversized Vaughn contingent. "We were used to watching the games on television, but now it was our brother out there. Who ever would have thought that he would be out there? We were just so proud and happy."

Her brother got his first big league hit the next day in Baltimore's Memorial Stadium. In the fifth, facing Todd Frohwirth, Vaughn took an offering the other way with a clean single to left. The Orioles, keeping with baseball tradition, tossed the ball into the Red Sox dugout, giving the rookie his first big league memento. Vaughn, after advancing to second on a groundball, was welcomed to the American League by a stranger, the Orioles shortstop, who later became a baseball legend. "Cal [Ripken] came to me and said, 'I hope you get three thousand more.' It was a classy thing to do and we've been friends ever since," Vaughn said during the 2000 season.

Ripken, the Orioles, the Red Sox, and all of America, courtesy of ESPN's *SportsCenter*, soon witnessed what all the Mo Vaughn excitement was about. In his fourth game in the major leagues, Vaughn led off the fifth inning against the Orioles' Jeff Robinson and gave a guy named Trump Vandrau his 15 minutes of fame. The postmaster from Chambersburg, Pennsylvania, was sitting in the 38th row of the right field bleachers, just five rows from the top of the stadium, when suddenly a baseball appeared in the Baltimore sky. "I wasn't even paying attention to who was hitting," Vandrau told the *Boston Globe*'s Steve Fainaru. "Then I turned around and it was coming at me. It hit me in the hand and fell and I picked it up."

Fainaru left his press box seat and went out to deep right field to check on the re-entry of Vaughn's monstrous shot, the second longest home run in Memorial Stadium history. Vaughn's teammate, famed baseball funny man Steve Lyons, could not believe how far the ball traveled. "Heck, I thought we were going to have to start the car to find it." In fact, Vaughn almost joined Hall-of-Famer Frank Robinson as the only player to ever hit a ball out of Memorial Stadium.

> "So much is expected of The Rook. He is expected to knock in runs, he is expected to hit home runs, he is expected to perform mouth-to-mouth on the Red Sox, lifeless for so long, he is expected to light a fuse in Boston, send off a rocket over Fenway and fire a flare or two over New England."
> — Michael Madden, Boston Globe

Vaughn, who also homered the next day in Milwaukee, had entered the major leagues with a bang, going 5-for-16 with two homers and six RBI. Life got even better a few days later when his childhood friend Kevin Morton entered the Fenway locker room to begin his Red Sox pitching career against Cecil Fielder and the Detroit Tigers. After driving 50 miles from Providence, Morton was immediately met by Vaughn. The two friends, who had spent hours together as kids, in college, and in the minors, shook hands, smiled and laughed about how they were now together on the big stage.

Morton, as was his makeup, always laughed, except when he got to the mound. Before the game, he told reporters that he was leaving 25 tickets for friends and family, but had no idea where they would sit. "I told them [my family] that this isn't like Pawtucket where you can pull up front and beep the horn,"

Morton joked. By gametime, Morton, then 22, was all business. His first pitch was a strike and his first inning went one-two-three. By the sixth inning, he had the Fenway faithful on their feet, having given up only two hits until Cecil Fielder welcomed him to the big leagues with a bomb. "It was the hardest ball I've ever *heard* off me," he said later.

Morton needed only 103 pitches to five-hit the Tigers in a 10-1, complete-game win. "How in the name of God did they ever hit him in the minors?" Red Sox manager Joe Morgan wondered out loud about his newest Seton Hall recruit.

"That was a beautiful night when Kevin and Maurice were out there," said Leroy Vaughn, who watched from what became his regular spot, 20 rows up behind the plate, said. "Maurice was so excited. He was pumping his fist to Kevin. Kevin was throwing that changeup up there and they couldn't touch it. It was a great feeling and I felt very happy for both of them."

"That was a great night," Mo Vaughn added, also remembering it as if it were yesterday. "Tony Peña kept going out to the mound and saying to Kevin, 'You listen to me. You throw what I put down, and you'll get through this thing!' That was the greatest day for us. That was my proudest day, the day we first played together in the big leagues."

By starting off so well, the two Norwalkers raised expectations leading to an inevitable fall. Morton's came first. In his third start, he was blasted for six runs in just two and a third innings and dropped to 1-2. Meanwhile, Vaughn headed into an 0-for-14 slump and his average dipped to near .200. "I've always stated that when I came up I was not going to tear up the league," Vaughn told the *Globe*'s Joe Burris. "I'm getting acclimated to a new situation, adjusted to a new league."

Vaughn was not given too much time to get used to his life as a major leaguer before the *Boston Globe* printed a series about black ballplayers in Boston. The kid knew his skin color would be topic for conversation in The Hub. His parents had prepared him for it. When Shirley and Leroy Vaughn first moved to Norwalk, they were met with a Confederate Flag on their front lawn, dead fish on their doorstep and taunting, racially-motivated phone calls. They told their children about the incidents and taught them to appreciate their heritage. Mo Vaughn also knew about Boston's problems with black players. He had been told the team had only 33 black players and was the last of the big league clubs to integrate in 1959. "I can handle it. I will handle it," he told the *Globe*'s Fainaru. "It's the way I am. What can you say about the situation? It's evident. It's a situation that has to be tackled in time. My approach to life is to go about it with an open mind, to not be biased about anything. I've got to make it right for the next man who comes along. I've got to make it a little easier for the next guy."

Rico Petrocelli, a two-time All-Star with the Red Sox, who had seen several black teammates struggle in Boston, thought Vaughn was the right guy to change things when he met the first baseman at a luncheon for inner-city school children. "Mo bridged that gap better than anybody I have ever seen," the former shortstop said. "He mentioned a number of times that he wanted to be the guy who kind of healed things regarding race relations. If there was anybody who really thought that way, as far as ballplayers were concerned, I think their thinking was really changed because Mo was just such a tremendous ambassador for African-American people, living here, playing here. He opened a lot of doors for a lot of kids playing here."

But before he could bring racial harmony to Boston, he had to first bring it to the Red Sox clubhouse. To do that, Vaughn had to overcome a pregame spat with teammate Mike Greenwell. The two teased each other during batting practice on August 24 in Anaheim. As the verbal jousting continued, Vaughn playfully poked Greenwell with his bat and soon it was "boys will be boys." By the time Morton arrived in the clubhouse to prepare for his start against the Angels, the tussle was over. "Jesus, what the hell happened here?" Morton asked himself as reporters swarmed the locker room to cover the fight's aftermath.

Morton found out what transpired and got a wink from his buddy. "Mo comes into the locker room and he's just smiling," Morton said. "I tip my hat to him because he was a rookie who acted like he was there for the long haul." Morton also pointed out that the problem between Vaughn and Greenwell was solved just as quickly as it began. "They ended up being friends and everything was good."

That night Morton was also good. He gave up only two hits, one being eventual Hall-of-Famer Dave Winfield's 401st career homer, in eight innings, but lost 1-0. He was hot again, allowing just two runs in his last 14 $^2/_3$ innings. He made Boston fans even giddier two weeks later with a 7-2 win in his first visit to Yankee Stadium. "Being from Norwalk, to pitch in Yankee Stadium..." Morton's voice trailed off as he thought of the significance. "When we were kids we would joke around and say, 'I'm in Yankee Stadium.' I wanted to be Ron Guidry. I was a skinny, small guy, just like him."

Mike Sheppard Sr. shared Morton's reaction. "When I was a kid, I went to Yankee Stadium all the time," Sheppard said. "Then, when Rick Cerone was with the Yankees, I started going again. It got to the point where I didn't need a pass because the guards all knew me. Now, here I was again, standing on the field in Yankee Stadium remembering all of those days as a kid sitting in the stands, and Mo and Kevin are warming up to play the Yankees. It was a great, great moment for me."

> "Mo was just such a tremendous ambassador for African-American people, living here, playing here. He opened a lot of doors for a lot of kids playing here."
> —Rico Petrocelli, former Boston Red Sox shortstop

Vaughn also enjoyed the Yankee Stadium debut. He remembered watching on television as his idol, Chris Chambliss, hit one of the most dramatic home runs in Yankee and baseball history to beat the Kansas City Royals in the bottom of the ninth for the 1976 American League pennant. Chambliss first learned of Vaughn's interest in him while coaching the Yankees in 2000. "It's flattering to hear that, because there were so many other great players that I played around and with," Chambliss said while dressing for an interleague game against the Philadelphia Phillies. "To think that I made an impact on somebody's life and then see them in the major leagues, that's really an honor for me."

Vaughn finished his rookie season hitting .260 in 74 games, with four homers, and 32 RBI. Good numbers, but certainly not the Rookie of the Year-type season Peter Gammons had predicted.

Rick Cerone, who was the first player from the 1975 draft to make it to the major leagues and the last to leave 18 seasons later, was thrilled with how his fellow Seton Hallers adjusted to the big leagues. "I was with Boston when they drafted Val, Kevin, and Mo and I saw them in spring training," Cerone said in November 2000. "I always told them the toughest thing is not to get to the big leagues, but to stay there."

After his rookie season season, Vaughn sounded just like Cerone. "The minor leagues and the major leagues are two different things," Vaughn said. "You can play well in the minor leagues, that is one thing, but when you get to the major leagues, then you want to stay there. I knew I would get there, but would I stay there? I knew that would be a totally different question."

MO VAUGHN: MAJOR LEAGUE MOMENTS HE'LL REMEMBER (Listed Chronologically)

Back to Triple-A: Just as he did the year before when Morton pitched, Sheppard, the Seton Hall coach, was in the Yankee Stadium stands rooting for the Red Sox on Opening Day in 1992. Vaughn gave his college coach another thrill when he hit a homer down the left field line to beat the Yankees. Unfortunately, the home run was one of Vaughn's few bright moments in the season's first month. Through 23 games, the slugger hit just .186 with two homers and 11 RBI. He even dropped a routine throw from shortstop Luis Rivera to cost the Sox a game in Kansas City. New Boston manager Butch Hobson had no choice. He was forced to send one of his all-time favorites to Pawtucket on May 4 while the Red Sox were visiting the Minnesota Twins.

Just like the first baseman thought, making it to the major leagues was one thing. Staying there was another. "He walked into my office and I told him," Hobson said in 2000 while managing the independent Nashua Pride. "He said, 'You're right. I need to go down there and get myself together.'" But Vaughn was seething inside. It was a blow to his pride to leave Minnesota no longer a major leaguer. He flew to Boston and contemplated not going to Triple-A, but his parents interceded. They sent a cousin, who lived in Brockton, Massachusetts, to personally deliver a message, "Get your stuff packed and show up." Their son heard them loud and clear and met his parents in a Pawtucket hotel the next day.

"We told Maurice that he had a long way to go," Leroy Vaughn said. "I told him about Wade Boggs, about Mickey Mantle, about how they went up and down. We convinced him, and he realized it, that he was there to get his work done." Although he did listen to his mother and father, Vaughn still vented to the media over his demotion. "I'm not trying to get into it with the manager or anything, but there were a lot of guys not hitting," he told the *Boston Globe*'s Nick Cafardo. "And when I made an error, they said it was because I wasn't hitting or that my concentration wasn't there. That's after making a million plays at first base without an error. That didn't matter." In the same article, Vaughn said Hobson had changed now that he was managing in Boston and that maybe the Red Sox should consider trading him.

> "I always told them the toughest thing is not to get to the big leagues, but to stay there."
> —Rick Cerone, former New York Yankees catcher

By the time Hobson heard about Vaughn's harsh words, the slugger was hitting .444 with three homers and seven RBI in seven Triple-A outings. "If saying things about me will ignite him to do the things he's doing right now and get up here where he belongs," the manager told the Boston media, "then go down and interview him every day."

Rico Petrocelli knew Vaughn was letting off steam, but he still wanted the first baseman to apologize to Hobson. "I said, 'Forget all of this stuff about being angry,'" the Triple-A manager said. "'That's not going to do you any good. What you need to do down here is to work hard, work on your fielding and also your hitting.' I also told him, 'The best thing you can do is to call Butch and tell him you are sorry and you just want to work hard and get back to the big leagues.' And he did it. That showed the character of the guy."

Petrocelli also discovered why Vaughn had dropped Rivera's throw. "He was taking his eye off the ball when he caught it from an infielder," Petrocelli noticed. "If the ball was above his head, he would look straight ahead, rather than up at the ball, so he wouldn't see it go into his glove and it would go off the top of this glove." Problem noticed, problem solved.

"You can't be pissed off about it," catcher Eric Wedge, who was in Pawtucket at the time before being promoted to Boston in August, told Vaughn. "You've got to get your focus back and prove them wrong and keep doing it, doing it, and doing it. He got right back up there." Vaughn played 39 games in Pawtucket and got his act together, hitting .282 with six homers and 27 RBI. Hobson brought him back to Boston where black "Hit Dog" T-shirts, in his honor, had been sold at concession stands to start the season. The shirts were hauled out of storage and back onto the concourse. Vaughn created the marketing buzz for the apparel, hitting .364 with a five-game hitting streak his first week back.

Mike Easler Enters His Life: The phone rang in Vaughn's home prior to the 1993 season.

"Hello?" Vaughn answered.

"Mo, this is the Hit Man," Mike Easler said in return.

"Oh God. What did I do?" the taken-aback first baseman said fearing for his life for a second.

"No, not that hit man. I'm Mike Easler, the Hit Man, the baseball player," Easler replied with a chuckle.

After the awkward introduction, Easler, who had just been hired as Boston's new hitting coach, continued, "Mo, you have so much ability, and right now, it looks like on the tape, you're fighting yourself. Your body is moving every which way, so it causes your head to move. What we have to do is establish a way of hitting where you're not moving as much and you're more balanced. If you just give me a chance, when I get to spring training, you're going to have the best year of your life and I think you're going to be the hitter that you never dreamed that you could be before at the major league level."

That phone conversation changed Mo Vaughn's life. "I was not calm until I met Mike Easler," Vaughn said about his coach, a former big leaguer who hit .293 over a 14-year career. "I was always on edge. When I met him, I began to prepare and understand what I had to do to be ready to play every day. He helped me relax."

Once spring training began, Easler got down to business with his eager-to-learn student. The two looked at tape and changed Vaughn's hitting style. "His big hero, at that time, was Cecil Fielder," Easler said about Vaughn. "Cecil had a slide with his front foot. He slid back and then he slid forward, and for Mo Vaughn, it just didn't work. Mo is better when his feet are more quiet and they're in a wider base with less movement. Doing it that way, he tracked the ball longer. I called it 'quiet explosion position.'"

Sheppard understood what Easler was talking about. "We had to discipline Mo mentally," the Seton Hall coach said about Vaughn's college days. "We tried to teach him that when he had two strikes on him, to just make contact and go the other way. I talked to Mike Easler about that. Easler said, 'Coach, I've been trying to teach that to him.' Easler loved to talk to me about what Mo used to be like in college. I told him that Fred Hopke [Seton Hall assistant coach] was always upset with Mo because he was always out in front, so I came up with a phrase, 'Wait on the ball, see it better and still be quick.' It was the same thing Easler was teaching him."

"Mo had so much ability that it was scary," Easler said in 2000 while working as the St. Louis Cardinals hitting coach. "It took one week for him to understand what we were trying to do. My God, I could just see it and said to myself, 'Oh, he's ready.'"

Vaughn was ready to the tune of .403 in the Florida practice games with six homers and 23 RBI. Fast forward to the end of the regular season. Easler's prediction of .300 with 20 homers in 1993 proved to be an undervalued projection. Vaughn rocketed to elite status with a .297 average, 29 homers and 101 RBI. He was named the team's MVP by the Boston chapter of the Baseball Writers Association of America.

First All-Star Game: Frank Thomas was named by the fans as the starting first baseman in the 1995 All-Star Game, but Yankees manager Buck Showalter tabbed Vaughn, with 21 homers and 50 RBI in the first half of the season, as a reserve. "I was in awe," Vaughn's sister Catherine said after learning of the selection. Once the Vaughn family descended on Texas, they were treated like royalty. "You walked into the hotel and there were people all over the place," Vaughn's other sister Donna said. "They would stay the night just to try and get an autograph. At the game, when they introduced him, I got a chill, watching him stand on the line. He was excited to get to go."

Vaughn was also proud to share the spotlight with his former college teammate, Craig Biggio. "When Maurice and Craig first saw each other, they were hugging," Donna said. "You could see the bond. I hadn't seen Craig in years. He was always so cute." Donna's brother loved Biggio for his style of play rather than his boyish good looks. "It was a great moment because I always referred to Craig as 'my captain.' He played as hard and as tough as anybody I'd ever seen play."

The next year, Vaughn, with a .350 average, 24 homers, and 73 RBI in the first half of the season, started in the 1996 All-Star Game in Philadelphia because Thomas, the fan's choice again, was hurt. Vaughn doubled in three at-bats. He also made the 1997 All-Star team, but was unable to compete due to an injury.

1995 MVP: Mike Easler lost his job in 1994 when Hobson was fired as Boston manager and his replacement, Kevin Kennedy, brought in new coaches. Instead of talking hitting in American League dugouts, Vaughn and Easler did it by long distance. "I was like a proud father watching his son go out there and mature and grow into a professional man and a complete player," Easler said. "Mo Vaughn and I had a very close relationship. It just kind of took off as he kept going on and on and on…"

Vaughn led the Red Sox to the 1995 American League Eastern Division title with 39 homers and 126 RBI in just 144 games with a .300 average and was listed by the media as a possible MVP candidate. Even though Vaughn publicly tried to downplay his chances, he was hopeful. "I knew I had a chance," he said. Hope turned to joy when his business advisor, Mark Gillam, called him at home on November 16 to give him the news. He was the American League MVP.

At the same time, Vaughn's sister Donna was listening to New York City's all-sports radio station, WFAN, while waiting in her car for daughter Courtney to finish dance class. The top-of-the-hour sports update came on with the American MVP Award as the lead story. "I called Mom and Dad. Then I called him on his cell phone and we talked in the car. He was happy," she said.

As usual, the MVP award was a family achievement. "No matter what Maurice does, he alone did it, but he always says *we* made the all-stars, *we* won the MVP," his mother, Shirley, says proudly. "When it comes to baseball, he always says 'we' to us."

200 Hit Seasons: "I can't run, so 200 hits was something to be proud of," Mo Vaughn said of his 207 and 205 hits, respectively, in 1996 and 1998. Of active players, only Derek Jeter and Alex Rodriguez each with three 200-hit seasons have more than Vaughn's two 200-hit campaigns.

Postseason Play: "My favorite times in baseball were running around the field after clinching in 1995 and 1998 to go to the playoffs," Vaughn said. His first chance to celebrate came on September 20, 1995, when Rick Aguilera struck out the Milwaukee Brewers' Dave Nilsson to clinch the American League East title. Vaughn enjoyed the moment, hugged Roger Clemens, and later hopped on a police horse, waving to a delirious crowd while sitting on the strong-backed stallion.

But Vaughn experienced no such joy in the postseason. He went 0-for-14 in the first round of the playoffs, a three-game sweep by the Cleveland Indians. "I don't think I'll ever close the books on what happened in 1995," Vaughn said. "I think I'll always refer back to it and learn from it because I think, as much as it hurts, you're always going to learn more from negative things than positive things."

Mike Easler had always said Vaughn was a fast learner and the 1998 playoffs proved that. After the Red Sox clinched a wild-card berth on September 24, the champagne flowed again. Vaughn immediately looked to a rematch with the Indians. In the first game, an 11-3 Boston win, he became only the fourth player in postseason history to get seven RBI in a game with a three-run homer, a two-run homer, and a two-run double. But that was it for Boston's run in the playoffs, with Cleveland winning the next three.

Honoring Jackie Robinson: Mo Vaughn knew a lot about the late Jackie Robinson before he decided to wear number 42 to honor the man who broke the color barrier with the Brooklyn Dodgers on April 15, 1947. Vaughn's mother once worked with Jackie Robinson's widow, Rachel, on a Connecticut-based charity, and each year the Vaughn family, along with thousands of others, attended a music festival at the Robinson's Connecticut estate.

When Vaughn chose to wear 42 when he first came to the majors in 1991, he never knew he would be one of the last players to ever wear the number. Major League Baseball, 50 years to the day Robinson first joined the league, declared that Robinson's 42 would be retired from the game. But those players who had 42 before the 1997 season would be allowed to wear it until they left the game. When they leave, so will number 42.

Vaughn, who was a highly visible black star, was a perfect player to speak about Robinson's importance to the game. "Black athletes ought to know about him," Vaughn told the *Globe*'s Larry Whiteside at a Jackie Robinson Foundation event. "Pay attention to the man. Make sure people appreciate what he went through and what his purpose was. They should be proud of his memory and his legacy. He broke the barrier and brought a lot of us along with him. None of us have gone through what he went through. I couldn't do it, and I wouldn't have tried either."

Since meeting Vaughn, Rachel Robinson had been equally impressed with what he had done. "When Mo Vaughn, the great baseball player, decided to wear number 42 on his uniform, I felt very pleased and hopeful," she said in the summer of 2000. "Hopeful because the choice Mo made meant to me that he was not simply paying tribute to Jackie Robinson, but was a young man committed to excellence and giving back to the society in some significant way. I'm proud of all Mo's achievements. Not only is he a superb athlete, but as I had hoped, he has been very generous in support of youth development programs. Like Jack, he is determined to make a difference in the lives of young people who need him."

Arrest and Innocence: On the ninth day of 1998, Vaughn, then 30, drove to the Foxy Lady, a gentlemen's club in Providence. "I was going through my contract negotiations and I was frustrated," Vaughn said. "I needed to get away. I lived in the same town I played in all year round, so my actions were reported every day. I fell asleep at the wheel on the way back. There was a car on the side of the road. I hit it. I got arrested for DWI."

Ironically, Seton Hall's Sheppard was in Providence at Big East Conference meetings and was within blocks of where Vaughn had started his night. Sheppard had always warned his players, Vaughn included, about how important it was to stay out of trouble. "When he was here, I spent a lot of time talking to the guys about not doing stupid things off the field," the coach said. "They had too much to lose. It was part of the discipline I tried to teach them."

Vaughn was somehow unhurt in the accident, which occurred on Route 95 near his home. The disabled car was destroyed in the crash and Vaughn's truck flipped at least once. His parents and sisters rushed to his side. "We believe that things happen for a reason," Leroy Vaughn said. "I believe this was a tremendous experience for him. We were very, very fortunate that nobody got hurt. Those type of things happen. They happen and now you have a new page in life."

But Vaughn, because of his celebrity status, had to endure the media spotlight throughout the ordeal and the ensuing trial. "The media really grilled me," he said. "It was like I had committed a mass murder." Vaughn and his lawyer, Kevin

> "When Mo Vaughn, the great baseball player, decided to wear number 42 on his uniform, I felt very pleased and hopeful. Hopeful because the choice Mo made meant to me that he was not simply paying tribute to Jackie Robinson, but was a young man committed to excellence and giving back to the society in some significant way.
> —Rachel Robinson, Jackie Robinson's widow

Reddington, fought the case and won, never needing Sheppard, who had agreed to be a character witness.

Vaughn, who was telling the story at his locker in the visitors' clubhouse in Baltimore's Camden Yards, paused for a moment to gather his thoughts before continuing.

"But as an athlete, do you ever really win?" said Vaughn, who took out full-page advertisements in two Boston papers to apologize for the incident. "That's the thing about athletes that we have to understand. It doesn't matter. Once the statement is made, it doesn't matter what the result is. If Chris Chambliss was involved in what I was involved in when I was a little kid, I wouldn't have understood. I remember when things happened to guys when I was younger and I would be like, 'Wow, how could he do that?' But now that I'm going through it, I know anything can happen.

"I apologized for it, because no matter if I was right or wrong, I was there. It can't happen to guys like us because right or wrong, you are still going to be wrong. We have no choice. That is the responsibility we have chosen to accept."

Signing with Anaheim: "I wanted him to stay in Boston," Leroy Vaughn said, "but after a while he really didn't want to. I kept telling him that, but finally, I recognized that he was right, that he wasn't being treated properly in Boston and it was time to leave. When I told him that, a huge weight came off his shoulders. He was very happy I finally agreed with him."

"This stinks," Dan Shaughnessy wrote in his *Boston Globe* column on November 12, 1998, immediately after Vaughn rejected a final offer from the Red Sox. "Vaughn put together six consecutive monster seasons for the Red Sox. He was a leader on and off the field — wildly respected by players all over baseball. Moreover, he was a black athlete who said good things about working and living in Boston. He's done legitimate community service and is an absolute kid magnet. His is a huge loss — worse than the departures of Roger Clemens and Carlton Fisk."

Boston was divided over whose fault it was that number 42 was gone. While Shaughnessy blamed Red Sox management and Vaughn equally for the discord that forced the separation, some, like the *Globe*'s Will McDonough, were pro-front office. "If you have a brain in your head or an ounce of common sense, you will go to the door or nearest window, open it, and shout at the top of your lungs, 'Thank you for sparing us five more years of Mo Vaughn's bull.' What a break we all just got. I'm closing in on 40 years of writing sports for this paper, and there was no bigger bore, or earache, over those four decades than Mo Vaughn." Later McDonough added, "Let's make it simple. Mo is about money ... wherever he gets the most is where he will end up."

McDonough had used a lot of his column space throughout the season to blast Vaughn for being critical of Red Sox management because they had not offered him a worthy contract extension. At one point, Leroy Vaughn grew so upset with McDonough's public lynching of his son that he sent the writer a note of complaint.

Red Sox management, and McDonough, seemed to tire of Vaughn's outspokenness about his contract and other issues. The big first baseman was the team leader and took that role seriously. "That's why they [Red Sox teammates] called me the Underboss," Vaughn said. "I was always the guy who had the eyes and ears. If there was a problem, it came to me. If it was a situation I thought needed to be addressed, then I addressed it. That's what I've always done. Me being who I am, my job is to make everyone feel as confident and comfortable as they can possibly be."

"Going into the 1998 season, even knowing he was entering his free agent year, Mo looked at himself as being solely the property of the Red Sox," Mark Gillam, Vaughn's business advisor, said. "Mo's desire was to sign a deal that would keep him in Boston while compensating him for what he could get as a free agent."

Spring training and some mid-season negotiations were fruitless. Gillam was hopeful things would pick up again during the World Series and a 14-day window of exclusivity Major League Baseball rules allowed teams to re-sign their own players. But during that time, Gillam's office phone, home phone, cell phone, and fax machine never rang with a call from the Red Sox and, as he said, "I'm a pretty easy guy to find."

While the Red Sox never surfaced during their two-week window of exclusive opportunity, the Anaheim Angels were chomping at the bit for a chance to get Vaughn. "Mark and I got to the office on the 15th day," Frank Cantone, Gillam's associate, said. "Mr. [Bill] Bavasi, then the Angels general manager, had faxed over a very impressive and persuasive letter. It was a very down-to-earth, candid letter about the Angels organization, their direction, and how good a fit Anaheim would be for Mo. We immediately faxed the letter to Mo and we entered into negotiations with the Angels."

"Had the Red Sox surfaced during that 14-day window, I am pretty sure Mo would still be in Boston," Gillam said. "Boston was a marriage made in heaven for him. He was Northeastern guy, his family was there, he loved the city, he loved the people, he had the Youth Center, he loved the kids. He was looking forward to a long, wonderful career in Boston. But when he looked at management, he got confused when it didn't naturally play out the way it should have.

"Mo would have felt validated if they had called," Gillam continued. "That is one of the most important things to him. We had a lot of late-night meetings and I could always tell that the biggest thing that mattered to Mo was what he called 'The Code.' He would say, 'You either follow it or you don't.' He loves a person or organization that operates with their palms out each and every day. When your palms are out, you are not hiding anything. He loves dealing with truthful, honest people."

After much discussion with family and friends, Vaughn rejected Boston's final offer of six years for $62 million, which came after the Angels had made their intentions known. "If they did not want Mo for the sixth year, they had an 'out clause' for $2 million, so that is why it was reported to be a $62 million offer," Gillam explained.

"It was never a personal issue," Red Sox director of communication Kevin Shea said in 2000. "It was strictly a business decision and I think our fans know it was a business decision. It was the terms and the conditions of the contract. At first, I think Mo thought it was a personal issue, but now I think he understands it was a business one. It was not a personal issue."

Vaughn agreed to sign with Anaheim for six years and $80 million. "By moving away he gave up his quality of life and he wasn't thrilled," Gillam said. "But he understood that sometimes in life you have to do things that are important for your business. The average career of a major league player is 3.5 years, so you have to maximize the value of your occupation. In this business, all of it is so perishable. One wrong swing…"

It was as if Gillam had a fortune-telling business. On 1998's Opening Day in Anaheim, Vaughn stumbled into the visiting dugout chasing a foul ball. He suffered a sprained ankle, missed two weeks and hobbled the rest of the way to hit .281 with 33 homers and 108 RBI.

Garret Anderson, one of the American League's rising stars, loved his new teammate. "He is definitely a person who has an impact on the guys in the lineup," the outfielder said. "He's definitely a guy who is positive about things and that does rub off on the other players in the lineup. He says, 'Go up there and have good at-bats. Make the pitcher pitch to everybody.' You have to think about what he says, because he goes up there and does it, puts good at-bats on the pitcher. He stresses that to a lot of guys on the team. He likes to talk about hitting and that is something a lot of guys don't like to do anymore."

Angles Manager Mike Scoscia agreed. "Mo is a presence and I think that besides the very talented ballplayer you see and the tremendous offensive player he is, you see a guy that is committed to winning and committed to making the organization successful. That is what you need in your franchise players. You need a guy who has that pride, who says, 'Hey, I'm not changing the way I'm playing because I'm making money. I'm playing the game the same way I did in high school, college, minor leagues, and the major leagues early in my career. That's to win.' That's what drives Mo."

Vaughn got that drive to win from Sheppard. "He stressed perfection," Vaughn said about his college coach. "I am now the same way. I've had some average years to me the last couple of years, years most guys would take. But I am not happy with them. I don't know how to be any other way."

Arm Injury: The 2000 Anaheim Angels were the first American League team to have four players with 30 or more homers. Vaughn [36], third baseman Troy Glaus [47], Anderson [35] and Tim Salmon [34], Vaughn's former teammate on the Cape Cod League All-Star team, led the Angels to a club record 236 homers. Left fielder Darin Erstad added to the offense with 240 hits, the most in the American League since Vaughn's former Red Sox teammate, Wade Boggs, hit the same number in 1985.

Vaughn never got the chance to join the 2001 hit parade because he learned prior to the season that the pain he dealt with during the previous season was a serious injury. He underwent surgery on February 6 to repair a ruptured biceps tendon in his left arm and missed the entire 2001 season.

Coming to New York: During a 2000 road trip to Yankee Stadium, the *New York Post*'s Barry Baum approached Mo Vaughn and asked if he would be interested in joining George Steinbrenner's crew. Vaughn's eyes lit up and a big smile came to his face. "If I get a chance to come over here I'd be far too excited," the Angels first baseman said. "I'd live right in the middle of the city." Fast forward to the beginning of 2002 and you can bet city realtors were knocking on his door. It was not the Yankees, but the New York Mets will certainly do.

Vaughn left Boston for the Anaheim Angels with hopes his East Coast roots would mesh with a California lifestyle. Although his Newport Beach home had a gorgeous view of the Pacific, it did not work. He missed his family and friends, along with the East Coast hustle-and-bustle that complimented his hard-charging approach to baseball. He tried to suppress those thoughts, but the terrorist attacks of September 11, 2001 brought them to the surface.

"Mom, I want to come home," Vaughn told his mother Shirley on one of their daily calls. "I don't want you and dad to take those flights anymore and I don't want [trainer] Pete [Rappoli] or anyone else flying out to Anaheim." Vaughn was especially spooked because he frequently took morning Boston-to-LA flights, the same ones that were hijacked from Logan Airport and crashed into the World Trade Towers.

Shirley Vaughn was not interested. "We like coming out to see you Maurice," she said about their every-homestand visits from Virginia. "The weather is great and we like playing golf." Her son replied that he was serious and by saying publicly that he wanted to come home, he hoped the Angels might listen to trade proposals from East Coast teams. And that is what he did on Boston's WEEI, sending more than a ripple through the baseball world. Vaughn also recognized that because his reasons were family-oriented, if a trade did not happen he hoped his relationship with the Angels would not be strained.

"We went back and forth about this for a while," his father Leroy said. "He knew he had an obligation to the Angels, but he is a big believer that family comes first. I'm not sure I agreed at first that leaving Anaheim was right, but he really wanted to come home. If he remained in Anaheim, Maurice said we couldn't come out as often as we did. I don't know who he thought he was, bossing his mother and father around like that, but I understood what he was talking about."

That is where Vaughn's agent Jeff Moorad stepped in and orchestrated the Mets-Angels Vaughn-for-Kevin Appier trade. As the deal neared fruition, Vaughn called his college teammate Dana Brown.

"He called me right after Steve Phillips [Mets General Manager], Omar Minaya (former Mets Senior Assistant General Manager] and Bobby Valentine [Mets Manager] went to Boston to watch him work out," Brown said. "He was pumped. I'd never heard him so excited. He could taste it and wanted it to happen so badly."

Three days after Christmas, Vaughn got a huge present. The trade went through and city's backpage headlines blared "Mo Town!" and "Just Say Mo!" Forty-five minutes away in Norwalk, Connecticut, Mets fans had reason to cheer.

"My phone has not stopped ringing," said Vaughn's 16-year-old niece Courtney Brooks, who once brought her uncle, then a minor leaguer, to kindergarten for show and tell. "People in Norwalk are so excited. One of my friend's brothers even called from Paris. I think the trade is great for personal reasons. We used to go to Boston on the weekends or close road trips and we would go out to the West Coast in the summer, but this is different. People don't understand how close our family is, how much fun we have together. Now we can see each other whenever we want. But one thing I won't do is bring him to my school again. That would be a mob scene."

KEVIN MORTON'S JOURNEY

Kevin Morton never pitched in the major leagues after going 6-5 with a 4.59 ERA in 1991. He was cut from the Red Sox during spring training the following year, and suffered in Pawtucket with a 2-11 record. He was put on waivers after the 1992 campaign and was claimed by the Kansas City Royals. Morton went to spring training with Kansas City, but developed tendonitis in his throwing elbow, and was sent to Double-A Memphis. "Mo and Val are running around on charters and I'm down sucking fumes in Memphis on buses where it's 9,000 degrees," he joked.

Morton then signed as a free agent in 1994 with the New York Mets and was assigned to Triple-A Norfolk. He pitched well enough to get a September call-up, but the major leaguers went on strike. No playoffs, no World Series and no big league revival for Kevin Morton.

A free agent again, Morton went to the Chicago Cubs minor league camp in 1995, but this time did everything he could to stay in the farm system. "I wasn't a scab," Morton said about the lingering strike which allowed minor league camps to operate while the big leaguers walked picket lines. "The Cubs manager, Jim Riggleman, and their pitching coach, Fergie Jenkins, were coming around looking for guys. They would say, 'Why don't you come up to camp and pitch a couple of innings.' I used to hide in the bathroom of the minor league complex every morning because I didn't want to go. They got to me a couple of times, but I said, 'Nah.' " Morton still believes he did the right thing, even though he was sent to Triple-A Iowa and never got a shot in Chicago once the strike ended.

He was 25, a former big leaguer who had not been back in three years. To revive his career, Morton headed to Taiwan in 1996 for what turned out to be a short-lived stay with the Sinon

Bears. "I was there a month and we won only two games," Morton said. "I was like, 'What the hell is going on here?' " He soon found out. "It turned out that half our team had been getting paid by the Taiwan mob to throw games. There was a huge gambling issue over there."

Morton returned home to Norwalk after just six and a half weeks overseas and spent the summer playing golf and training to run with a friend in the New York City Marathon. A day after completing a run and 36 holes, Morton could not get out of bed, in pain with a severe back injury which proved to be a herniated disk requiring surgery.

He returned in time to sign with the expansion Tampa Bay Devil Rays, who had a working relationship with the Mexico City Tigers. With Morton's back hindering him, the Mexican League hitters had a field day. "I knew I was wasting my time," Morton said of his final days in baseball. "The hitters were not that good, but neither was I." Morton left after just six weeks, flew back to Connecticut, and began his life after baseball.

VAL GETS THERE TOO

Scranton, Pennsylvania, was a magical city for Mo Vaughn and John Valentin, but not because the Harry Houdini Museum was located there. The two baseball players remember the city well because it was where each pulled a "disappearing act" from the minor leagues. It was where they first learned they had been chosen to play in the major leagues. Thirteen months after Vaughn got the news while in town to play the Philadelphia Phillies' Triple-A affiliate, the Scranton magic had worked again.

"When John called me to tell me he got promoted to Boston, I was basically all alone in Pawtucket," Valentin's wife Marie said. "I was so excited, but I could only share the news with a couple of the players' wives who were my friends."

The next day, the entire Valentin family was reunited in the major leagues. "It was amazing," Arnold Valentin Jr. said about arriving at Fenway, just like his brother, for the first time. "It was the ultimate excitement. It was a great, great feeling."

Red Sox manager Butch Hobson, always a John Valentin fan, did not give his newest rookie a chance to learn the new routine. "I flew into Boston, it was around 4 in the afternoon, and I was starting to worry that it was getting close to time to get on the field," the infielder said. "I took a taxi to the park and Butch said, 'You're in the lineup.' I said, 'I'm in the lineup?' Everything hit right away. All I remember was worrying about going out there and not making an error. It was exciting, but it was so close to gametime, so I didn't get a taste of what it was like." Prior to the game he selected a number and posed with the team for its official 1992 team photo. "I had a choice of numbers and I picked 13," he said. "It was [Dave] Concepcion's number and it was Arnold's favorite number when he was a kid."

In his debut against the Texas Rangers on July 23, 1992, the new Red Sox shortstop made several strong defensive plays, while Vaughn kept shouting encouragement to him from first base. "It was a bit weird looking over and seeing Mo," Valentin said. "It was like Seton Hall and Pawtucket all over again. That helped me a lot to keep calm." Offensively, Valentin, who came up after hitting .290 with nine homers and 29 RBI in Pawtucket, started 0-for-3 against All-Star right-hander Kevin Brown.

His fourth at-bat came in the eighth against Terry Mathews with a runner on second base. Valentin delivered an RBI single to center that scored the last run in a 7-5 Boston win. In Boston for less than seven hours, John Valentin earned his first standing ovation from the crowd of 32,927 while the Rangers tossed the souvenir ball into the Red Sox dugout. "It was a lot more overwhelming than I thought it would be," Valentin told the *Boston Globe*'s Michael Vega after the game.

Up in the stands, Arnold could sense his brother's discomfort. "I could tell he had nervous energy," he said. "After the game, he told me that he couldn't hear anything. He said it was a 'loud quiet.' He had tunnel vision and that is how he got through the night."

Less than a week later, the Valentin clan, along with much of Jersey City, invaded Yankee Stadium to see their conquering hero. The shortstop went 2-for-4 in the series' opener to increase his hitting streak to six games. "I got a hit and was standing on first base next to Don Mattingly, a guy I had seen play a thousand times," Valentin said. "He was the first Yankee player I met. He said, 'Way to hit, kid.' He was a nice man, friendly, but very businesslike. It was an incredible feeling. When I play the Yankees, it's always special."

It took Valentin nearly a month, until August 22, for him get his first major league home run in a 10-8 win over the Seattle Mariners in Fenway. With the Red Sox down 7-3 and the bases loaded, Valentin hammered an 0-1 pitch from Mike Schooler. "I hit a slider into the net," Valentin remembered. "It was a perfect scenario. Fenway Park, the history, great tradition, great park, the wall, the net. Me. I was just thinking flyball. I ended up hitting a grand slam."

The grand slam was the big moment in a solid rookie season. Valentin hit .280 in 58 games with 13 doubles, five homers, and 25 RBI. He returned home to Jersey City after the season and finally let it sink in that he was a major league shortstop. "It was something that didn't hit me right away," Valentin reflected. "It wasn't like I finally made it. It wasn't until I went home that it hit me that I played in the major leagues with Roger Clemens and Wade Boggs. It was a lot more special to reflect on it in the off-season. But I knew I still had to *stay* in the majors."

While home, just as Rick Cerone had done while Valentin was in college, the Red Sox shortstop returned to Seton Hall bearing gifts of bats, batting gloves, and other equipment for the current Pirates. "I always thought it was great when Rick came back and had all of that stuff with him that he gave to us. I always said that if I ever made it to the major leagues, I would do the same thing for the guys."

JOHN VALENTIN: MAJOR LEAGUE MOMENTS HE'LL REMEMBER (Listed Chronologically)

First Game Back in Fenway in 1993: Valentin broke a finger in spring training and missed the first month of the 1993 season. He returned in late April with a 1-for-21 start. That slump ended in a 6-1 win over the then California Angels. Valentin had his first "career" game. He hit two homers over the Green Monster — a two-run job in the second and three-run blast in the fourth — to give him a career-high five RBI in a single game. It was the first two-homer game at Fenway for a Boston shortstop since Valentin's Triple-A manager Rico Petrocelli did it against the Yankees on June 18, 1970.

Vaughn, who had two doubles in the game, was happy Valentin was back in the swing of things. "I saw him do that stuff at Seton Hall all the time," Vaughn told the *Boston Globe*'s Vega before reciting a familiar theme inspired by Seton Hall coach Mike Sheppard Sr. "I think struggling at this game is good for you. It builds character. If you can get through the bad times, which Johnny has done, it's going to make you a better player."

Meeting Mike Easler: While most thought it was Vaughn who Mike Easler helped the most upon his arrival as Boston's hitting coach in 1993, some would argue that his biggest success story was John Valentin. This was the year Valentin became an everyday shortstop, holding off challenges from Luis Rivera and Tim Naehring, who eventually became the team's third baseman.

"Johnny Val is a special person," Easler said in 2000 while working as the St. Louis Cardinals hitting coach. "He is a special competitor and is sometimes very difficult to work with because he's a perfectionist. He wants everything to be just right. He won't take no for an answer. He always would say, 'I know I can do it. I know I can do it.' He's very intense — sometimes too intense — but John and I worked beautifully together. It would take just one week with John Valentin and he'll go on a tear forever and ever. I really understand John more than almost anybody that I know in baseball."

Valentin hit .278 in 1993 with a team-leading 40 doubles, 11 homers, and 66 RBI. In the off-season, he worked with Easler and Vaughn to better his swing. "Val took his hitting to the next level when I was working with him," Easler continued. "Sometimes at Mo's house, Val used to come over and we used to all work together in the batting cage. Val had the same passion, the same thing that Mo had, but Mo had a different ability than him."

Easler wanted to develop Valentin's hitting stroke and get him away from being strictly a pull hitter. "That's his strength," Easler said, unaware that Valentin had learned to pull the ball as a child to avoid the dogs in Jersey City. "That's just his swing, but I had to break him and I did break him. He wasn't convinced he could hit the ball out of the ballpark the other way. That was the problem. He wanted to hit for power. When he was the seventh or eighth hitter, I told him, 'Val, you're gonna be one of the best second hitters that ever played the game. You're gonna be one of the best in Red Sox history to hit second.'

"He had a short, quick swing. He could pull the ball, perfect in Fenway, but once he learned to go to right field ... He could hit behind runners really well. He could bunt just as well. I just knew that he was a perfect second hitter, and he turned out to be that."

Unassisted Triple Play: July 8, 1994, was a historic day, and not because 18-year-old Alex Rodriguez, now baseball's $252 million man, was making his major league debut with the Seattle Mariners. It was historic because Red Sox shortstop John Valentin made it that way. With Mike Blowers on second and Kevin Mitchell on first with none out in the top of the sixth, the Mariners were leading 3-0 and threatening to add more. With designated hitter Marc Newfield at the plate, Seattle manager Lou Piniella called for a hit-and-run. Newfield promptly drilled a line drive to Valentin near the second base bag. Valentin calmly caught the shot, stepped on second to double-up Blowers and then tagged Mitchell, who never even tried to get back to first.

> "I think struggling at this game is good for you. It builds character. If you can get through the bad times, which Johnny has done, it's going to make you a better player."
> — Mo Vaughn

With the three outs recorded, Valentin calmly and routinely tossed the ball towards the mound, but the umpires realized how rare Valentin's feat was and retired the ball. It was only the 11th unassisted triple play in major league history and the first by a Red Sox player since George Burns did it in 1923. Ironically, Mickey Morandini, Valentin's teammate on the 1988 USA team which went to Cuba, had been the 10th major leaguer to record an unassisted triple play on September 20, 1992.

But Valentin was not finished. Just as it always seems to happen in baseball the guy who makes a great defensive play to end an inning is usually the first guy up to begin the next inning. That is the way it was for Valentin. With the Fenway Park crowd still buzzing over the triple play, Valentin came to the plate and sent a Dave Fleming full-count offering over the Green Monster. The solo shot, which required a curtain call from Valentin, was followed in the same inning with a two-run blast by Tom Brunansky and another solo job by Rich Rowland. The power surge gave the Red Sox a 4-3 win.

It was the first time in more than 10 years the Red Sox had blasted three homers in the same inning. The last time was September 18, 1984, when Dwight Evans, Tony Armas, and Easler went deep against the Blue Jays.

"They were probably the most humongous plays I've ever seen in my life," Alex Rodriguez said about the sixth inning triple play and the trio of home runs.

Three Homer Game: It was supposed to be Roger Clemens' night. The certain Hall-of-Famer had Fenway filled with more than 33,000 on June 2, 1995, when he made his season debut after coming off a shoulder injury. But the 10-inning, 6-5 win over the Mariners ended up being John Valentin's night to remember. He went 5-for-5, with three homers and a double, for 15 total bases, one off Fred Lynn's American League record-tying effort in 1975.

Hitting for the Cycle: John Valentin had a knack for doing unique things. He had already hit a grand slam for his first big league homer, had an unassisted triple play, and a three-homer game. Now, on June 6, 1996, he had the Fenway faithful on their feet when he became the 19th Red Sox player to hit for the cycle. It was the first time in his baseball career that Valentin achieved the milestone.

Valentin was later immortalized in a *Did You Know?* segment on ESPN's *SportsCenter*. Network researcher Todd Snyder uncovered this gem: "Did you know the only player in Major League Baseball history to record an unassisted triple play, hit for the cycle, and have a three-homer game during his career is John Valentin." The graphic also pointed out that all three had come during a three-year period — the triple play in 1994, the three homers in 1995, and the cycle in 1996.

Meeting Kevin Kennedy: Butch Hobson was fired as the Red Sox manager immediately after the 1994 season. The same thing happened to Kevin Kennedy with the Texas Rangers. As is usually the case with baseball managers, Kennedy got a second chance. The Red Sox hired him. One of the Boston players who intrigued him greatly was John Valentin. "John was very interesting to me because I wanted to hit him second with his offensive production," Kennedy said during a break from his broadcasting job at Fox Sports Net in the summer of 2000. "John had hit sixth or seventh for Boston in previous years. I was well aware of what he could do. I always envisioned John, especially in Fenway Park, hitting second."

Valentin began the 1995 season in the second spot, but did not do well in spring training, forcing Kennedy to use some tough love with the shortstop. "He finally came into my office and said, 'Hey Skip. I think I can drive in 60, 70 runs if I get back to my normal sixth spot. Right now I'm struggling a little bit.' I said, 'I feel you can drive in 100 runs if you stay in the two spot because you are going to get more fastballs hitting in front of Mo and [José] Canseco.' By the time our conversation was over, he understood the point and, lo and behold, he went out and he hit 27 home runs with 102 RBI, and hit .298. It was the best year of his career." That year, Valentin became the first Red Sox shortstop to hit more than 20 homers since Petrocelli had blasted 29 in 1970.

> "They were probably the most humongous plays I've ever seen in my life."
> —Alex Rodriguez, former Seattle Mariners shortstop

Moving to Third: John Valentin and Mo Vaughn knew Nomar Garciaparra had Seton Hall ties. While at Georgia Tech, and in his first few years as a pro, Garciaparra dated Jaime Keating, a Georgia Tech volleyball player and the daughter of then Seton Hall athletic director Larry Keating.

"Every time Larry saw me, he would tell me there is this young guy coming up who is dating my daughter," Vaughn said. "Larry would always tell me, 'You think Val is good? Wait until you see Nomar.' Once Larry told me there was this kid that he knew well, I knew I was going to take care of him."

Garciaparra did challenge Valentin for the shortstop job. It happened towards the end of the 1996 season when Garciaparra was promoted from Triple-A. "The first game he played in the major leagues, I was at short and he was at second," Valentin said about Garciaparra's arrival. "He looked very uncomfortable. He wasn't a second baseman. He was a gifted, talented shortstop. You knew he was a shortstop. He was awkward at the different position. I knew, because he was a number one draft pick, that they were either going to move him to another position or I would get traded or moved."

After Valentin hit .298 with 13 homers in 1996, he met with General Manager Dan Duquette. "I told him that if he was thinking about moving me to a different position so Nomar could play shortstop, just tell me so I can go and practice. I can play second or third. I'd like to know so I can go home and prepare." Valentin was not happy with the meeting, which left him unsure of what position he would play. During the off-season, he wrote a letter to Duquette, asking to be traded.

When word got out to the media about the note, Valentin stated his position. "Honestly, I don't want to leave, but when I'm in a meeting with the general manager and I ask him where I'm playing and I can't get an answer ... I felt embarrassed," Valentin told the *Boston Globe*'s Nick Cafardo. "I'm not trying to make waves. If the Red Sox feel Nomar is their shortstop, then tell me that. I can take it."

The Red Sox entered 1997 spring training with their middle infield in disarray. Tim Naehring had accepted a new contract and was set to play third. Valentin and Garciaparra were shortstop candidates with Wil Cordero and Jeff Frye prepared to battle at second. Eight games into spring training, the decision was made about the infield. Vaughn would be at first, Valentin at second, Garciaparra at short, and Naehring at third. "I thought that was a raw deal in a sense because I had played shortstop really well," Valentin remembered. "Maybe not All-Star caliber, although in 1995 I played All-Star caliber baseball, but I didn't get picked to the All-Star game. I wish they had been up front with me." Valentin was angry with the decision and bolted camp.

"I took the next day off," Valentin continued. "At that point,

I didn't want to come in. I wanted to be traded. I wanted to be a shortstop and wasn't ready to move to a new position. There were 25 other teams I could play shortstop for. Because they lied to me, I no longer trusted the Red Sox. I wanted a day off so I could decide what to do, whether I wanted to put my foot down and demand to be traded or go play second base. I decided to go play second base because I really enjoyed playing in Fenway Park. It was a park I hit well in. I loved the park. I loved the fans. I loved the city. I loved my relationship with the Jimmy Fund and all the people I had to deal with. I just wasn't too happy with the organization."

Valentin was characterized by fans and the media as another example of a spoiled millionaire ballplayer. He strongly denied that was the case. "Am I concerned that people are going to think I'm selfish? Well, sure," he told the *Globe*'s Bob Ryan. "I think if I could sit down with every fan individually, I'd get them to come away sympathetic to my position. But we know that just isn't possible."

Valentin never held Garciaparra responsible for his move to the right side. "Val at no point, ever, did not show respect for me," Garciaparra said. "Val was never mad at me. He was never like that. I always thought Val was the classiest person in the world. He was upset with the way they handled the situation, not that I was the person involved. I owe Val an awful lot to this day. He's taught me so much at that position. Now we talk all the time, I'm always talking to him about the position. We can joke now about it. — 'I took your position.' I look at Val almost like a big brother. He's a guy I can turn to and ask questions and it helps me out an awful lot. I felt that way from the first day. He never made me feel like I couldn't go talk to him about the position."

Once the 1997 season began, Valentin started just 15-for-94. "Obviously, I wasn't happy with the way I started," Valentin told the *Boston Globe*'s Larry Whiteside in July. "During the course of spring training, I went through the whole situation of not wanting to move from short. It was very emotional for me. It was a difficult time. It's hard to understand, but I consider it behind me." Once he did put the position move behind him, Valentin started to hit again, .324 in May and .373 in June.

Valentin then moved to third base when Naehring had elbow surgery in mid-July, an injury that forced him to retire. Jeff Frye, Valentin's former summer ball teammate, became the second baseman with Wil Cordero moving to the outfield.

Valentin continued to hit and won the American League Player of the Week award in mid-August. He ended with a .308 average, a career-high 47 doubles, 18 homers, and 77 RBI, good enough to earn a four-year, $24 million contract prior to the 1998 season. His new friend Garciappara, who made the All-Star team, won the Rookie of the Year award by hitting .306 with 30 homers and 98 RBI.

CHAPTER 17

BACK IN THE GAME

The Scottsdale, Arizona, Police Department headquarters on Civic Center Boulevard stands down the left field line right next door to Scottsdale Stadium, the spring training home of the San Francisco Giants. When spring rolled around during the mid-1990s and the Cactus League started up, the place got hopping. But fans never noticed the police officer standing beyond the left field fence who arrived for work each day wishing he was someplace else. This was the time of year when his body craved baseball, but the addiction went unanswered. As the cop stood in the police department parking lot, a long home run away from baseball, he dreamed of what could have been. He was not in the right uniform. He was not in the right line of work.

After helping Seton Hall win its first Big East title with an unheard of .529 average, after becoming a top-round draft pick and climbing the Oakland chain to Double-A, Marteese Robinson was out of baseball. Rather than the gold and green of the A's, he wore the tan of the Scottsdale PD. He had turned in his bat and glove for new tools of the trade, handcuffs and a Glock 40 gun.

"I have to admit, those days were tough," Robinson said. "I knew what all of the guys I watched were thinking, since I had once been in their shoes trying to make it to the big leagues. Usually I was okay being out of baseball, but spring training was always hard. I couldn't avoid it because my job was right there and sometimes I was even assigned to work the games. Every spring, the baseball bug came back. I would see people I knew, saw guys I had played with and got the itch again. But I knew it couldn't last. I had made the decision to become a police officer."

He had become involved in law enforcement by default. He had married the former Charlotte Gray and had a daughter, Bria. To support his family, Robinson needed steady work. He saw a job in the paper for a detention officer in the Maricopa County Sheriff's Office. "I always wanted to be an FBI agent when I was little," Robinson said. "When I saw the ad, I was intrigued. I figured it would be a stable job and I would be in law enforcement." He did not know the success rate for applicants was just as low as it was for minor leaguers trying to get to the majors. Robinson was shocked when more than 600 showed up to take the required exam to fill fewer than 10 jobs. But he passed the test, interviewed and was hired. Robinson joined the judicial system and was given the entry-level, graveyard shift where he processed and booked prisoners and watched over them until they were arraigned by a judge the next morning.

Two years later, Robinson's marriage fell apart. "Charlotte came home one day and said she didn't love me anymore," Robinson said. "I was devastated. I continued to try, but it didn't work out."

Robinson kept his mind off the divorce with a new job. After two and a half years serving with the county, he took a similar detention officer position with the Scottsdale Police Department with an eye towards eventually becoming a cop. Eight months later, his supervisor, Wilt Davis, convinced him to enter the police academy. The grind of police work never fazed Robinson.

"It was relatively easy for me," the former first/second/third baseman said. "I was used to being pushed. It was also easy for people from a military background who were used to being pushed. Baseball wasn't the military, but I was used to pushing myself to the limit as a baseball player. Police work paralleled baseball. Just like no game is ever the same, I never knew what I would get day-in-day-out as a cop. I had a bunch of teammates who each had an important role. We were a team and we backed each other up. In baseball, even though you are on a team, when the ball is hit to you, you have to do your job and catch it. It's a team thing, but it is individualistic. It was so comparable to baseball."

A smile crossed his face. "You know, it just hit me now that I'm talking about it, but in college, Shep [coach Mike Sheppard Sr.] treated us like we were in the military," Robinson said. "He pushed hard and he taught us discipline. Maybe for me, the stuff he taught me was better used when I became a cop. Maybe all of it sunk in after I left baseball."

Even though Robinson had a new job, he still missed the game, especially when he saw the Red Sox or Astros on television. "I watched Craig on TV. I watched Mo and Val on TV," Robinson said. "I watched them all the time. Every chance I could. I was always so proud of them, but I always felt that I should have been there with them. I tried to keep that thought deep down, but I wished I was there."

Although he had been friendly with all three stars, Robinson did not let them know his whereabouts. He only stayed in contact with Dana Brown, then a scout with the Pittsburgh Pirates, but made his former Seton Hall teammate swear not to let anyone know what he was doing. "They had their lives and I had mine," Robinson said. "Yeah, I missed them, but I thought it would have hurt too much to speak to them because they had made it and I didn't."

"Marty tried to hide it from me, but I could tell he missed it," Brown said. "Every time he talked to me he always wanted to know what was going on. I always would say, 'Marty, you belong back in the game. When I get in a position of hiring, I'm coming after you.'"

Brown, who was a 35th-round draft pick in 1989, rose as high as Double-A in the Phillies' organization before being released in 1991. During his minor league career, Brown sent Sheppard, his former college coach, a letter chastising him for the way he treated his players. "I wanted him to know that in the pros they do a lot more teaching than they do yelling. If you do something wrong, it gets pointed out, but you never get screamed at the way Shep did to us. The reason I wrote the letter is because I cared for Shep. He always told us that he was preparing us for pro baseball, but I wanted him to know that in pro baseball, no manager or coach treated his players like Shep did. I wanted him to know that he is a great coach who helped all of us, but he didn't need to be as loud as he was."

"At first the letter was hard on me," Sheppard said. "I was upset that he said I was too tough on them. For the most part, the kid was right. I shared the letter with the team. I told the guys that I didn't want them to worry about the messenger, but listen to the message. I thanked Dana for the letter. I think he was amazed that I thanked him. I changed for better after I got the letter. I had a little too much football coach in me."

Brown, who maintained his good relationship with Sheppard after he sent the letter, stayed in baseball following his playing career. He spent two seasons serving as a hitting and base-running coach for Philadelphia's rookie team in Martinsville, Virginia. Brown then entered scouting with the Pittsburgh Pirates where he was given the team's Northeast region and has since progressed to become the team's East region scouting coordinator.

Like Brown, Robinson's boss, Sgt. Doug McCumber, recognized Robinson's passion for baseball and allowed him to work spring training, Phoenix Firebirds (San Francisco Triple-A) or Fall League games at Scottsdale Stadium whenever possible. "One thing was always interesting with Marteese," McCumber said. "He always wanted to work inside the games even though if you worked traffic detail outside you got paid more. The closer he was to the game, the happier he was."

> "I watched Craig on TV. I watched Mo and Val on TV. I watched them all the time. Every chance I could. I was always so proud of them, but I always felt that I should have been there with them. I tried to keep that thought deep down, but I wished I was there."
>
> —Marteese Robinson

Robinson often told his friends how well Biggio, Vaughn, and Valentin were doing in the major leagues. "I was so proud of Craig when he moved from catcher to second base and started winning Gold Gloves and making the All-Star team every year. The minute they moved him to the infield, I knew he would do well because he was a great athlete and could do a lot of things. I took pride in what he did."

When Vaughn won the 1995 American League Most Valuable Player Award, Robinson could not wait to share the news. "I was ecstatic," Robinson said. "Someone I had played with, was friends with, was the MVP. I always knew that joker would have a MVP-type season because he could hit for average as well as power. It was just a matter of time and getting on a winning team. That year, Val had his best season too."

Robinson was also putting up good numbers. He went 2-for-2 in capturing wanted murderers. His first high-profile collar came after a high-speed car chase ended in the arrest of a double homicide suspect. His next major case came on a routine traffic violation. After pulling over a vehicle, Robinson watched as the driver opened the door and ran into the night. Robinson took off after him just as Keith Swanson arrived as backup. "I have no chance of catching up with 'Teese because I'm just a chubby, little bald guy, but I kept running," Robinson's good friend said. "As I'm running, I see 'Teese's flashlight so I pick it up. Then there's his radio. There's his gun belt. The shit was just falling off of him because he was running so fast. With all his stuff falling off of him, 'Teese could have had a damn yard sale chasing the guy. By the time I caught up with him, I expected to see him running down the street in his underwear. I was laughing so hard I was lucky I could run." By the time Swanson found his friend, Robinson had the suspect in handcuffs. They booked him, ran his fingerprint, and learned he was wanted for murder in California.

> "Marty tried to hide it from me, but I could tell he missed it. Every time he talked to me he always wanted to know what was going on. I always would say, 'Marty, you belong back in the game. When I get in a position of hiring, I'm coming after you.'"
> — Dana Brown, Montreal Expos amateur scouting director

Robinson's job was good and so was his personal life, which included his marriage to the former Charlene Coulombe. With love back in his life, his first love — baseball — would also soon return. Dana Brown never let up and continued his onslaught when he visited Phoenix on a scouting mission. Charlene was surprised to see her husband so animated when he talked about baseball with his college friend. "Marteese never mentioned

Dana to me," she said. "He doesn't like to talk about the past. Dana was the first person I met from his baseball life and I saw that bond. But Marteese tried to dismiss Dana. He would say, 'No, no, no.' every time Dana brought up returning to baseball."

After returning home to New Jersey, Brown ran into Chris Buckley, then the assistant director of scouting for the Toronto Blue Jays, and the two talked about Robinson. Buckley, who had coached Robinson in American Legion and was a former volunteer assistant coach at Seton Hall, had available scouting positions.

"Dana was going to give him my number on the spot, but he didn't know it by heart," Robinson said. "He was going to break the promise, but he didn't care because he knew I wanted to be in baseball, even though I didn't think so. So instead, Dana called me and asked if it was okay if he gave Chris my number. I said he could." Buckley called and spoke to his former player for a while, relived old times, and caught up before getting to the reason for the conversation. Buckley, who is credited with being the first to discover Mo Vaughn as a potential Seton Hall recruit, wondered if the cop might be interested in a baseball job. Robinson agreed to at least listen to a Blue Jays' sales pitch and Buckley turned him over to Mark Snipp, the team's national scout.

> "He always wanted to work inside the games even though if you worked traffic detail outside you got paid more. The closer he was to the game, the happier he was."
> —Sgt. Doug McCumber, Scottsdale Police Department

"Chris wanted me to call him because he was too close to Marteese," Snipp said. "He wanted somebody else to speak with him and make an honest decision. We had a number of lengthy telephone conversations. It is not the way I like to hire people, but he was so impressive on the phone. He spoke well. He was very intelligent. It was obvious he knew baseball. I thought it was obvious that he wanted to get back into baseball. I had never recommended anyone for a job before based on a telephone call, but I recommended Marteese Robinson."

That was music to Buckley's ears. He immediately called

Robinson to tell him that he was coming to Phoenix to watch the Arizona Fall League, the Instructional League's new name, with Blue Jays director of scouting Tim Wilken, and wanted him to come by their hotel. "I drove up in my squad car and knocked on the door," Robinson said. "Tim had never met me and he saw a guy in a police uniform and sunglasses through the peep hole. When he opened the door, I could tell he was a little nervous. A cop knocking on your hotel door can't be for anything good. I said, 'Hello, I'm Marteese.' I could see him let out a little sigh of relief."

After the initial shock of first impressions died down, the three discussed scouting opportunities the team had in Oklahoma and Kansas. Robinson politely described his current situation. His mother had moved out to Phoenix in 1995. He had a daughter from a previous marriage who lived there and he had just gotten married. Moving was out of the question. He also told them he would suffer a 50 percent pay cut from his police officer's salary if he joined the scouting ranks, but if he could remain in Phoenix, that would be acceptable because Charlene's salary would keep them financially solid.

"I had to turn it down, but I told Tim I wanted to get back into the game to learn about scouting, to learn everything I could about the game," Robinson said. "I told him I wasn't getting into it to be a scout. I wanted to get into it, climb the ranks, and do what he did. I knew I wanted to be one of the decision-makers. He seemed surprised that I said it, but he also seemed impressed by it. I'm not sure anyone had ever said that to him."

"I was impressed by Marteese right away," Wilken said by cell phone from the Arizona Fall League in 2000. "He had a pretty good idea about players. He could break down their skills and see the tools each had. Even though he was out of the game for about eight years, he still had that. By being a cop, he also learned how to read people's body language. He could watch a baseball player and learn a lot about them, just by watching how they carried themselves. That is a great sense to have."

Three months after the initial meeting in Phoenix, Buckley left a message for Robinson to call. Robinson called back and learned that Toronto's Arizona-area scout, Chris Bourjos, was being promoted to the major league scouting department and his position was now open. Would Robinson want the job? "I told him yes, but that I had to talk with Charlene," Robinson said.

"His happiest time was when he was playing ball," Charlene said. "He wasn't happy anymore as a cop. But taking the job would be a huge pay cut. He would be on the road a lot. I was pregnant, and Bria was with us. I knew he wasn't satisfied with his life and he wanted me to say yes." She did.

Betty Robinson, Marteese's mother, was happy with the news. "He missed baseball," she said. "That's all he talked about. In the beginning, when he first became a cop, he was happy. But then that faded. I could tell he really, really missed it."

"He needs to be in the game," Mo Vaughn, Robinson's college teammate, said emphatically years later. "Dana and Marty are putting their mark on the game. When people deal with them, good things are gonna happen. They are both where they should be — in the game and making a difference."

Robinson had not seen Vaughn in seven years, not since Dana Brown's wedding in 1992. "I remember the wedding vividly because Mo, Dana, Val, and Eric Young were all over me to try to get me back into baseball," Robinson said. "They were mad that I had given up."

Their friendship was rekindled when Robinson was running errands in Scottsdale in March 1999. While stopped at a light, Robinson could not help but notice a big Lexus SUV had pulled up next to him, rap music blaring. Robinson looked over to his left. "I figured the guy was a football player," Robinson said. "He looked pretty big." The driver also looked, lowered his window, and peered back again.

"Marty is that you!?" the driver screamed.

"Mo!" Robinson yelled, instantly recognizing the familiar voice.

Robinson followed Vaughn to Tempe Diablo Stadium where the major leaguer was scheduled to work out. "He hadn't changed," Robinson said. "I said it looked like he was doing okay for himself and he said sheepishly, 'Yeah,' but he was more excited to hear about me with scouting. He said Dana had told him about me with scouting and he was happy. He said that is where

I belonged. He was proud. The friendship had never left; we picked up right where we had left it. I watched him work out. It was a good feeling watching him interact with everyone, seeing him as a superstar."

Vaughn understood that timing had played a crucial role in Robinson's baseball demise. "Marty had more talent that any of us," Vaughn said years later. "But I wouldn't be here today if a friend of mine, Carlos Quintana, didn't break his arm in a car crash. He was a great first baseman. Timeliness is the essence of everything. Marty was behind Big Mac [Mark McGwire] for all of those years. It's not always the most talented to make it. You have to be at the right place at the right time."

A month after reconnecting with Vaughn, Robinson was back on the road when he picked up the April/May 1999 edition of the Holiday Inn Express *Navigator* magazine, the type of periodical that sits near televisions in every hotel room in America. Bored, he skimmed through the magazine and noticed an article that appeared to be about baseball. He looked at the pictures first and then was stunned to see his name included in the story. The author, *Sports Illustrated*'s Mark Bechtel, wrote about watching baseball in Huntsville, Alabama. Bechtel mentioned guys he had seen play for the Double-A Stars — Jose Canseco and Terry Steinbach — and against the Stars — Al Leiter and Turk Wendell.

After the writer recounted a discussion he had with Wendell, he wrote: "A few weeks later, during the 1998 playoffs, I was sitting in a café in Boston reading a story about Red Sox teammates John Valentin and Mo Vaughn. The two all-stars were reminiscing about their days at Seton Hall in the late 1980s and they recalled how neither was the best player on the team. The best guy on the squad, according to both of them, was Marteese Robinson, a first baseman who never got out of the minors.

"Marteese was a [Huntsville] Star in the early '90s and one day he promised Boz [Bechtel's friend and the Stars clubhouse attendant] he would buy him a Rolex when he got to the majors. Boz harbored an unnatural fixation on watches — he referred to his as his 'sleek, elegant timepiece' — and a Rolex certainly would have made him even more obnoxious. I think he was more upset when Marteese was released than Marteese was."

Robinson was shocked. "Are you kidding me?" he asked out loud. He called Charlene and told her that he was in the article. A proud wife, she told him to bring copies home.

As it turned out, she did not have much time to show off the magazine because it, along with the rest of their possessions, would soon be packed for a move. Buckley promoted Robinson to cover the fertile Southern California region.

"Chris then called me to tell me that something else was going on and not to jump the gun with Southern California," Robinson said. "I thought something might have happened with the job." Instead, Buckley told Robinson that there was talk of promoting him to Toronto.

Robinson had impressed Toronto General Manager Gord Ash during the team's pre-draft meeting in May. Ash had wanted to create a coordinator of scouting position under Assistant General Manager Dave Stewart, the former Oakland 20-game winner, All-Star, and 1989 World Series MVP, and was waiting for the right candidate to come along. Ash thought Robinson might be suitable for the job and asked Wilken and Buckley for their input. Robinson was brought to Toronto for an interview.

"To me, it was all happening too fast," Robinson said. "It is like playing A ball and then all of a sudden finding yourself in the big leagues. I found myself questioning if I was ready for it. I finally realized they would not have been giving me a shot if I wasn't ready. They wanted me there for a reason."

As a player, Robinson had envisioned what it would be like to get a call telling him he was going to the major leagues. Back in Phoenix, Robinson thought about that as he sat at his kitchen table in July 1999. The job was his if he wanted it. "I was shaking when I called Chris back," Robinson said. "We talked for a while about some of the details and what the job would entail. I told him we wanted to come to Toronto. When I hung up, I looked at Charlene and yelled, 'We're going to the major leagues!' I couldn't believe it. I had waited my whole life to say that!"

Several days after he accepted the position, with his wife in Phoenix to handle the move, Robinson returned to Toronto and became the fifth member of the 1987 Seton Hall Pirates to reach the major leagues. He arrived at the team's SkyDome offices at One Blue Jays Way, got settled, met a bunch of people, and patiently waited for a free moment so he could take it all in. "The press box area sits behind home plate," Robinson said. "I walked in and looked around the ballpark. It was a great moment for me, knowing I was in the major leagues. It wasn't in the capacity I had envisioned, but nevertheless, I was there. I had made it. It was a great feeling."

Charlene noticed a difference in her husband. "Once he left for Toronto, I noticed that every picture of him as a cop, he had a straight face," she said. "Every picture I found of him in baseball, he was smiling. He didn't talk about baseball much before because he felt like a failure, but now everything was different. He was so happy."

> "I walked in and looked around the ballpark. It was a great moment for me, knowing I was in the major leagues. It wasn't in the capacity I had envisioned, but nevertheless, I was there. I had made it. It was a great feeling."
> —Marteese Robinson

Now, just like Biggio, Vaughn, Valentin, and Morton had done before him, Robinson had to prove he was worthy of staying in the big leagues. He attacked the scouting budget, instituted computer programs and a cell phone distribution system for the team's scouts, processed scouts' expenses, and guided the day-to-day operations of the 28-member department, which included scouts in the United States, Canada, and Latin America. He also developed a scouting manual which described, in 110 pages of full-detail, everything a Blue Jays scout needed to know.

"We were looking organizationally to find a guy who could handle the responsibilities of coordinating our scouting," said Stewart, now the pitching coach for the Milwaukee Brewers. "Marteese had been in scouting, but we felt that he was smart enough, and with his knowledge of scouting, had the leadership qualities." Robinson arrived in an age when minority hires in the front office were being championed. "I think with his ability to absorb and sponge knowledge, he is the type of person to move up in the organization," Stewart continued. "Marteese is a very smart man. The least of our worries is that he will advance. We expect that to happen. I don't think we are ever going to worry about the direction Marteese is going to take us in. He is a guy we count on and depend on in this organization. From a minority standpoint, I think he is going to make us proud."

Snipp also thought the Toronto position would allow Robinson to thrive and eventually move up the ladder in baseball. "In my opinion," he said, 'I think, someday, general manager will not be out of the question. I don't think it is tomorrow. If he keeps doing what he's doing, learns the rules and becomes assistant general manager, from there that is a stepping stone to general manager. He has the look, he has the image, he has the polish. He has the qualities you need to have that job. It certainly wouldn't be out of the question."

The job in Toronto took its toll on Robinson's new marriage because Charlene could not work in Canada without a sponsor. "I interviewed with a law firm in Toronto and took the baby [son Marteese Jr.] with me," Charlene said. "After the interview, we talked more on the phone and they said they had opportunities, but because of the legal issues, it would be difficult to hire me."

> "I noticed that every picture of him as a cop, he had a straight face. Every picture I found of him in baseball, he was smiling. He didn't talk about baseball much before because he felt like a failure, but now everything was different. He was so happy."
> — Charlene Robinson

The couple agreed that Charlene, rather than sit around unable to work, would move to Florida for a time, get a job, and let her grandmother assist in watching their son. "We had no option financially," she said about what turned out to be a year-long move.

Robinson's entry into the major leagues caught the attention of *Baseball America* columnist Alan Schwarz. In February, after speaking with the reporter, Robinson flew to Florida to scout during spring training and spend six weeks with his wife and son. He also got reacquainted with another member of "The Hit Men."

One of Robinson's assigned teams was Craig Biggio's Houston Astros. He drove to Baseball City in Davenport, Florida, to see the Astros against the Kansas City Royals. As usual, Robinson arrived at the ballpark early, settled into a seat behind homeplate, took out his notepad and started to scribble notes to himself as the Astros took batting practice.

"Craig finished his swings and looked towards the stands," Robinson said. "He shielded the sun from his eyes with his hands and he was looking right at me. He knew he knew me from somewhere. Finally, he yelled out 'Marty!?' I yelled 'Craig!' He told me to come down. We talked for a while and he introduced me to Jeff Bagwell. He said, 'Bags, remember the guy I was telling you about?'"

Biggio had told Bagwell that a guy he had played with at Seton Hall was just like him. "One day Marty would get four hits," Biggio said in 2000. "The next day, you never knew what he was gonna do. Probably get five hits. I played with Baggy during his MVP year [1994] and it was the same kind of thing. You would think you'd seen it all and then the next day something better would happen. Defensively, Marty had it all, just like Baggy."

Biggio had read Schwarz' *Baseball America* article, which had hit the newsstands that same week. "I hear you are a bigwig now," Biggio said to his friend. Robinson sheepishly smiled and told Biggio he had nothing to fear in the fame department. "Craig had that trademark smile going," Robinson said. "I could tell he was happy for me. He was proud of me."

The article sent quite a buzz through baseball circles. "His name is legendary among those who followed college baseball in the late 1980s," Schwarz wrote. "Sure, Seton Hall had Craig Biggio, Mo Vaughn, and John Valentin, but for one year those stars were mere moons revolving around Marteese Robinson — the guy who hit .529."

Scott Brosius, who had played in the minors with Robinson, also knew about his former double play partner's new career. "Marteese was an intelligent person and he was capable of making adjustments," the former New York Yankees third baseman said. "Those are qualities that will help you in any job you are doing. He's obviously been around baseball quite a bit. I'm sure he will do that job quite well."

Ozzie Canseco agreed with Brosius' assessment. "Marteese is very intelligent. As a professional ballplayer who was very talented himself, he knows talent. He's a hard worker. He's clean cut. He's well-spoken. He has a great sense of humor. What more can you ask? I see him doing very well." Mike Bordick agreed. "I think he will be great at it. He was a very intelligent kid and he's obviously been around the game."

"If you give him an opportunity to be a general manager," Mo Vaughn said with a proud smile, "he will put the right team out there to win a World Championship. I also know one other thing, with Marty in the front office, I know I'll always have a job in this game."

Back in Arizona, Robinson's police buddies were thrilled that he had made the move and was back in the news. "I'm extremely happy for him and proud of him for making it back to what he loves," Sgt. McCumber said. "If he goes on to become a general manager, that would be a kicker. I expect to be the security director of that team!"

First the Holiday Inn magazine, then *Baseball America*. The legend of Marteese Robinson then hit ESPN. It was the third inning of the May 28, 2000, *Sunday Night Baseball* battle between the Yankees and the Red Sox at Yankee Stadium when Charley Steiner, who was calling the game for ESPN Radio, told a story abut the 1987 Seton Hall Pirates. When Valentin came to the plate, the announcer explained that Valentin, Biggio, and Vaughn all had played on the same college team, but they were not the best player. "That was a kid named Marteese Robinson," Steiner told America, "but he never made it."

Steiner was well prepared, but he did not take the credit for uncovering the nugget of information. He admitted later that he had never heard of Robinson. "I once approached Craig about his college days and he confirmed that all three played there," Steiner said. "He also said there was another guy who was better than them, but he never made it. I asked Craig, 'How did you ever lose?' He laughed and said, 'Not enough pitching.'"

Prior to the New York-Boston game, Steiner repeated the story to ESPN Television coordinating producer Phil Orlins, a South Orange, New Jersey, native. "I knew all about those guys," Orlins said. "They were incredible. I knew about Marteese so I filled Charlie in."

The story was worth telling, but it did not end there. As Dave Stewart predicted, Robinson was on his way up the baseball food chain. St. Louis Cardinals General Manager Walt Jocketty, who had been Oakland's assistant general manager when Robinson was playing, called Toronto general manager Gord Ash after the 2000 season and inquired if Robinson would be interested in working for the Cardinals as the team's director of pro scouting.

"My first reaction was no," Robinson said. "I was happy in Toronto, although it was hard not having Charlene and the baby with me. But then I realized it would be a great opportunity to further my career. If I was going to progress in baseball, I probably would have to leave Toronto eventually."

> "I also know one other thing, with Marty in the front office, I know I'll always have a job in this game."
> — Mo Vaughn

Robinson agreed to an interview and got the job. He now heads a five-person team responsible for evaluating all talent in pro baseball, from the major leagues to the lowest level of rookie ball. "Marteese has been on the fast track," Cardinals Director of Baseball Operations John Mozeliak said. "He has been exposed to scouting and the administrative side of the front office. When we decided to separate pro, amateur and international scouting, we spoke to numerous people about the position. Marteese is a great fit for us. He is a sharp guy."

Robinson, who assists Mozeliak and Jocketty in evaluating talent for trades and free agent signings, joins pitcher Matt Morris as the second Seton Hall product working for the Cardinals. "I have to meet Matt Morris and share the Seton Hall bond and we both have good Shep stories to tell," Robinson said after getting the job. "I'm sure we'll have plenty of time to share them."

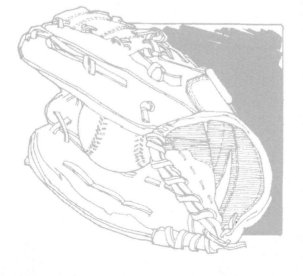

LEAVING A LEGACY

Following in Their Footsteps

Matt Morris was a highly-touted pitcher out of Central Valley High School in Montgomery, New York. He had been offered a full scholarship by Seton Hall and had also been taken in the 25th round of the 1992 draft by the Milwaukee Brewers even though he had only pitched for a year in high school. Morris had a tough decision to make: go to Seton Hall and hope he improved on his 5-3 record as a high school senior or accept an offer from the Brewers and begin a pro baseball career.

"Now everything is kind of hard," Morris told Bill Burr in his hometown *Times Herald-Record*. "If the offer is there ... to tell you the truth, I don't know what I'm going to do." It took him 15 days to decide that Seton Hall held the key to his future. "It was tempting," Morris told the paper's Thomas Hill on June 17, 1992. "But I'm better off holding off to my junior year [at Seton Hall], when I'll be more ready. There's always a chance I'll blow my arm out, or not get any better. But since I've only been a pitcher for one year, I feel I'm going to get better and improve my velocity. I'm pretty positive I'll get drafted again."

Morris was certain he made the right decision, largely because of the guys who came before him at Seton Hall. On his recruiting visit, the first thing Morris noticed when he walked into the school's baseball office were the photos on the wall of major league and minor league players Seton Hall coach Mike Sheppard Sr. had produced. The powerful right-hander tried hard not to look at the wall while he listened to Sheppard's initial sales pitch. But the coach, knowing the photos were a huge selling point, let Morris take a look. Sheppard first pointed out some of the great ones he had coached who went on to the major leagues — Rick Cerone, John Morris, Charlie Puleo, Pat Pacillo, and Rich Scheid.

Matt Morris had the same gleam in the eyes that Sheppard had once seen in Craig Biggio, Mo Vaughn, John Valentin, Kevin Morton, Marteese Robinson, Dana Brown and the rest of the guys on his 1987 squad. But back then, it *was* Cerone, Morris, Puleo, Pacillo, and Scheid who had the newcomers believing they too could make it to the big leagues. But now, Biggio, Vaughn, and Valentin were *the* Seton Hall heroes and Morris wanted to be just like them.

"I think it is a big reason why the guys my age and younger chose Seton Hall," Morris said by phone from the St. Louis Cardinals clubhouse in the summer of 2000. "Just for the fact that Mo Vaughn, Craig Biggio, and John Valentin were in the big leagues and were stars. It had a lot to do with me going there. Knowing you're going to Seton Hall to play baseball and knowing there is a future. These guys passed through the same uniform and made it to their eventual goal.

"They walked in the same office I did. They all went through the same things that I did at Seton Hall and they are at the top of the game right now. They paved the way for guys like me."

Morris followed in many of the same steps Biggio, Vaughn, and Valentin had taken during their college careers. He pitched in the Cape Cod League All-Star Game after his freshman year and after his sophomore season made the United States National Team which traveled to Nicaragua for the World Amateur Baseball Championships. By the time he was eligible to be drafted again as a college junior, Morris was All-Big East and the second-rated college prospect by *Baseball America*. He was also a first-round pick, the 12th overall pick, by the St. Louis Cardinals.

Morris got the chance to meet a few of his Seton Hall idols, Valentin and Morton, but he learned the most from Biggio. "Mike Moriarty [now in the Minnesota Twins' organization] and I went to lunch with Coach Sheppard and Craig when I was a junior," Morris said. "We were two shy kids not asking much. Really the only thing we had in common was Seton Hall. We didn't talk too much about the big leagues, more about Coach Sheppard and what Craig's time was like at Seton Hall and what he got out of it."

Biggio remembered the conversation. "I told them that the main thing about Seton Hall is that it is not a country club-type school. You are not going to get everything handed to you. It has a lot of great things about it, but you are going to have to work for it. Shep makes you a better person when you come out of there. The way Shep runs the program, when you accomplish something there, it is a great feeling."

Matt Morris was brought up to the St. Louis Cardinals on April 4, 1997, and started his first game against the Astros in the Astrodome. He walked to the mound to throw his first big league pitch and staring out at him from the batter's box was Craig Biggio. "He was the first guy I ever faced and he singled and stole second," Morris said. "Then I got one out and he scored on a single. It was kind of ironic. He didn't say anything, but he showed me what it's about."

"The kid had nasty stuff," Biggio said a year prior to Morris making the 2001 National League All-Star team. "I knew he was going to have a tremendous future. He threw 97 miles-per-hour, had a great hook and was learning how to throw the slider."

> "They walked in the same office I did. They all went through the same things that I did at Seton Hall and they are at the top of the game right now. They paved the way for guys like me."
> —Matt Morris, St. Louis Cardinals pitcher

Maybe Biggio should join Marteese Robinson and Dana Brown in scouting. Morris blossomed into a National League All-Star in 2001, finished 22-8 with a 3.16 ERA and battled the Arizona Diamondbacks eventual World Series co-MVP winner Curt Schilling pitch-for-pitch in two memorable playoff outings.

That effort paid off for Moris. He signed a new three-year, $27 million contract and also earned a prominent place on Sheppard's "Wall of Fame."

HELPING CHILDREN WITH CANCER

BIGGIO AND THE SUNSHINE KIDS

CHAPTER 19

The awestruck, bright-eyed eighth-grader could not believe his luck. His idol and big brother-figure, Craig Biggio, had asked if he wanted to be a bat boy for the Houston Astros when they visited Shea Stadium. Of course he said yes! Three years into Biggio's major league career, Chuck Alben was dressed in a gray, Astros uniform, sitting the closer to Major League Baseball than any kid could ever dream of being.

During the game, he sat with Biggio on the bench. "It was unbelievable sitting in the dugout," Alben said. At one point, Biggio told Alben to rub his bat for good luck. "He struck out, came back, and said, "Don't ever touch my bat again,' " Alben said laughing.

This was just one example of how Biggio liked to include his young friend in his life. Biggio and Alben had come a long way since the loss of Alben's brother, Chris, to childhood leukemia 11 years before. "Leukemia was something that was new to me," Biggio said, now a 35-year-old father of three. "I didn't know much about it. When leukemia hit back then, they [doctors] knew a little bit about it, but not a lot about it. They have come a long way in the last 20 years, but there is still a lot more that we don't know about it."

Biggio knew about the research through his involvement with the Sunshine Kids, the Astros' official charity and the group Biggio has dedicated his off-the-field life to, largely because of Chris Alben. Biggio saw how leukemia, a form of cancer, ripped the life out of his young next-door neighbor and the heart out

207

of the Alben family. Biggio decided, even at that early age, that whatever he did in his life, he was going to help, in some way, sick children.

"I think he was so impacted by what happened in his life," said Sunshine Kids Associate Director Shannon Lillis, who only knew bits and pieces of the Chris Alben story. "Anything he could do with his celebrity status and who he is as a person, he wanted to give back. Craig really does truly care. He gives of his time and he knows that these kids look up to him. They get close to him. That's what makes the kids feel so good. They know someone is looking over them, so they think, 'I can beat this.' "

The affiliation between the Sunshine Kids and the Astros dates back to 1982 when Astros pitcher Joe Sambito welcomed some children with cancer to his team's Astrodome clubhouse. The charity, started by Rhoda Tomasco, does not raise money for cancer research. Instead, it raises funds to better the lives of childhood cancer victims and their families. "Our goal is to get kids out of the hospital and to get them to be kids again, doing fun things like going to an Astros game," Lillis said. "We take them on trips across the United States for a week. We take them skiing in Aspen, Colorado. We take them to Texas hill country where they get to ride horses and river raft. We give them a break from the hospitals, from the treatments, and let them just be kids."

Biggio remembered his introduction to the charity. "Larry Andersen used to bring the kids out to the field," Biggio said in October 2000. "It was something Joe Sambito had started. They would bring the kids out to the field and get them some hot dogs and Cokes and they would watch the games. He did that a couple of times a year. It was pretty cool. They would rope it off in the Dome, bring down 20-25 kids, and they could sit and watch batting practice. Both teams would come over and sign stuff for them. When Larry got traded, I said, 'Hey, I don't want this good thing to go to waste. It was a good program with a great bunch of kids and I wanted to keep it alive."

He and teammate Pete Harnisch took the reigns, but, when the pitcher joined the New York Mets after the 1994 season, the Sunshine Kids became Biggio's baby. "I got my hand involved in it more," Biggio said. "We started doing the same thing —bringing the kids to games — but then we started to do more."

Biggio, who also works with other Houston charities, schools, and churches, along with the Jersey Spinal Cord Center, was not content to offer a couple days a year to the cause. Instead, he made the Sunshine Kids part of his life. He donated the pool table in the game room, the deck, swing set, slide and barbecue pit at the group's administrative offices. More importantly, he is with the kids as often as he can be. On teen nights, Biggio sits and joins the discussion. He attends Halloween and Christmas parties, weekend events, fundraisers, golf events and, of course, hosts the Sunshine Kids at Astros games. "Behind the veneer of a 'hell bent for leather' ballplayer, there is a caring person," former Astros manager Larry Dierker said.

Games, golf events, and pizza parties are the fun part, but Biggio also helps during the trying times. "A lot of people don't know this, but he's gone to the hospital when a child has had a bone marrow transplant," Lillis said. "He's gone and seen kids in the hospital wards, the clinics. He's gotten close to several children."

One of those kids is Julian Zagars, who was diagnosed with cancer in 1988. He was sent to Seattle's Fred Hutchinson Cancer Research Center, named after the former Detroit Tigers pitcher who later managed the Tigers, St. Louis Cardinals, and Cincinnati Reds from 1952-1964. The boy, then 13, underwent radiation treatments and a bone marrow transplant which not only rid his body of the cancer, but also depressed his immune system. Upon returning home, Zagars was forced to wear a mask to be protected from other people's germs. The youngster did not have the life of a normal kid, but Biggio was there to change that.

"It is hard to put into words how much Craig helped me," Zagars said. "When a young person has cancer, to meet a person like Craig and get the encouragement that he gives you is incredible. An individual with cancer is less likely to go to a ball game, or do anything, if they have to wear a mask or not have hair because of radiation treatment. But to Craig that really didn't matter. We knew Craig was there for us.

"You have a fear, not of what the cancer is going to do to you, but the fear of acceptance, especially from your peers. That time in your life when you are young, when you are trying to develop friendships, it is a tough time in anyone's life. But when you have cancer thrown in on top of that, it is a big, big challenge. It's almost an insurmountable obstacle. But it isn't when you have somebody like Craig in your life. He helps you through it. It is kind of cool to know that you know a baseball player. Knowing that a guy like Craig has time for me is a great feeling. It really helps."

Zagars was a baseball fan who regularly took advantage of the Sunshine Kids trips to the Astros games. "When I first met him, and he does this with each of the kids, he remembers your name," Zagars said. "I would say, 'Hi Craig,' but I didn't expect a celebrity-type person to remember my name. You kind of just expect they are there to say hello, or there because of the media, but that is not Craig. Each time he saw me, each time he saw the other kids, he always remembered our names."

Once a year, besides welcoming monthly Sunshine Kids visits, Biggio and the Astros also host a Sunshine Kids Baseball Party where the children get to play a baseball game with the pro players. "About a hundred Sunshine Kids in Houston go to the baseball field, the Astrodome and now Enron Field," the group's associate director Lillis said. "A hundred kids running around the baseball field with Craig. The kids just love it being on the field. It just makes their day."

Biggio's mother was visiting her son a few years back and went with him to the annual party. She was totally amazed by the impact her son had on the children and their families. "I'm in total awe of what he does with the Sunshine Kids," Johnna Biggio said. "To see the light in these children's eyes and how much they admire and respect Craig and then have the parents come up and tell me things is just amazing."

But, as Zagars knows, cancer is not fun and games. It has claimed the lives of many of the children Biggio has gotten close to. Where most people are afraid to even enter a hospital, let alone a children's cancer unit, Biggio summons the strength to handle the emotional trauma the disease brings. "We've talked and prayed a lot," Astros chaplain Gene Pemberton said.

"I don't care how strong you are, it's still tough when one of those kids passes away."

Zagars, 25, who is in remission and working for mutual fund firm AIM in Houston, knows Biggio is now much more capable of handling the emotional strain cancer presents. "In the early years, when he first got involved in the Sunshine Kids, I don't know if he knew what he had gotten himself into," Zagars said. "But we helped him to realize what each individual goes through. Each child has a unique set of experiences with cancer. It is not going to be the same each time. Each child Craig meets and each friendship he makes with a child, he learns a little more about what the kids go through. Maybe he learns a little more about what it means to be special in someone's life and give back to indi-viduals who are currently dealing with cancer."

"I consider myself very lucky to be associated with children like this," Biggio reflected. "Kids never ask to be sick. You never meet a kid who is sad. They always have a smile on their face. They are always happy. I pinch myself because I'm lucky enough to be able to hang out with them. It is hard, though. You see a lot of the kids you get to know, and some of them don't make it. But on the flip side, some of the kids diagnosed are not supposed to make it, but they graduate from high school. That's cool. It's a tough and emotional ride, but you have to do the best job you can with it. I bring my sons, Conor and Cavan [daughter Quinn is still too young] with me sometimes. They don't ask many questions, except, 'Who are those kids?' I tell them, 'Those are my friends.' "

While he works to help his friends deal with cancer, Biggio has also helped the Sunshine Kids gain funding and national

> "You have a fear, not of what the cancer is going to do to you, but the fear of acceptance, especially from your peers. That time in your life when you are young, when you are trying to develop friendships, it is a tough time in anyone's life. But when you have cancer thrown in on top of that, it is a big, big challenge. It's almost an insurmountable obstacle. But it isn't when you have somebody like Craig in your life."
> —Julian Zagars, Sunshine Kids

attention. With Biggio heavily involved, the golf tournament annually raises more than $200,000, but Lillis points out there is no way to measure Biggio's importance to the group. Besides the work he does for the Sunshine Kids, the second baseman has been seen time and time again wearing the yellow Sunshine Kids starburst pin on his Astros cap. "Everyone at the Astrodome, and now Enron Field, asks for the Sunshine Kids pins. They'll ask, 'The pin that Biggio wears on his hat, what is it for?' They learn it's for kids with cancer and they will ask where they can we get it. People from across the United States will call us. They will make donations just to get the pin. It's for a great cause and they know Craig is involved in it. The exposure Craig has given us has been phenomenal. You see him on TV and in magazine and newspaper pictures with the pin in his hat. He's showing, 'I'm with the kids. I'm supporting the kids.' We didn't ask him to do it. He did it himself."

> "...I didn't expect a celebrity-type person to remember my name. You kind of just expect they are there to say hello, or there because of the media, but that is not Craig. Each time he saw me, each time he saw the other kids, he always remembered our names."
> —Julian Zagars, Sunshine Kids

All the work Biggio did, and still does, for the Sunshine Kids, was recognized by Major League Baseball at the conclusion of the 1997 season. He won the Branch Rickey Award, sponsored by the Rotary Club of Denver and the Major League Baseball Players Alumni. Biggio was named the sixth recipient of the prestigious award that previously went to noted stars and community contributors Dave Winfield, Kirby Puckett, Ozzie Smith, Tony Gwynn, and Brett Butler.

"As I told him at the time," Astros owner Drayton McLane said from his office three years later, "the Branch Rickey Award that Craig won was just as important to us as the MVP award Jeff Bagwell won a few years before."

Bagwell was happy his friend won the award. "He is proud of the Branch Rickey Award and he should be very proud of that," the All-Star first baseman said. "His peers, and the people in the game, recognize what he does in the community. They can't bestow a higher honor than the Branch Rickey Award. Great people have won it and Craig is just another great person on that list."

Just as Biggio was once moved by others' charitable efforts, Bagwell, who works with numerous Houston charities, is equally touched by Biggio's involvement with the Sunshine Kids. "As an athlete you always want to get involved," he said. "When you see a guy as involved as Craig, you kind of really appreciate that. I don't feel I give enough of my time. I give a lot, but when I watch what Craig does, I say, 'Man I need to give more.'"

Another of Biggio's friends, Bill Spiers, who occasionally reminds Biggio that his Clemson team beat Seton Hall in the 1987 NCAA Tournament, also helps with the Sunshine Kids. "We see those kids smile even though they are going through the worst of times," Spiers, who retired after the 2001 season, said. "It certainly brightens your day to see those kids smile and he does that to them. We as players come to the ballpark every day and play a game. We get in such a routine. It gets put into perspective when you take time to be with those kids. It is hard. For me, you hate to see anybody go through that, especially these kids. God does things in mysterious ways, as they say, and it is unfortunate to see them go through it."

> "It's a tough and emotional ride, but you have to do the best job you can with it. I bring my sons, Conor and Cavan with me sometimes. They don't ask many questions, except, 'Who are those kids?' I tell them, 'Those are my friends.'"
>
> —Craig Biggio

Matt Galante, who left the Astros for the New York Mets after the 2001 season, was impressed with the efforts his former players give towards the sick children. "Baseball is a game," the third base coach said. "It is our livelihood, but it is a game. We lose a game and we are devastated. But these people are in way more trouble than we are. You see some of those kids and you feel for them. I have a tough time with kids being sick and realizing that they probably will not live the lifetime that we have experienced and the joys that we have in life. It is tough for me to see an eight-year-old, knowing that he is not going to make it much longer. Craig does a great job with that. It is touching to see Patty and him work with those kids. The other guys learn from it. They participate in it with him. All of these guys do great things that most people don't know about."

Zagars thought celebrities got involved in charities to help their image. He was shocked to find it was not true. "The one thing about Craig is that he didn't do this for the attention," Zagars said, pointing out that Biggio shared in his high school graduation activities. "Whenever we have an event at the house, there is never any media there. That is not what it was all about."

BASEBALL IS PUT IN PERSPECTIVE

Alexandria and Francesca Valentin were two excited kids, bouncing around their home in Hazlet, New Jersey. They were going to be on television later that afternoon and were waiting for the network-sent limousine to pick them up. They kept peeking out the windows and yelling, "Is it here yet? Is it here yet?" Liz Valentin, who would also appear on the show with her husband Arnold, had her hands full trying to dress her daughters while also getting ready herself.

Finally the limousine pulled into the driveway and the girls went nuts. It was the biggest, white limousine they had ever seen. They flew out the front door and inspected the car. Finally they were allowed to get in when their parents came out and told the driver they were ready to go. This was June 2000, and the frightening, emotional moments the family had endured the past year were in the rear view mirror. Mom and Dad could only smile as they watched their girls frolic in the back of the oversized car.

Television producer Lisa Spagnuolo heard the story of how brain cancer survivor Alexandria Valentin wanted to help other kids who had the deadly disease. She asked Liz and Arnold if they, along with their daughters, would be willing to come on regional cable television and tell their story. "Of course," was the reply, as long as Alex could promote the charity at the hospital which had cared for her and give out an address where kids could write to her.

Ten-year-old Alex Valentin is an amazing, awe-inspiring child who speaks as though she has already lived a full life into adulthood. Fourteen months prior to the television appearance, Alex suffered from headaches that often had her in tears. Visits to the doctor proved nothing until an MRI was taken. The news was shocking. Alex, a previously healthy child, was suffering because a golfball-sized tumor had formed in her brain.

For a family that had lived on a high since Alex's "Uncle Johnny" had become a member of the Boston Red Sox in 1992, this news quickly put baseball, money, stardom, and fame into a new light. "Baseball means nothing," John Valentin told the Boston media. "A situation like this puts things in perspective."

Valentin had started 1999 spring training in a great mood. He was healthy after an injury-plagued 1998 season and had just visited Disney World with his wife Marie and their two kids, Justin and Kendall. The warm Florida sun and expectations of the coming season, along with celebrating Justin's birthday, had him in high spirits. But all of that changed with one phone call.

Upon getting the shocking MRI results, Liz Valentin immediately called the hotel where her brother-in-law was staying. She got no answer in his room and left an urgent message for him to call immediately. "When John called the hospital, the first thing he wanted to know was how Alex was," Liz Valentin said. "Was she comfortable? How were we doing? How were we holding up? Had we spoken to the doctors yet? He said, 'I'll be there on the next flight. Don't do anything until I get there. Everything was going to be OK.'" Valentin told Red Sox manager Jimy Williams that he had to leave camp for a family emergency. The manager quickly agreed and told his player to go and return only when he was ready. John Valentin, his wife, and children were back in New Jersey several hours later.

Arnold and Liz Valentin waited nervously, but made no move until John arrived at Riverview Medical Center. "John was able to hold it together for us," Arnold told the Newark *Star-Ledger* several months later. "He just took charge of the whole situation."

John Valentin could take charge because he had been down this road before, although admittedly, on the outside looking in. As one of the most active Red Sox players ever involved with the

Jimmy Fund, the Boston Red Sox' official charity since the days of Ted Williams in 1952, Valentin often met children suffering from cancer and their parents.

Before leaving for New Jersey to see Alex, Valentin immediately made countless phone calls to his friends in the Jimmy Fund office to learn which area hospitals could best care for his niece. The decision was made to have her transported by ambulance to Beth Israel Medical Center in New York City. "I was able to help Liz and Arnold emotionally because of all the experience I'd had in dealing with these types of cases," John said.

While the adults wrestled with the decision making, all Alex Valentin had been told was that she had a "boo-boo" on her head. But she knew something was very wrong just by looking at her parents' faces. "I could tell they were scared," she said. Three days after the diagnosis was made, seven-year-old Alex underwent surgery. "We had a good sense that she would be okay when the operation was performed," John Valentin said. "They said they got 99 percent, nearly 100 percent of the tumor out. It was a case they had seen before. She would have to go through chemotherapy. After the surgery was done we were pleased, but in a state of shock."

Knowing his niece was in good condition and receiving great care, Valentin headed back to spring training. His disappearance from camp, listed by the Red Sox as being "for personal reasons," led the media to speculate that the third baseman was being traded. Instead, when he returned, they were stunned to learn that he had gone to New Jersey to care for his niece.

Larry Whiteside of the *Boston Globe* was one of the reporters who covered Valentin's impromptu press conference on his arrival back in Fort Meyers, Florida. "Sometimes it's pretty hard to relate to today's major league baseball players, what with their pampered lifestyle and multimillion-dollar contracts," he wrote. "But every once in a while, a dose of sobering reality strikes a player and we all are reminded that ballplayers suffer sometimes, too."

Whiteside also mentioned towards the end of his article that the Red Sox player was active in the Jimmy Fund. But the media did not know to what extent, something Valentin was happy about. "I do things there without anyone knowing," Valentin said. "I don't want attention for it because the attention is not what it is about. Me helping someone else, who needs help, why should I get credit? It's ridiculous. I go unannounced most of the time to the Dana-Farber Cancer Institute. I call in before I'm coming so they can tell the kids they have a guest coming. What is so amazing about these kids is that they don't even feel like they are sick. They have great attitudes. They have better attitudes than we as people who are healthy have. It puts everything in perspective. I give them hats, T-shirts, pictures. I'll sign anything for them."

Valentin began his love affair with the Jimmy Fund shortly after arriving in the major leagues. He knew, because he was a big leaguer, that people looked up to him. He also knew how privileged he was to be a member of the Boston Red Sox and wanted to be involved in the community. "I wanted to sink my teeth into something that would help people, but I didn't know what to do. I didn't know how to go about it," Valentin said prior to the 2001 season. "Every so often the team would get together and go to the hospital to see these sick kids, and I knew right off the bat that I wanted to share my life in the Red Sox uniform with them. I went to the hospital just like any other player, but it hit me kind of differently. It has put another focus in my life.

"When I was starting out, the kids didn't know who I was. They wanted Roger Clemens to come. But I developed a relationship with all types of sick kids and their families and I wanted to do more, so I set up ticket programs so they could see us play."

Valentin went on to do much more than just provide Red Sox freebies. He has served as chairman of the organization's "radiothons" and "stairclimb" fundraisers, visited the hospital

> "Sometimes it's pretty hard to relate to today's major league baseball players, what with their pampered lifestyle and multimillion-dollar contracts. But every once in a while, a dose of sobering reality strikes a player and we all are reminded that ballplayers suffer sometimes, too."
> —Larry Whiteside, Boston Globe

hundreds of times and has even gone to visit sick children at their homes. "I can remember him during a snowstorm actually going out because he had promised a young Jimmy Fund patient that he would come to his home," Jimmy Fund Executive Director Mike Andrews said. "John has made himself so available. He clearly feels very strongly about the Jimmy Fund."

Andrews is one of the few who can appreciate Valentin's efforts because he has seen it from both sides, as a player and administrator. Andrews spent five of his eight-year major league career as the Red Sox second baseman from 1966-to-70. "John has done things for those children that our doctors, as great as they are, aren't able to do. When John Valentin goes in to see a patient, sometimes we don't have a medication that can do the same thing to make them feel better."

Valentin has gotten personally involved with many kids, including Lucas Bartlett, who wore Valentin's number "13" during T-Ball games before passing away at age six. The two number "13s" spent hours together, playing and talking. "He was one of my best buddies, but I knew he was going to pass away," Valentin said. "Getting close to family and kids can be really difficult. I like to keep that inside me."

Valentin, who had always tried to help others, was now personally affected by his niece's cancer. While he continued to help the sick children in Boston, he put almost all of his energy, through occasional visits and constant phone calls, to helping Alex get through the dreaded chemotherapy treatments which caused her hair to fall out.

"I used to have to go to the hospital and it drove me nuts because I had to go there and get a needle, and it was pretty shocking, especially all the way in New York," Alex remembered. "I was scared because all I knew was that I had to go. I couldn't say, 'Mom, I don't want to go.' I had to go. It was pretty weird when I was going through it, and it didn't hurt, but I never knew what kind of pain I was going to feel. When I was going through radiation I would lay on the bed and they would take pictures of my head, but I didn't realize it was so bad for me, so that was the good part. I didn't realize it was so bad."

But her parents knew how debilitating the treatment was and

they continued to give their daughter reassurance that everything would be okay. But Alex, who appreciated her parents' efforts, was not interest in sugar-coated discussions. "My parents were really good to me," she said a year later while sitting on a couch in the living room at her home. "The things that were different between my parents and Uncle Johnny is that Uncle Johnny was more realistic. He said everything like it was really going to happen. I wouldn't have been able to get through this if I didn't have my uncle. He always used to say to me, 'Don't give up. Don't give up.' It made me always warn myself that I won't give up so if he didn't say that to me, I wouldn't feel as good. He's amazing. It's like he's a genie and he can make me feel better in a minute."

> "John has done things for those children that our doctors, as great as they are, aren't able to do. When John Valentin goes in to see a patient, sometimes we don't have a medication that can do the same thing to make them feel better."
> —Mike Andrews, Jimmy Fund executive director

Valentin might have been able to prepare Alex for the chemotherapy sessions, but no one was able to guide her through the emotional pain of watching others suffer. "The hardest thing is to make friends and have friends pass away," Alex said. "I know this person and she had it before me. She was so good to me and she was only three or four…" Alex then went silent for a moment. "Once I heard that something happened to her I was upset and mad. I was really upset. She fell asleep and God just told her, 'You did a good job in this part of your life.'"

Alex was determined to help the other kids fight through cancer. Each time her uncle called with words of encouragement, she quickly shared them with her friends. Magic Johnson came to the hospital to see the children during one of Alex's chemotherapy visits. "He was doing the same thing that my uncle does, visiting kids in the hospital," she pointed out. "But seeing my uncle was much more exciting."

As is usually the case, it was the child who calmed the adults through the entire process. "Alex is a mature kid," John Valentin said. "It is amazing how she has handled her situation, but it is not surprising. Kids, when they get sick, just seem to take the sickness and run with it. I've never seen kids wallow in it. Alex is just so mature. She's handled it really, really well. I don't know, maybe she was the right person to have had this problem."

Valentin suffered through the entire 1999 regular season knowing what was going on back home. "It was very hard to play that year," he continued. "I am her uncle and we are a tight-knit family. I talked to her almost every night. It wasn't a good thing a lot of the time to hear them on the phone. I was hurting too. My knees were hurt, but I didn't care. I didn't care anymore how I felt or how I was playing. I was really focusing on getting Alex better." At the start of the season, Valentin took a thick, black magic marker and wrote "ALEX" on the green underside of his Red Sox cap. It was his way of honoring his niece and letting her know that he was thinking about her.

In between chemotherapy visits, Arnold and Liz took their daughters to Boston so Alex could go to Fenway Park for her favorite activity — watching Uncle Johnny play baseball. "Me and my uncle got a big thing about baseball," she said. "I love baseball. It's my favorite, favorite sport."

> "I wouldn't have been able to get through this if I didn't have my uncle. He always used to say to me, 'Don't give up. Don't give up.' It made me always warn myself that I won't give up so if he didn't say that to me, I wouldn't feel as good. He's amazing. It's like he's a genie and he can make me feel better in a minute."
> — Alexandria Valentin

By October, Alex's chemotherapy treatments reached the halfway point and her family's spirits lifted. "It got much better to deal with halfway through," Alex said. Not surprisingly, her uncle rebounded from a regular season where he hit just .253 and put on a postseason show. He erupted with two homers and seven RBI to help beat the Cleveland Indians, 23-7, on October 10. Valentin joined his former Seton Hall and Boston teammate Mo Vaughn as one of only four players in major league history to have seven RBI in a playoff game. After the Red Sox disposed of Cleveland, they faced the Yankees and Valentin's ex-teammate Roger Clemens. Valentin hit a two-run homer against him too. In seven postseason games, Valentin had four homers and 17 RBI, but the Red Sox failed to get by the eventual World Series champions in a five-game series.

Valentin's late-season knee injury was worse than originally thought, so after the season he underwent surgery and rehabilitation in New Jersey. He returned for the 2000 season, but tendonitis in mid-April forced him out of the Red Sox lineup until May 19. Eleven days later, with Alex Valentin watching with her family in New Jersey via satellite television, his season ended. Kansas City's Carlos Beltran hit a second-inning chopper right at him. Valentin took two steps toward the ball and suddenly fell to the ground, screaming in pain as his left knee collapsed.

"He kept saying to me, 'I'm done, I'm done,' " Valentin's teammate and friend, left fielder Troy O'Leary told the *Boston Globe*. "I said, 'No, you'll be able to come back next year.' He had to wait for his wife to come in. I had to get out of there [trainer's room] because I was going to start crying."

Back in New Jersey, his family watched in stunned silence as Valentin was carted off the field. They were unable to do anything for him. All except Alex, that is. Now finished with her chemotherapy treatments, she went to her room, shut the door, and prayed. Ten minutes later she came back into the family room and calmly told her family not to worry. "Uncle Johnny will be okay," she announced.

The next day, Arnold and Liz flew to Boston to see John and told him what Alex had said. "She prayed," John Valentin said. "She believes a higher power talked back to her and said that I was going to be okay, so she wasn't worried about it anymore. Everyone else was upset that I was hurt, that my career might be over, but not Alex."

Valentin had suffered the same injury that forced NBA star Charles Barkley to retire in 2000, but surgery and an exhaustive rehab assignment had him back with the Red Sox nine months later, at least three months ahead of schedule.

But not even Alex's prayers could prevent her uncle from suffering another season-ending injury. This time, his overworked knee led to a heel injury, ending his 10-year Red Sox career. He later signed with the Mets, bringing him closer to one of his favorite people.

Even with frequent visits to the disabled list, Valentin could still smile with thoughts of his niece, including memories of the trip Alex and her family had made to the television station. Back then the Red Sox third baseman did not want to upstage his niece, but still agreed to do a brief interview by telephone.

Throughout the one-hour taping, Alex calmly explained her illness and treatment and, when asked, explained to host Mary Amoroso how important her famous uncle was in her recovery. At that point, the host told Alex a "surprise" caller wanted to speak to her. The youngster's eyes lit up as she quickly recognized the familiar voice. "This is really emotional to talk about," Valentin told Amoroso. "She's such a special kid and has been through so much. We are all really proud of her."

After John hung up, little sister Francesca joined her parents and Alex on the set. The five-year-old proceeded to clown around, waving and making faces at the camera. "She told me she was going to behave herself, but it didn't matter, it was fun," Alex said.

After the show, the two girls got big hugs from their parents, said thank you to the TV show staff, and bounded for the door. Outside was the limousine and they could not wait for the ride home.

THIS ONE'S FOR JASON

It was the summer of 2000 and Sue Leader was at home with her children when the phone rang. She expected it to be another annoying telemarketer to bother her on a Saturday afternoon. Instead it was a stranger who, at Mo Vaughn's mother's urging, wanted to talk about Sue Leader's late son Jason. Leader had thought about Jason every day since he lost his fight to cancer in 1994, but she had not done so yet that day. She agreed to the interview and began to talk, noting, "I might have to stop sometimes. Is that okay?" She continued to talk for 15 uninterrupted minutes until a downpour of tears made her speechless. "I'm really sorry," she said in between short sobs. "If you don't mind, can we continue this another day?"

A week later, she answered the phone again and was better prepared to talk. She had tissues next to her this time but wanted to get through the story without crying again. "I guess you can tell how difficult it is talking about this," she said. "Jason was such a good kid and he just loved Mo."

Sue Leader, along with her since-divorced husband Phil, became regulars at the Boston-based Jimmy Fund and Children's Hospital where Jason received treatment for neuroblastoma, a tumor affecting the adrenal glands and nervous system. The Jimmy Fund provided the Leaders with home away from home, three-plus hours away from their home in Niverville, New York, a half-hour south of Albany, where Jason's sisters, Jamie and Jenna, and brothers, Jesse and Justin, often remained with family and friends.

Jason had been in and out of the hospital since being diagnosed when he was eight. As his 11th birthday approached, he was back in again. His ideal birthday present would have been to go home, but the doctors knew that could not happen. Instead, they arranged for the Jimmy Fund to give him another birthday gift. "The day before Jason's birthday, Jeff Hubbard from the Jimmy Fund came over and talked to Jason," Sue Leader said. "He brought a ball signed by Roger Clemens for Jason because he felt bad for Jason that he was in the hospital on his birthday."

Thinking the boy would answer the same way all the other kids in Boston did, Hubbard asked, "Who is your favorite Red Sox player?" He was stunned by the answer, "Mo Vaughn." "Mo Vaughn, huh?" Hubbard asked smiling inside. It was the end of April 1993 and Vaughn was not yet the well-known commodity he would soon become. Ironically, Jeff's father, Miles Hubbard, had coached Vaughn at Trinity-Pawling School. "I'm not going to make any promises, but I'll try to set up something with Mo," Hubbard said, knowing the player would come through for him.

"When Jeff left the room, Jason felt really, really badly," Sue Leader said. "Jason said, 'Mom, I should have said Roger Clemens because he had the ball.' I told him, 'No Jason, you shouldn't have done that. You told the truth. He wasn't hurt by it.'" Hubbard returned to the hospital later that day with some Mo Vaughn baseball cards. Although he did not say anything to Jason, he arranged for Vaughn to speak to the boy the next day — Jason's birthday.

That next night, prior to the Red Sox-Angels game in Anaheim, Red Sox broadcaster Joe Castiglione called the hospital and spoke to a stunned Jason Leader. After a few moments, Castiglione passed the phone to Vaughn who wished Jason a happy birthday, told him to keep fighting, and added that he would *try* to hit a home run for him. "Jason was excited, he was so excited." Sue Leader said. "He couldn't believe that he actually got to talk to Mo. We were in the hospital and we didn't have a radio and we couldn't get it on TV, they didn't have cable in the hospital, so Jason was a little disappointed because he couldn't see the game."

Jason Leader did not know it, but after midnight on the East Coast, Vaughn connected on a seventh-inning, 3-1 pitch from Ken Patterson and hit the birthday homer for Jason. Castiglione told his radio listeners about the earlier conversation between Vaughn and a sick boy in Boston. Jason Leader awoke a few hours later in the center ring of a media circus. "The next morning, we woke up in the hospital and the nurses came in and told us what happened," Sue Leader said. "The public affairs people were on the phone because they wanted to talk to Jason. When Mo hit the home run, Joe talked about the promise Mo made."

While the phone call and home run certainly lifted the spirits of her son, Sue Leader later learned Vaughn had also gotten something out of it. "At the time, Mo was in a batting slump and was kind of down, but here was Jason who was battling cancer and he was so upbeat. Mo was very impressed with Jason." Vaughn enjoyed talking to the youngster and worked with Jimmy Fund officials to get Jason to Fenway Park where the youngster would throw out the first pitch and meet Vaughn face-to-face.

The *Boston Globe*'s Larry Whiteside was there to record the meeting, which took place a week later. "As he [Vaughn] came down the steps of the Red Sox dugout, a big smile came across the face of Mo Vaughn," Whiteside wrote. "Slowly, his eyes focused on those of the thin young man who had been patiently waiting for him for about 15 minutes. 'How you doing?' said Vaughn in an effort to break the ice. 'You doing all right? Everything all right? These guys [the media] aren't bothering you? You let me know.'"

"It was a Fenway moment, one you'll see on news reels and highlight tapes 20 years from now," Whiteside wrote in his article. "Mo Vaughn meets Jason Leader. Film at 11. Sure, it's corny to compare this to the story of Babe Ruth allegedly hitting a home run for a bedridden boy in the 1920s, an episode dramatized in the William Bendix movie, *The Babe Ruth Story*. Vaughn wants the new movie to be accurate. He did talk with Leader on the phone. Honest. 'But I didn't make a promise,' said the Red Sox first baseman after escorting Leader into the clubhouse and introducing him to several players. 'But I did tell him I'd try. It's a situation that just worked out. I'm not Babe Ruth at all.'"

He did not have to be. Jason Leader did not know much about Babe Ruth, but he knew a lot about Mo Vaughn. Vaughn, who had been given the home run ball by the Angels fan who caught it, presented Jason with it and inscribed it, "*To Jason, stay strong, my friend. Mo Vaughn.*" The little boy got a standing ovation from the Fenway faithful when he walked out to throw the ceremonial first pitch to his hero.

"When Jason was sick, he would be so sick and yet, when he went to Fenway, he was so comfortable," Sue Leader said. "He just enjoyed Fenway and seeing Mo. Just being there helped him out and made him feel so much better." The original meeting also allowed Sue Leader to meet Vaughn's parents, Leroy and Shirley, to begin a friendship that continues to this day.

"Mo reminded me of the gentle giant," Sue Leader said. "You could tell he had a really, really, good heart. He gave Jason his home phone number and told Jason to call him any time. Even if he didn't want to talk, just give him a call. It surprised me. It impressed me. You think they [baseball players] are so popular, they have their own lives and don't get involved in anything else, but Mo was not like that."

Mike Andrews, the former Red Sox second baseman who heads the Jimmy Fund, marveled at the effort Vaughn put forth into the friendship. "Mo's relationship with Jason Leader is a perfect example of an athlete giving a young man some of the finest moments of his life, even though it was inevitable where it was going to end," he said. "What he did for that young boy was something no doctor could touch."

"People didn't know how often Mo called to say, 'How is it going?' " Sue Leader said. "They only saw it when the media was around. He did it because it was explained to him that there was a little boy in the hospital who can't go home on his birthday and you are his idol. He did it out of the kindness of his heart. He was very touched by Jason. Mo would call Jason at home and in the hospital just to see how Jason was doing. On Jason's 12th birthday, Mo sent him baseball cards, balloons; it was a care package."

That care package, sent a year after the two first met, was one of the few times the *Boston Globe* followed up on the Leader-Vaughn story. "Jason Leader, the young cancer patient for whom

Vaughn hit a home run last season, celebrated his 12th birthday Saturday, and Vaughn still is thinking of him. The first baseman sent a package of flowers and balloons, along with the best wishes of the Red Sox and their fans, to Jason Leader." It was a public moment to what had become a very private friendship that went beyond the player and the boy.

Sue Leader and Shirley Vaughn talked often about Jason's treatments. They shared a lot of laughter and a lot of tears. The tears grew more frequent when doctors found the cancer had spread to Jason's spine. "Jason was the type that didn't want Mo to see him suffering," Sue Leader said. "He didn't want sympathy from anyone. He didn't want Mo to see him that way. Towards the end, Jason was in a wheelchair and I know that upset the whole Vaughn family. It was tough for Mo to see Jason go downhill."

> "Mo's relationship with Jason Leader is a perfect example of an athlete giving a young man some of the finest moments of his life ... What he did for that young boy was something no doctor could touch."
> — Mike Andrews, Jimmy Fund executive director

The family learned from the doctors that there was nothing more they could do. Jason watched his family try to rally around him and, while he never told them he knew he was dying, he did ask to go to Fenway Park one more time. "We got permission to take him out for the night to Fenway Park," Sue Leader said. "We took him to Fenway and met Mo, Shirley, and Leroy after the game. Shirley talked to me and asked me how things were. I told her that they had given us the news; we both sat there and cried. I hugged her. I didn't tell Mo. I left that up to Shirley."

"After the game, we told Maurice what was happening," Shirley Vaughn said. "We were all crying. Jason was better than any of us. That was one of the most miserable nights in my life. Watching Jason say goodbye to Maurice. It tore Maurice up. Maurice gave him a shirt to take with him."

"Jason knew," Sue Leader said, "but he was such a strong fighter that he would never think this was his last time. Mo knew it and I knew it."

Jason Leader died on August 15, 1994, and was buried in his hometown. Vaughn made the long drive to Niverville by himself. "Mo came to the funeral," Sue Leader said. "It showed a lot. Jason meant a lot to him. The hardest part was we tried to keep the media out of it so it would be a family thing. He wasn't there as a baseball player. He was there as a friend, but it didn't work. It was a very difficult time. My family is so close and was so upset. He was just one of us. It wasn't a baseball player doing something because of his status. He was just Maurice the human being."

With Jason gone, the two families worked together to launch the "Jason & Mo Friendship Fund" in the boy's memory. The charity allows Sue Leader and her family the opportunity to help others the way Mo Vaughn helped them.

In 1998, Shirley and Leroy Vaughn were named the honorary starters for the Jimmy Fund Walk-a-thon where they helped raise money for the Jimmy Fund and the Jason & Mo Friendship Fund. Their son could not be there. He was in Baltimore wrapping up the regular season with his 40th homer of the season to send the Red Sox to the playoffs on a high note. Joe Castiglione, the broadcaster who made the initial phone call to Jason in 1993, reported that as Leroy Vaughn crossed the finish line, he said, "This one's for Jason."

Leroy Vaughn's son, one of baseball's most community-minded citizens, admits that losing Jason to cancer had a profound impact on him. While speaking at a corner locker in the New York Yankees' visiting clubhouse during the 2000 season, Mo Vaughn's voice quieted noticeably when talking about the little boy. "It was a great relationship between the two of us. After him it became very, very difficult for me to get involved with kids like Jason who were sick. It became too tough for me to watch these kids in that situation because they don't know what's going on. They just think they're living," Vaughn paused, "but they're dying. But they really think they're living. I had to stop doing that a lot because it was messing with my mind a little bit."

But do not get the idea that Vaughn has given up providing a helping hand. He cannot say no and has done an incredible amount of charity work even as his career has taken him to

Anaheim and now New York. "I try to tell him that even though he wants to help everyone he can, he won't be able to solve all of the world's problems by 10 AM," Vaughn's business manager Mark Gillam said. "One thing people should really know about Mo is that he has a heart the size of Texas."

Vaughn showed his passion for helping others when he first arrived in Boston and recognized that he might have an opportunity to assist children. By 1994, he opened the Mo Vaughn Youth Development Program and Center in the basement of the Harvard Street Health Adolescent Child Life Center in the Franklin Field area of Dorchester, Massachusetts. He called on Norwalk friends Roosevelt Smith and Bryan Wilson to start the program.

"Mo always wanted to do things with kids, so once he got to Boston, he said that he wanted me to start a Youth Center," Wilson said. "He wanted to run it, but he knew that would be tough because he was running all over the place. We had a lot of talks about what he wanted. He said, 'Everything you don't learn in school that is important. Life skills, like balancing a checkbook. It's not going to be just rolling out basketballs and letting them play.' He really wanted a structured environment for the kids." Vaughn was not interested in "A" students. He thought those children were doing fine on their own. He wanted to help the average kid who could be swayed by the lure of the street.

With government approval in place, Wilson, Smith and other volunteers began circulating flyers throughout the community, advertising the five-hour, after-school sessions that would include tutoring, hot meals for dinner, speakers, and field trips. Soon the group started interviewing kids and their parents, judging if the program was suitable for them. "We were expecting a lot from the kids," Wilson said. "We also needed the parents to be on the same page as we were so we didn't teach the kid one thing and the parents another."

Sasha Link, then a middle school student, noticed the flyer and thought the idea sounded interesting. But Mo Vaughn was not the draw for her. "Some of the kids knew of him and wanted to meet him, but a lot of us didn't," explained Link, who is now on a Mo Vaughn Youth Program scholarship at Bridgewater

State College as the group's first college student. "I was like, 'Who's he?' Somebody told me and I still didn't know because I wasn't into baseball." Still, she became one of the core of 30 who attended each day.

Vaughn, who also "adopted" and often visited the elementary school children at Dorchester's Taylor School, increased his community activity. Soon Vaughn was giving away a thousand circus tickets and offering another thousand at reduced prices to Dorchester residents. He also brought the children to the Ice Capades, Boston Pops concerts, and other cultural events.

Vaughn was honored numerous times for his charitable contributions, but before October 2, 1995, his actions had only been recognized in New England. *Sports Illustrated* let America in on the secret, putting him on the cover: **"MO VALUABLE. NO ONE IN BASEBALL IS MORE IMPORTANT TO HIS TEAM — AND HIS CITY — THAN BOSTON'S MO VAUGHN."** The article, written by Gerry Callahan, claimed Vaughn should win the American League MVP Award, if not for his 39 homers and a major league-leading 126 RBI, than for his community work.

> "I try to tell him that even though he wants to help everyone he can, he won't be able to solve all of the world's problems by 10 AM. One thing people should really know about Mo is that he has a heart the size of Texas."
>
> —Mark Gillam, Mo Vaughn's business manager

Several years later Vaughn remembered the article and pointed out that he never got involved with children to gain a reputation as a good person, but the media grabbed hold of his daily feel-good efforts. "I had no idea that this stuff was gonna get that big," he said. "I went out there with these kids and they responded which was good. It just snowballed and it got crazy — it got out of hand."

Vaughn went on to win the MVP Award and held the press conference at the youth center so he could share it with his kids. "That was a really nice day," Vaughn said. "The kids really enjoyed being a part of it, with all of the television cameras and media there." Two months after being named the MVP, Vaughn went to New York for the annual, star-studded Baseball Assistance Team dinner, which raises money for former players in need. Vaughn was there to accept the Bart Giamatti Humanitarian Award for his community work.

The MVP was in the spotlight, but he paled in comparison to others in the room — former greats like Yogi Berra, Steve Carlton, Joe DiMaggio, Ted Williams, Duke Snyder, Pee Wee Reese, Robin Roberts, and Warren Spahn.

"That dinner was really, really nice," Vaughn said. "There were so many all-time greats there and they were honoring me with such a nice award. I've said it before, and I'll say it again, because I am a baseball player, I have the status in the community where I can be a positive force. I can pull some strings to get things done easier than other people. I enjoy what I do for the kids, but I really don't deserve credit for it."

One of the board members of the Mo Vaughn Youth Development Program and Center, Boston businessman John Connors, asked Vaughn to assist him in another charitable endeavor. The St. Francis House, which sits in the heart of downtown Boston, had grown from providing two meals a day for the homeless to offering a full range of services, including clothing, medical services, counseling services, job training, legal services, and GED courses.

Vaughn agreed to meet Connors at St. Francis House and created a "Homers for Homeless" program. Vaughn agreed to donate $1,000 for every home run he hit. "When he walked into the day center, which is the hub of activity, our guests looked in disbelief," St. Francis House Director of Communications Debbie Farrell said. "They were dumbfounded. They were tentative at first to approach him because he was Mo Vaughn. They couldn't believe a guy like him wanted anything to do them. But Mo solved that problem really quickly when he went right over to three guys who were playing dominoes, sat down and said, 'So how do you play this game?' They taught him how to play and he won. To this day, our guests still talk about how Mo Vaughn beat them in dominoes even though he never played before."

Once the 600 guests saw that Vaughn was a down-to-earth

superstar, they began to ask for autographs. "They ran out of paper, so they were grabbing anything they could — paper bags, garbage bags, napkins and somebody even had him sign her baby!" Farrell said.

Once word spread that Vaughn would donate money for every home run, box scores were read in the shelter the way stock quotes were scanned at financial firms. The guests understood how important Vaughn's donations, which totaled about $111,000 for every home run he hit through the 2001 season, were to the program. Along with continuing programs, the shelter now offers hot breakfasts, more clothing, and more counseling.

"When Mo left to go to Anaheim, our residents were devastated," Farrell said. "They thought it was the end. He was their personal hero. But once they found out he was going to continue the 'Homers for Homeless' program, they went right back to the papers and kept track."

Besides making sure children and the homeless are taken care of, Vaughn has also been heavily involved in giving a lesson or two about baseball. After Vaughn got his youth center off the ground, he asked Paul Rappoli, a former Red Sox minor leaguer he befriended in 1989, if he might be interested in working with him on baseball clinics. Rappoli, who now runs Vaughn's 17,000-square-foot Hit Dog Training Center in Stoughton, Massachusetts, had been doing his own youth clinics and one-on-one tutoring. He knew a Mo Vaughn Hitting Clinic would have more clout with the kids and parents than one named after a career minor leaguer.

> "I've said it before, and I'll say it again, because I am a baseball player, I have the status in the community where I can be a positive force. I can pull some strings to get things done easier than other people. I enjoy what I do for the kids, but I really don't deserve credit for it."
>
> —Mo Vaughn

The new partners held their first clinic over the 1995 Thanksgiving holiday at Northeastern University for 170 kids. The second clinic was a couple of months later during the Martin Luther King Jr. Day school vacation at Springfield College. One of Rappoli's friends in the minor leagues, a shortstop named Nomar Garciaparra, was invited to be a counselor for what Vaughn jokingly called "minimum wage."

"I called Nomar and he came out from California," Rappoli said while laughing at Vaughn's minimum wage mention before confirming that Garciaparra did not take any money. "He had some friends on our staff, guys like Lou Merloni, so it was a nice time to hang out with his buddies during the off-season, spend time with Mo, and teach," Rappoli said. "The first year, they had no idea who Nomar was," Rappoli said. "They got his autograph, but, then again, they got everyone's."

That was the start of Vaughn's friendship with Garciappara. "I have so much respect and I love that man so much," Garciaparra said about Vaughn during the 2000 season. "He's not just a role model to people, he's a role model to players, to his peers. That says a lot because he does so much. He's not just a great ballplayer, but he's a great man, a great person. He helped me a lot coming up. He would come and he'd have to have a talk with me. We still do this to this day. It is like an annual talk right before the season. And he prepared me."

Vaughn enjoyed being the youngster's baseball father-figure. "Every year we would talk," Vaughn said. "I would talk to him about the attitude and what it takes to be successful, especially in Boston where the lights are big and the pressure is always on. I would tell him the only way you could feel good going to the park each day is if you were prepared. You are only as good as your last at-bat. If you do it once, you have to do it again and again. Do it two times, you have to do it three times. The expectations are always there. Now he turned out to be a superstar and knows how to do his thing. I hoped I helped him, but I don't know if I did or not."

Vaughn's words to Garciaparra proved he had been listening to Mike Sheppard Sr., his college coach at Seton Hall. "I was 7-for-7 in a doubleheader and the last time up, I hit the ball as hard as I could and the shortstop made a great play for an out," Vaughn remembered. "At our postgame meeting, Shep singled me out. He said, 'Our guy Mo Vaughn is supposed to be an All-American, but he couldn't get that last hit to go 8-for-8. He had to settle for 7-for-8 because he did not want to concentrate on that last at-bat.' I wanted to kill the guy. At the time, when it was going down, I wanted to fight him. But as I got older, I understood what he was trying to do and I appreciate it."

Garciaparra appreciated Vaughn's words too. "I never had a role model or hero growing up as a kid," the 1997 American League Rookie of the Year said. "I just played the game. But if you ask me, 'Who is your hero now, who do you watch?' Mo Vaughn would definitely be one of those people who I actually watch now, cheer for and want to see do well. And that is because of him as a person."

Garciaparra is not alone.

DONATIONS

If you would like to make a donation to the charities mentioned in this section, here are their mailing addresses and other information:

<u>In honor of Craig Biggio:</u>
The Sunshine Kids Foundation
2814 Virginia
Houston, TX 77098
1-800-594-5756
www.sunshinekids.org

<u>In honor of John Valentin:</u>

The Jimmy Fund	*Making Headway Foundation*
375 Longwood Avenue	(Alex Valentin's charity)
Boston, MA 02215	115 King Street
800-52-JIMMY	Chappaqua, NY 10514
www.jimmyfund.org	914-238-8384
	www.makingheadway.org

<u>In honor of Mo Vaughn:</u>

Mo & Jason Friendship Fund	*St. Francis House*
c/o The Jimmy Fund	39 Boylston Street
375 Longwood Avenue	Boston, MA 02112
Boston, MA 02215	617-542-4211
800-52-JIMMY	www.stfrancishouse.org
www.jimmyfund.org	

Donations

CONCLUSION

TOGETHER AGAIN

CHAPTER 23

Mike Sheppard Sr. took the phone call as he always does — "Pirate Baseball." He heard the familiar voice on the other end and agreed to a meeting. The "Old Man", as Seton Hall baseball players affectionately call their head coach, then turned to his assistant coach and youngest son, Rob, and said, "I'm going to see Rick on Monday down in Newark." Rob Sheppard smiled.

The plan was working perfectly. Rob's dad was going to start the next week with a bang. A meeting with his first major leaguer followed by a surprise visit from "The Hit Men" and a former shortstop who once hit ninth.

During the 2000 major league season, Craig Biggio, Mo Vaughn, and John Valentin, along with Marteese Robinson, agreed to meet during the winter and take the cover photo for this book. Although each had said okay, no date was ever established. But Biggio, ever the captain, took charge of the situation. "I'll be back in New Jersey for Thanksgiving so we can do it then," Biggio said from his Houston home. "Let's do it at Seton Hall so Shep can benefit from it, but let's make it a surprise for him." And so the wheels went in motion.

When November 20, the day Biggio suggested, rolled around, the eldest Sheppard thought he had a quiet day planned. A morning meeting with Rick Cerone followed by an early Thanksgiving lunch with fellow Seton Hall Athletic Department staffers. He would end his day with a late-afternoon meeting, arranged by Rob Sheppard, with his Seton Hall team. He had no idea his day would also include an emotional reunion with four of the greatest players he had ever produced.

Although Biggio, Vaughn, and Valentin carry the Seton Hall torch in the major leagues today, along with Matt Morris and Florida Marlins pitcher Jason Grilli, Sheppard's favorite Seton Hall big leaguer will always be Rick Cerone. The All-American led the Pirates to the 1974 and 1975 College World Series. He was Sheppard's first first-round pick, taken by the Cleveland Indians in the 1975 draft, and then became Sheppard's first major leaguer when he was called up that same year at the tender age of 21. For those reasons, Sheppard calls Cerone "The Standard Bearer."

Eight years removed from his major league playing career, Cerone was hard at work in his new job as the owner and president of the Newark Bears, one of eight teams in the independent Atlantic League. Cerone, who grew up in Newark, was principally responsible for bringing baseball back to the city for the first time since the old Newark Bears were the Yankees top farm team before they left for Springfield, Massachusetts, in 1949.

Cerone asked for the meeting with Sheppard because he wanted his old coach to bring his Seton Hall team to Newark to play. Cerone, having once toiled in relative obscurity at Seton Hall, knew the college players would greatly enjoy the minor league experience, and Sheppard could recruit with Riverfront Stadium as a bargaining chip. But Cerone was also thinking with his business hat on. He needed to expose The Bears Den, as his stadium is affectionately known, to as many people as possible.

After the morning meeting to discuss scheduling details, Sheppard was caught off guard when Cerone said, "Tell Rob I'll see him later." Cerone quickly remembered the afternoon activities were a surprise and recovered. "Don't worry," he replied to Sheppard's puzzled look. "He knows what it is about."

"When I left Rick's office, I was guessing that Rick was trying to get Rob to come and work for him in Newark," the Seton Hall coach said. "I would never stand in Rob's way if that is what he wanted to do, but I was a little pissed that he had not told me that he was interested in working for the Bears. When I got back to Seton Hall, I asked Rob why Rick was coming to see him, but he waved it off and said it was nothing."

Sheppard could not put his finger on it, but he knew something was up and, whatever it was, his son was a part of it. "People seemed more excited than usual and they kind of smiled at me in the halls," Sheppard said. "What they were excited about? I had no idea."

As Sheppard sat upstairs in a conference room eating lunch, his surprise was walking in the door a floor below. First, Marteese Robinson. Then in walked a combined 34 years experience in Major League Baseball and $27 million in annual salaries — Biggio and Valentin, then Vaughn. It was as if they never had left. "Bidge," "Val," "Marty," and Mo were back where it all began, and the afternoon-long reunion began with hugs, laughter, jokes, and memories.

"I have never been around a team with so many tough guys," Vaughn said about the 1987 Pirates. "I'm the youngest. They taught me how to play. We used to go out there and beat people up. It was the best then and it is still the best team I have ever been a part of in my baseball career."

Biggio and Valentin began a technical discussion about their respective season-ending knee injuries and rehab assignments. But the Astros second baseman quickly realized he should speak guardedly about his progress. "We better be careful what we say around Marty," Biggio said about Robinson while Vaughn and Valentin laughed loudly with him. "He's a front office guy now!"

Back on campus and all together for the first time since the late 1980s, they were college teammates again. They talked baseball. They talked hitting. Biggio explained the nuances of hitting in Enron Field compared to the Astrodome. Vaughn mentioned that it had taken a while for him to learn how to adjust to Edison Field after years in Fenway. Valentin insisted Fenway was still the best hitter's park around.

They began playfully attacking each other in ways only old friends can do. Valentin was blamed for Robinson's broken arm in 1986. Valentin ripped Vaughn for his collegiate fielding deficiencies. They made fun of Biggio for being the smallest of the group and chastised Vaughn for being the biggest. Robinson made certain his three multi-millionaire friends recognized that he was the least paid in the bunch.

A few moments later the joking died down if only for a minute. In walked Sheppard, who had just been summoned from his office and told that Biggio, Valentin, Vaughn, and Robinson were on campus and wanted to see him. He got teary-eyed outside the room and again when he walked in. "Holy mackerel," he said quietly over and over again as he shared emotional embraces with his former stars.

This was not the Mike Sheppard the former Pirates were used to. He was no longer the in-your-face drill sergeant, but instead, as he called it, "a more cerebral coach who can get deeper into every kid." Sheppard, now 65 and recovering from a stroke, even admitted to tiring easily in the afternoon. Still, he tried to retain his tough guy image with his former pupils, even as tears of joy welled up in his eyes.

> "I have never been around a team with so many tough guys. I'm the youngest. They taught me how to play. We used to go out there and beat people up. It was the best then and it is still the best team I have ever been a part of in my baseball career."
> —Mo Vaughn

Vaughn could not resist and yelled out, "There's no crying in baseball," Tom Hanks' famous line from *A League of Their Own*. Sheppard responded, "Hey Mo, I can take you on one at a time or all together and the result will still be the same." The players howled with laughter.

Sheppard was no longer their coach. He no longer held the reigns and drove them hard, but still Sheppard had their respect. That was evident when the entire group moved to an upstairs conference room for a "Welcome Back" press conference. The players eagerly answered questions about their 1987 team and then showered their former coach with praise.

"Talk about toughness?" Vaughn said. "Any one of us could play for anyone because we played for him. He knew playing for him would be the toughest thing for us. Going to the next level would be easier for us to succeed because nobody would do or say the things he did to push us. He tried to make us men at an early age, but it helped all of us in our lives. He was instrumental for all of us here today and for the other guys who are out there living their lives."

Sheppard responded, "You're ahead of schedule. It usually takes guys to be about 40 before they figure it out." Vaughn could not resist another dig at Biggio and Robinson, who along with Valentin, also sat in front of the media. "Well, Marty and Craig are pretty close to that," he laughed. "At least I *still* look young," Biggio, 35, fought back with a smiling face that still had him looking not a day over 20.

Biggio followed: "He's a really tough guy. When you are 18 years old and you think you know everything, but you really don't know everything, you need a guy like him to keep you in line. When you are here, you clash. You go head-to-head. But when you leave, you hug him and say, 'Thank you.' You didn't realize what he was doing for you. I owe that man everything. It was only three years, but it was three critical years."

When it was Valentin's turn to speak, he broke up the room. "These guys are not really telling the truth," the major league veteran told the media. "All we wanted to do is get drafted and get away from Shep!" Everyone laughed and Biggio followed, "Three years and out! That's the truth!"

"You know what?" Sheppard countered. "When you guys were here, I said to myself that it was my job to make you tough. If I made it too tough on you, I don't apologize at all. Look where it got you!"

On the way to the press conference, the players had stopped to admire the plaques identifying the school's Athletic Hall of Fame members. Biggio, Valentin, and Vaughn were all on the wall and Vaughn noticed an empty spot near theirs. "Marty," Vaughn yelled. "We need to get you up here with us! That is your spot!" None of the players knew it, but Seton Hall officials felt the same way.

Two days shy of six years after the dinner to induct Vaughn, Biggio, Valentin, and Sheppard into the Seton Hall Athletic Hall of Fame, Robinson was inducted and also had his number retired, an honor Seton Hall baseball had bestowed on only one other, Rick Cerone.

"I know now why they didn't put me in with the other guys," Robinson said. "Mo, Craig, and Val are big stars and the school was looking for a little pop by having them back. I can't blame the athletic department for that. As for Shep, he should have been in a long time before then. In fact, they should probably name a building after the guy. It is really nice that I am going to be in the Hall of Fame."

A year-and-a-half earlier, after speaking to the reporters, Sheppard escorted the magnificent four to meet his team. The coach made the unnecessary introductions and Biggio, Vaughn, and Valentin took turns talking baseball with the 2001 Pirates, who looked on with complete and undivided attention. "We've been in the exact spot where you guys are now," Vaughn told the team. "We were just like you. We were just a bunch of guys who had fun and loved the game. We worked hard, learned from Shep and from each other and now we are in a position where you guys want to hear from us. The man made us tough and I would go to war with any of them."

The major leaguers took questions and laughed as they shared Sheppard stories with the current crop of Pirates — Does Shep still do this? Does Shep still do that? Everyone was amazed that the coach had never changed his ways. As long as he was the coach, discipline would be the overriding theme for Seton Hall baseball.

"I tell the kids about how Mo Vaughn worked by himself fielding in the squash courts," Sheppard said. "I tell them that Valentin was a walk-on who batted ninth, how Biggio was a retriever who became a receiver, how Robinson broke his arm badly but came back to win the Player of the Year award. Now here they were, talking to them. Holy shit, you could have heard a pin drop. That did more good for the team than anything I could tell them. It's the best part of the program when the pros come back."

As the day that Sheppard called one of his career highlights wound down, Biggio, Vaughn, and Valentin signed autographs for the team, shared some more hugs with each other, and headed home. On the way out, Robinson spoke to an old friend.

"You know, we all thought Shep was crazy when we were

here," the former All-American said. "We could never understand why he was so demanding of us. We had so much talent and we just crushed people. But it was never enough for him. He demanded perfection, but perfection in baseball was impossible. But you know what? By instilling that toughness into all of us, he made certain that in whatever we went on to do after college, we would be able to be good at it because nothing would ever be as hard as what we went through at Seton Hall. In my job now, I am amazed at how often my eye is drawn to the dirtiest, most hard-working and toughest guy out there. That was the kind of guy Shep loved. I guess, as the old saying goes, 'The apple doesn't fall far from the tree.' "

To Sheppard, things had come full circle. Biggio, Vaughn, Valentin, and Robinson had returned together and provided valuable lessons for the new generation of Seton Hall baseball. The message was heard. So much so, that even with Sheppard sidelined for the 2001 season while recovering from triple-bypass heart surgery, the Pirates, led by interim-coach Rob Sheppard, won the school's second Big East title.

The 2001 Seton Hall Pirates seemed to remember Vaughn's parting words, "If we could do it, why can't you?"

ABOUT THE AUTHOR

David Siroty was the Assistant Sports Information Director at Seton Hall University from 1986 to 1990 and promoted the school's baseball program, including the 1987 Big East Champions.

After graduation from Syracuse University in 1985, Siroty worked for a year at The Big East Conference before landing at Seton Hall. He next served as Assistant Commissioner at The Northeast Conference where he earned the Mike Cohen Good Guy Award from the New York Metropolitan Basketball Writers Association. Siroty has also held public relations positions at CN8-The Comcast Network, the DVC Group, and currently serves as Director of Public Affairs at Saint Peter's College in Jersey City, New Jersey.

Siroty previously was a freelance writer for *Eastern Basketball* and *Basketball Times*. This is his first book.

He and his wife Jill reside in Westfield, New Jersey. They welcomed the arrival of their son, Matthew Braden, in August 2001.